THE MARCH OF ISLAM

AD 600-800

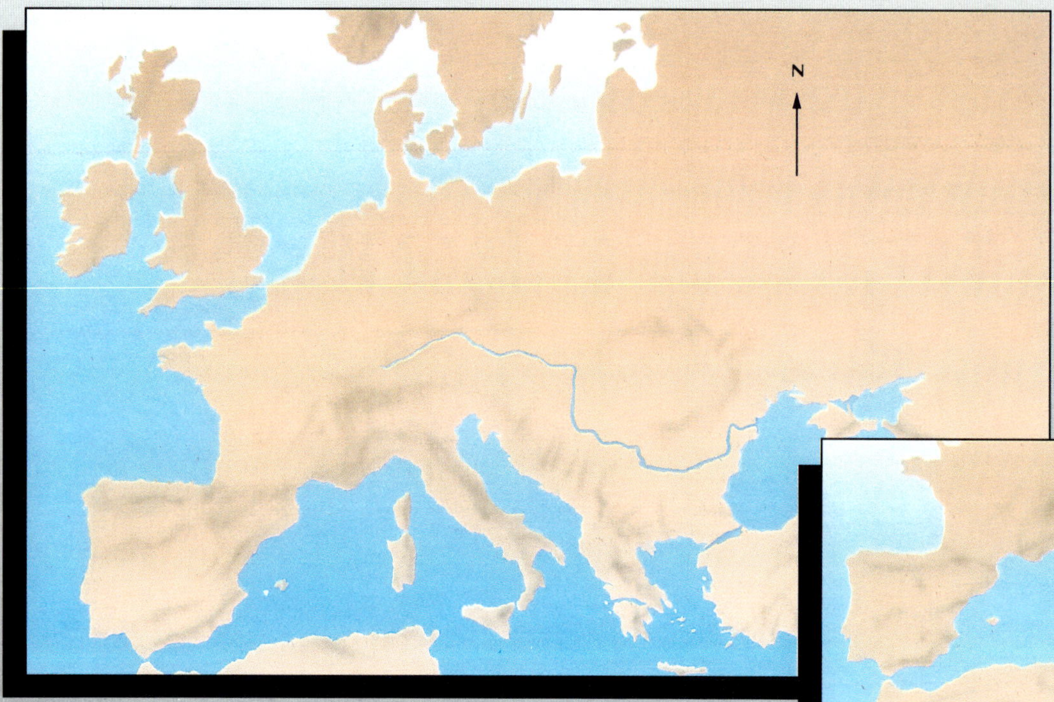

EUROPE AND BYZANTIUM

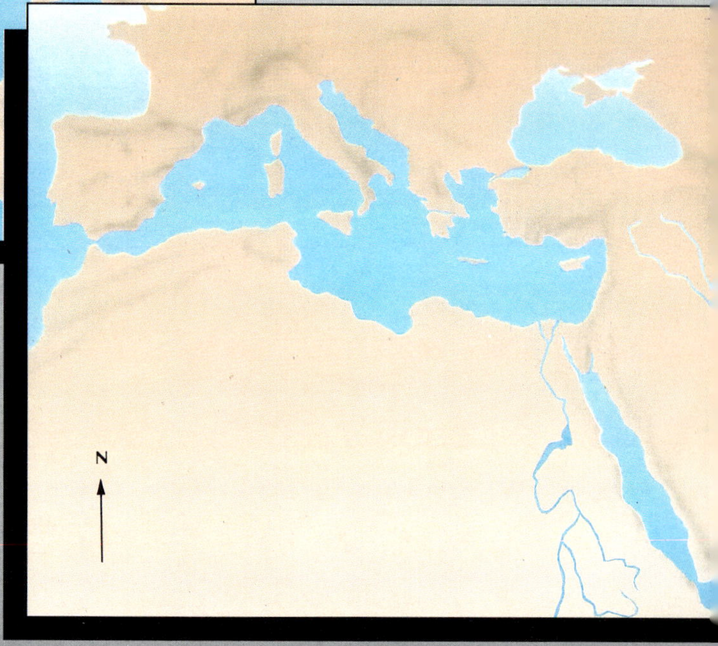

THE ISLAMIC EMPIRE

AD 600-800

JAPAN

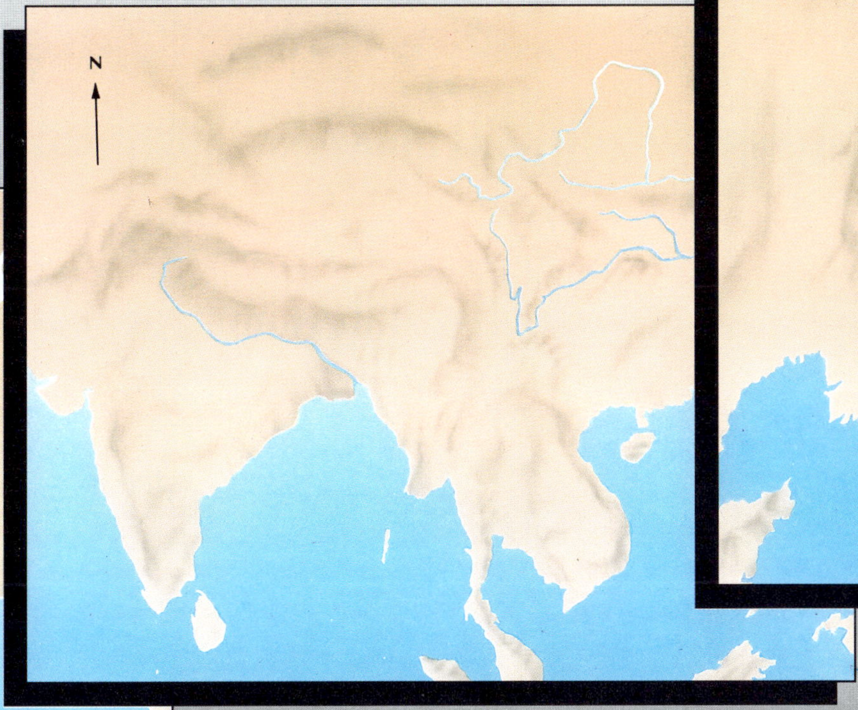

INDIA, CHINA AND SOUTHEAST ASIA

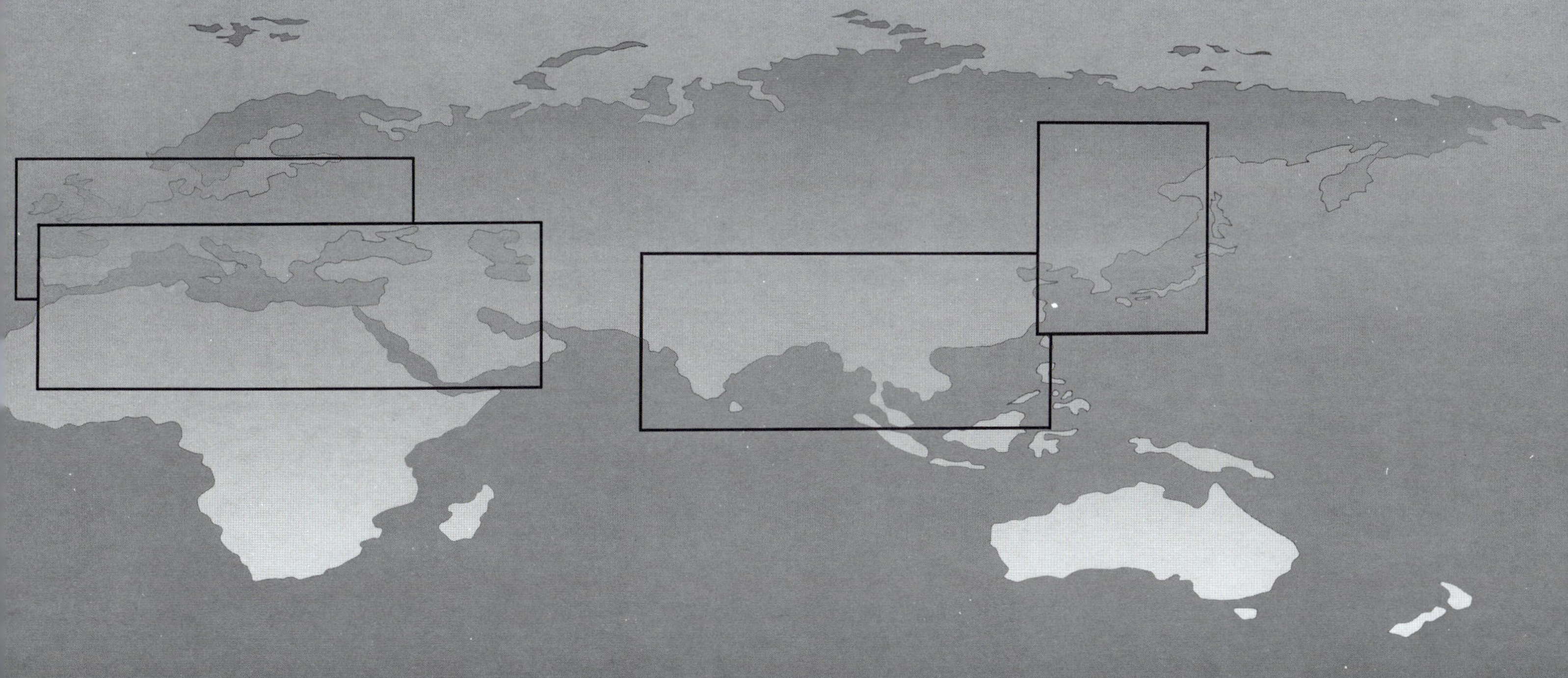

TIME
LIFE
BOOKS

LOST CIVILIZATIONS
HOW THINGS WORK
SYSTEM EARTH
LIBRARY OF CURIOUS AND UNUSUAL FACTS
BUILDING BLOCKS
A CHILD'S FIRST LIBRARY OF LEARNING
VOYAGE THROUGH THE UNIVERSE
THE THIRD REICH
MYSTERIES OF THE UNKNOWN
TIME-LIFE HISTORY OF THE WORLD
FITNESS, HEALTH & NUTRITION
HEALTHY HOME COOKING
UNDERSTANDING COMPUTERS
THE ENCHANTED WORLD
LIBRARY OF NATIONS
PLANET EARTH
THE GOOD COOK
THE WORLD'S WILD PLACES

This volume is one in the Time-Life series
HISTORY OF THE WORLD

THE MARCH OF ISLAM

AD 600-800

BY THE EDITORS OF TIME-LIFE BOOKS

TIME-LIFE BOOKS, AMSTERDAM

TIME-LIFE BOOKS

EUROPEAN EDITOR: Ellen Phillips
Design Director: Ed Skyner
Director of Editorial Resources: Samantha Hill
Chief Sub-Editor: Ilse Gray

TIME-LIFE HISTORY OF THE WORLD

SERIES DIRECTOR: Henry Woodhead
Series Administrator: Philip Brandt George

Editorial Staff for *The March of Islam:*
Designer: Tom Huestis
Associate Editors: Jim Hicks (text); Sally Collins (pictures)
Writer: Stephen G. Hyslop
Researchers: Karin Kinney (text); Jane Martin (pictures)
Assistant Designers: Alan Pitts, Rebecca Mowrey
Copy Coordinator: Jarelle S. Stein
Picture Coordinators: Renée DeSandies, Betty H. Weatherley
Editorial Assistant: Lona Tavernise

European Edition:
Sub-Editor: Diana Hill
Chief of Editorial Production: Maureen Kelly
Production Assistant: Samantha Hill
Editorial Department: Theresa John, Debra Lelliott

ISBN 0 7054 0975 9

CONSULTANTS

Europe and Byzantium:
WALTER GOFFART, Professor of History, University of Toronto, Toronto, Canada.

KLAUS WINANDS, Institut für Baugeschichte und Denkmalplege, Universität Aachen, Aachen, Federal Republic of Germany.

India:
VIMALA BEGLEY, Research Associate, University of Pennsylvania Museum, Iowa City, Iowa.

Islam:
JOHN ESPOSITO, Director of International Studies, Holy Cross College, Worcester, Massachusetts.

GEORGE SCANLAN, Professor of Islamic Art and Architecture, The American University in Cairo, Cairo, Egypt.

PRISCILLA P. SOUCEK, Hagop Kevorkian Professor of Islamic Art, Institute of Fine Arts, New York University, New York, New York.

YEDIDA K. STILLMAN, Associate Professor Classical and Near Eastern Studies, and Director of the Judaic Studies Program, State University of New York at Binghamton, Binghamton, New York.

Southeast Asia, Japan and China:
CHARLES A. PETERSON, Professor of History, Cornell University, Ithaca, New York.

SPECIAL CONTRIBUTORS: Ronald H. Bailey, Champ Clark, George G. Daniels, Charles Hagner, Brian McGinn, Charles Phillips, Brian Pohanka, David S. Thomson, Bryce Walker (text); Cecile Ablack, Marie F. Taylor Davis, Mariana T. Durbin, Roxie France-Nuriddin, Feroline Burrage Higginson, Cindy Joyce, Sara Mark, Deborah D. Richardson, Jayne Rohrich, Jacqueline Shaffer, Corinne Szabo, Marilyn Murphy Terrell (research).

Correspondents: Elisabeth Kraemer-Singh (Bonn); Maria Vincenza Aloisi (Paris): Ann Natanson (Rome). Valuable assistance was also provided by: Wibo Vande Linde (Amsterdam); Jaime Florcruz, Jane Zhang (Beijing); Janet Huseby (Berkeley); Barry Iverson, Nihal Tamraz (Cairo); Barbara Gevene Hertz (Copenhagen); Jo Chang (Hong Kong); Marlin Levin (Jerusalem); Caroline Lucas, Linda Proud (London); Arti Ahluwalia, Ross Munro, Deepak Puri (New Delhi); Christina Lieberman (New York); Ann Wise (Rome); K.C. Kwang (Seoul); Dick Berry, Alison Hashimoto, Mieko Ikeda (Tokyo); Traudl Lessing (Vienna).

CONTENTS

Warriors and Warlords

"Ever since I buried my lord, I must mourn alone," a vanquished warrior laments in an eighth-century Anglo-Saxon tale. "Now I have left my homeland. I sail the icy seas in search of a new lord, a generous giver of gold, a lord who will welcome me into his drinking hall and divert me from my grief."

This fighting man's quest for a strong and generous leader was a search shared by fellow warriors throughout the world. But nowhere was the liege-to-lord bond fiercer than where rulers claimed to act upon divine authority. The Arabs who abandoned raiding to wage war for Islam's lords did so in the belief that the struggle would yield both earthly prizes and heavenly rewards. Rapaciousness and piety also motivated the knights who helped the Frankish monarchs to repel the Muslims in Europe, as well as the imperial guards of China and Japan who defended the sacred confines of their masters against profane intruders.

The more idealistic soldiers never demanded payment for their efforts, yet shrewd rulers were quick to compensate their men. "May God keep you safe and bring you much booty," Muhammad once told one of his commanders. When the warrior protested that he had not become a Muslim "for the sake of wealth", Muhammad reassured him. "Honest wealth," the Prophet avowed, "is good for an honest man."

The caliphs of the aristocratic Umayyad clan, who gained control of the Muslim world in the mid-seventh century, raised the sword of Islam against infidels from the Indus River to Gibraltar. Chief among the rulers' assets in these wars were mounted nomadic tribesmen, who adapted the hit-and-run tactics of desert raiding to large-scale campaigns.

The age of chivalry was born in Europe in the eighth century when lords wealthy enough to secure war-horses, weapons and armour pledged allegiance to the Frankish kings in their struggle against Islamic control of the Iberian Peninsula. Such support enabled Charlemagne not only to contain the Moors but to forge an empire from the Pyrenees to beyond the Rhine.

The emperors of China's Tang dynasty wielded the sceptre of power with a firm hand. Wary of the civil strife that had brought previous regimes to ruin, they established an elite imperial guard consisting of six regiments of infantrymen – all with halberds at the ready – and six regiments of cavalry; another three regiments of each protected the crown prince.

Following the example of Chinese rulers across the sea, the emperors of the Nara dynasty, which came to power in Japan in the eighth century, commissioned a corps of guards. Some of these defenders put up a fine front, but the practice of giving the posts to aristocratic youths with no military aptitude undermined the corps, and the dynasty ultimately paid a price.

THE PROPHET'S QUEST

1

Across much of the world, from the twilight forests of northern Europe to the golden plains of northern China, the opening decades of the seventh century echoed with the clash of swords and the cries of embattled armies. In Britain, long since abandoned by the legions of Rome, Angle and Saxon princelings fought among themselves for territory and supremacy. Visigothic invaders had seized much of Spain, and former barbarians called Lombards were expanding in Italy, threatening Rome itself. Far to the east, in India, the resplendent empire of the Guptas had shuddered into collapse. Some 70 local potentates now split the rich subcontinent among themselves, forming a mosaic of squabbling antagonism. China was deep in a stew of political turmoil as an unpopular emperor vainly tried to hold his throne in the face of dozens of rebellions flaring up simultaneously.

And in the age-old lands of the Middle East, two great imperial states confronted each other in mutual envy and suspicion. The empire of Byzantium – champion of Christianity, heir to ancient Rome – held sway over the eastern Mediterranean from its capital at Constantinople. Much troubled in the west by Germanic invaders, it was still the world's mightiest power – lord of Anatolia, Egypt and Syria and of all eastern Europe south of the Danube River. In AD 600, citizens of Constantinople firmly believed they resided at civilization's heart.

This conviction was hotly disputed by Byzantium's chief rival, the empire of Persia. From their capital at Ctesiphon on the Tigris River, in the Mesopotamian birthplace of human culture, Persia's rulers controlled a realm that stretched eastwards from the borders of Byzantium to the steppes of Russia and the mountains of Afghanistan. The scope of their power and the splendour of their court harked back to the days of Persia's first world empire a thousand years before. So did their conflict with the West. Successive Persian regimes had fought the Greeks and then fought the Romans. And now the Sassanians, as members of the current Persian dynasty were called, were caught up in a debilitating, off-and-on tug of war with Byzantium for ultimate control of the Middle East.

While the great powers fanned the flames of their antagonism, a mood of smouldering discontent spread through their subject populations. It expressed itself, partly, in religious strife. The Christian church had begun to dissipate its youthful vigour, squandering its energies in doctrinal disputes. Conflicts broke out between Christians and Jews, with murders and reprisals on both sides. Expectations took on an apocalyptic hue. When you see the kingdoms fighting among themselves, ran a popular Jewish adage of the time, "then look for the footsteps of the Messiah".

A messiah would indeed soon appear – though the deliverance he brought bore little resemblance to what the Jews had in mind, and they would never recognize him as a messenger of God. In a western Arabian trading city, on the dry stony

Less than a century after the prophet Muhammad proclaimed the new faith of Islam, Muslim armies had conquered an empire that stretched over 6,000 kilometres from the Indian Ocean to the Atlantic. The first four Muslim rulers — called caliphs — who succeeded Muhammad sent Arab forces bursting from the Arabian Peninsula to overwhelm Syria, Iraq, Palestine, Egypt and much of Persia. The caliphs of the ensuing Umayyad dynasty (661-750) extended the empire beyond the Indus River and fabled Samarkand to the borders of India and China in the east and across North Africa to Morocco and Spain in the west. In their conquests, Arab armies destroyed the Sassanid empire of Persia, severely crippled the Byzantine Empire and spread Islam through three continents.

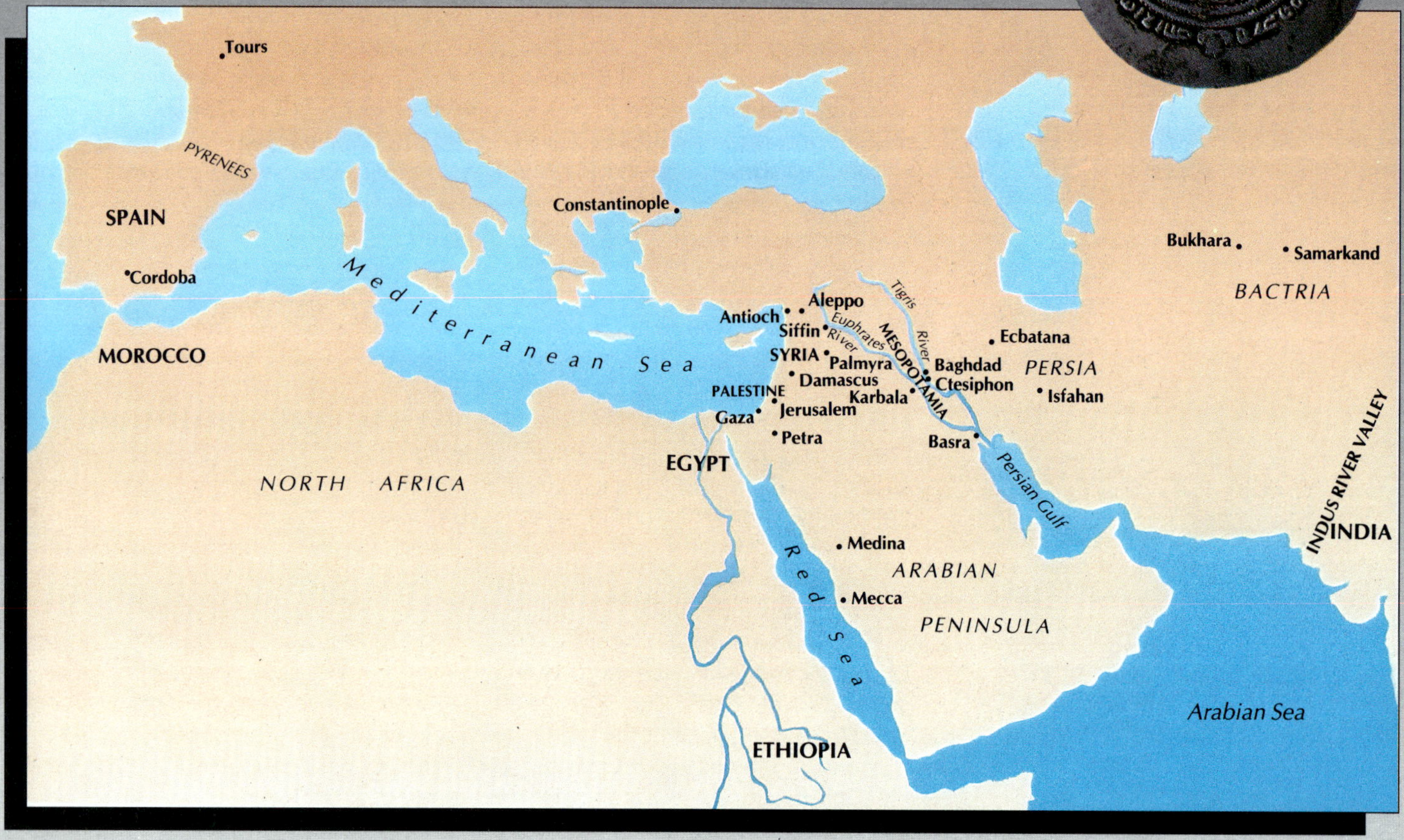

margin of the civilized world, an obscure middle-aged caravan trader named Muhammad ibn Abdulla was touched by divine inspiration and began to preach. His message was simple: submission to the will of a single, universal god, a promise of a judgment day of reward and punishment, and charity to the poor. But the repercussions of that message were profound. For Muhammad's words, caught up by his fellow Arabs, would resound throughout the hemisphere and shake the existing order to its foundations, shifting the balance of power in the Middle East and reshaping the outlines of world politics from his day until modern times.

Islam exploded upon the world with the sudden force of a desert whirlwind. With the cry *Allahu akbar* – God is great – ringing across the sands, Arabian armies began to sweep through Syria and Mesopotamia in 633. Within a decade, they had conquered Persia and Egypt and taken the holy city of Jerusalem. In 674, they were poised at the gates of Constantinople. By the early 700s, Islam's banners fluttered in the wind from Spain in the west to India in the east – an expanse of territory that made all previous empires seem minor by comparison.

Arab administrators ruling the countries conquered by Islam issued a variety of coinage – some of it adopted from the native money and some purely Muslim. The gold coin on the upper left portrays in Byzantine style the Umayyad caliph named Abd al-Malik, who holds the Sword of Islam, a symbol of Arab power. The silver dirham below it, minted in Persia, bears in Arabic script the name of an Arab governor, al-Hajaj ibn Yusuf, but the image is that of a Sassanian emperor. The gold coin on the right, shown front and back, carries Arabic writing rather than figurative decoration. Part of the inscription on the front says, "There is no God but God alone." The margin on the reverse announces that the coin was struck in Damascus in the year 78 of the Islamic calendar (AD 697-698).

This rapid triumphal expansion of Arab power was as breathtaking in its unexpectedness as in its scope. Nothing in the nature of Arabia's land or people seemed to suggest a capacity for zealous world conquest. Few regions on earth were so bereft of natural advantages. The Arabian Peninsula lay wedged between Africa and Mesopotamia like a forgotten appendage – more than 2.5 million square kilometres of sand wastes, gravel flats and lava fields, creased by dry riverbeds and dotted at rare intervals by date-palm oases. An L-shaped rim of mountains along the west and south coasts trapped a modest annual rainfall and offered reasonable, even inviting, living conditions. But most of the peninsula was bone dry and searingly hot. Years might pass before a single raindrop fell upon the Nafud Desert in the north, with its 90-metre-high sand dunes, or in the vast Rub al-Khali – the Empty Quarter – in the centre. When the rain did come, it fell in torrents, causing devastating flash floods. Yet no permanent river flowed within the peninsula.

Life under these conditions tended to be a hand-to-mouth scramble for existence in mud-brick settlements in the oases or among tent-dwelling herdsmen and camel drivers. No clear-cut indications survived to tell future generations just where Arabia's inhabitants came from, although the people were clearly Semitic in origin. By Islamic tradition, they traced their lineage back to Abraham, the ancestral patriarch of both the Arabs and the Jews.

Some time during the second millennium BC, the story went, Abraham left his family home at the ancient city of Ur in Mesopotamia (called Ur of the Chaldees in the Bible) and went to dwell in Palestine. His aged wife, Sarah, appeared to be barren, so at her urging Abraham wed a slave by the name of Hagar, who bore him a son, Ishmael. A number of years later, Sarah gave birth to a son of her own, Isaac. Because this second birth caused friction between the two women, Abraham took Hagar and Ishmael to the Valley of Mecca, an isolated caravan stop situated on the edge of Arabia's western mountains. He left them there with provisions and then returned to Sarah. Before long, Hagar was frantic with worry; she and her son were running out of water. But one day Ishmael dragged his heel through the sand and a spring of clear, cool water bubbled up beneath his foot. The spring became the well of Zamzam, which would later be a landmark to Muslim pilgrims. The new water source attracted other settlers, giving birth to the city of Mecca. Abraham visited Hagar and his eldest son, and with Ishmael he constructed the shrine that centuries later was to be the holiest place in Islam, the Kaba, embedding in its wall a sacred black stone of meteoric origin.

Ishmael married a woman from among the new settlers. According to tradition, his offspring became the Arabs, while the children of Abraham and Sarah's son Isaac became the Israelites. Some of Ishmael's descendants wandered down to the peninsula's southern extremity and settled among the people who dwelt in the rugged, 3,660-metre-high mountains of what would become Yemen. There they found conditions more amenable. The summer monsoons would sprinkle the land with a relatively generous 50 to 75 centimetres of rain a year, moisture enough to sustain agriculture. People caught the runoff in reservoirs and irrigation channels and led it to terraced fields on the mountain slopes, where they grew wheat, barley, melons, almonds, fruit trees and other staples of a prosperous, sedentary life.

As the centuries wore on, the farming villages grew into cities and the cities into kingdoms. Stone palaces of great luxury and sophistication rose among the mountain peaks, including a walled citadel at Sana that was 20 storeys high. Vast irrigation works transformed the high-country landscape. The people of a kingdom called Saba built an enormous dam at Marib, their capital, in about the year 750 BC, that controlled the region's water supply for the next thousand years.

Besides their agriculture, the South Arabians had another source of wealth. The region lay at the junction of several major trade routes, along which the luxuries of the East would be ferried to the growing empires of the eastern Mediterranean. Lateenrigged Arab dhows with their ballooning triangular sails — vessels that would remain almost unchanged into the modern era — would arrive from the Indian Ocean carrying gems, textiles and spices from India and China. Some might sail through the narrow straits between Yemen and Ethiopia and into the Red Sea. But to avoid areas troubled by conflict between the Byzantines and Persians, most merchants shifted their cargoes to caravans at the entrance to the Red Sea and travelled north overland, along the interior edge of the mountains to Palestine and Syria.

These caravans were enormous communities of people and animals, with as many as 300 merchants, drivers and guards and 2,500 camels. The value of the goods they hauled was staggering. In one venture, recorded in the Bible, the queen of Sheba — presumably Saba — arrived by caravan at King Solomon's court in Jerusalem with a royal ransom in gold, and more rare spices and precious stones than the Judeans had ever seen. The delighted king gave her "all that she desired", including, by one tradition, a son who founded a dynasty that ruled Ethiopia.

For all the riches shipped from the East, Arabia's most valuable trade goods for centuries were of local origin. On the dry inland slopes of the southern coastal mountains grew two varieties of gnarled, scrubby balsam trees. The resins that oozed from their trunks, frankincense and myrrh, were among the most precious items of the ancient world. Each had dozens of uses: in perfumes and cosmetics, in medicinal ointments, dissolved in wine as healing tonics, and in religious rituals. Dried and powdered frankincense was cast on to the coals of sacrificial altars so that the offerings would rise to heaven in a nimbus of fragrant smoke. The Romans used frankincense and myrrh in cremations to disguise the stench of burning flesh.

With firm control of the caravan trade and a monopoly on the production of the aromatic resins, South Arabia strode from prosperity to riches. Greek and Roman chroniclers of the first and second centuries AD marvelled over its wealth. The historian Strabo spared no adjectives in describing the "costly magnificence" of its palaces, with their alabaster statues and interior trim set with jewels. Scholars, relying on dubious hearsay, turned out multivolume studies of its geography and people. When Ptolemy of Alexandria, the most eminent cartographer of his day, mapped out the peninsula, he labelled the region *Arabia Felix* – Arabia the Blessed.

Few of civilization's refinements penetrated to Arabia's barren interior, however. This was the realm of the Bedouin, the true desert nomad, for whom life continued as it had for several thousand years: in an endless pilgrimage from pasture to oasis and back again, its rhythms as predictable as the march of the seasons.

In this desiccated land, the basic equation between human needs and natural assets tilted heavily on the side of hardship. Life was possible largely through the agency of a remarkable creature – the camel. It served the Bedouins as transport and provider of food and materials, as warhorse and as unit of exchange. A healthy adult camel could travel up to 100 kilometres a day across the desert carrying loads of about 180 kilograms. It could survive for three days without water in summer's blistering heat and even longer in winter. The Bedouins wove tents and ropes from its hair, tanned its skin into leather, burnt its dried dung as fuel, drank its milk and on occasion feasted on its flesh. Large sums – the dowry of a bride, or the payment to requite a blood feud – were computed in numbers of camels.

The other mainstay of Bedouin life was the date palm, its nourishing fruit obtained through trade with the oasis settlements. Besides providing an easily preserved food, the dates could be fermented into beer, the stones crushed into camel feed, and the palm fronds woven into baskets or used as construction material. The date palm, a proverb maintained, was "the mother and the aunt of the Arabs".

Despite its footloose habits, Bedouin society was knit together into a tight fabric of tribal loyalties and alliances. Clan members always tented together, gathering round clan wells and oases in the dry season and moving out to the same area of desert pasture when winter rains carpeted the sands with a thin, fleeting green. If several clans had a common ancestor – and most Arabs could trace their lineage back many generations – the clans together formed a tribe. The Banu Harith were descendants of Harith; the Banu Bakr descendants of a patriarchal Bakr.

Nothing in life was more important to an Arab than tribal allegiance; it was both law and religion. "Be loyal to thy tribe," sang a desert bard, "its claim upon its members is strong enough to make a husband give up his wife." In return for fealty, the tribe was honour bound to protect its members and succour them in time of need. An insult to one was an insult to all and demanded vengeance in kind. Yet within the tribal embrace, each member had a proud sense of independence and equality. The desert held no second-class citizens: all were subject to the same law of survival and the unbreakable ties of custom and lineage. Even the tribal sheikh held his position not by hereditary right, but by the agreement of his tribesmen.

The hard desert life led inevitably to competition among the tribes for the limited number of wells and grazing areas. A Bedouin might kill his last camel to feed a stranger, for that is what the desert code bade him do; but if he needed another camel, he simply took it. So armed bands were constantly galloping across the dunes to rustle the livestock from a rival's encampment or to waylay stragglers along the caravan routes. The object was plunder, not combat. Blood called for blood in the tribal ethic, and the random spilling of it could spark a feud that no one wanted. Even so, tribal feuds were constantly breaking out. One of the most famous, celebrated in song and legend, erupted in the fifth century between the

Muhammad's Mecca

In the early 600s, when Muhammad lived in Mecca as a trader, the city was a small but crowded place of about 3,000 inhabitants, most of whom lived in a cluster of flat-roofed dwellings made of stone and sun-dried brick. Mecca lay in a forbiddingly dry and sandy valley that was virtually surrounded by a double range of desolate, treeless hills. The only thing, in fact, that made life possible in this parched Arabian landscape was the fresh water bubbling from the well of Zamzam in the centre of Mecca. Next to the well in the town's square was a modest shrine known as the Kaba, a small box-like structure dedicated at that time to local Meccan deities. The Kaba would one day become the holiest place in the world for the followers of the new Islamic religion of which Muhammad was to be the prophet.

As an oasis, Mecca was a natural stopping place for the camel caravans taking goods from South Arabia to the bazaars in the great cities of Syria and Babylonia to the north and east. The people of Mecca doubtless profited from commerce with the caravans – and from fees that they charged the caravan owners to pass through – as well as from trading expeditions of their own. And Mecca already attracted pious folk who were intent on praying at the Kaba. After Muhammad's radiant faith burst upon the world, swarms of pilgrims would seek out the city where the Prophet was born.

Caravan tracks converged on Mecca from all points of the compass. At the centre of the oasis, a warren of narrow streets, was the clearing in which stood the Kaba and the well of Zamzam.

Bedouin nomads from the desert bartered with local traders in the arcaded shops of Mecca, placed at some distance from the Kaba *(background)*. In Muhammad's time the city's main products were woollen cloth and various leather goods, such as sandals, belts and saddles, as well as utilitarian articles used by passing caravans – basins and skins for water and oil.

Housing a sacred black stone – a meteorite – and covered by a woollen cloth with zigzag stripes, the Kaba stood about 3.5 metres tall as rebuilt in 608. Its door was elevated to make entry difficult for intruders. Its walls were made of alternating layers of stone and wood – an unusual method of construction in Arabia but common in neighbouring parts of Africa. Because Mecca lacked trees, the wood undoubtedly came some distance, probably from a ship wrecked on the Red Sea shore somewhere west of the city.

Taghlib and Bakr tribes and lasted for 40 years. Its cause: a Taghlib chieftain had accidentally wounded the favourite she-camel of a Banu Bakr matron.

Such incidents were the raw material for the desert Arabs' most highly developed art form. Always on the move, unable to experiment with architecture or other visual arts, they vented their creative energies in one direction only: the power of the spoken word. The classic Arabic of the desert was an extraordinarily expressive medium. Chanted by the fire at night, under the sweeping canopy of desert stars, and in the glimmering shadow of the dunes, the stately rhymed prose of the Bedouin saga took hold of people's souls and would not let them go. "The beauty of a man lies in the eloquence of his tongue," one adage declared. And any Arab so endowed was looked upon with awe, as if possessed by some supernatural force. So it would be with the words conveyed by Muhammad. Their resonant power would be seen as a miracle, conclusive proof that they were of divine origin.

Fiercely independent, proud of their skill at arms, the nomadic desert Arabs looked down their noses at their sedentary oasis cousins but could not have survived without them. The oasis settlements were the desert's gardens and marketplaces, supplying apricots, oranges, sugar cane, watermelons, pomegranates and, of course, the essential products of the date palm. Some oases were caravan stops, with bazaars where the Bedouin purchased weapons, tools, milk basins, clothing and many other necessities of desert life. In return, the nomads offered camels, milk, hides, and protection from raiders – or, to be precise, they agreed not to raid the place themselves. Alliances developed between certain oases and particular tribes, and a desert sheikh might keep a permanent dwelling in his adopted oasis.

Beliefs in the desert tended towards spirit worship. The landscape was said to be haunted by demons called jinns. There were evil spirits to guard against with amulets and charms, and tribal gods that required a token obeisance. The moon was seen as a benevolent spirit, and various stars were identified with clan deities. Certain natural features – trees, caves, desert springs, rocks of unusual aspect – were also venerated. Some achieved the status of shrines, within whose precincts all life was held sacred and all swords were kept sheathed.

The most important sanctuary was the Kaba at Mecca, with its sacred black meteorite. Mecca had arisen as a caravan stop in a barren ravine of the Hijaz, Arabia's mountainous western region, and in spite of its bleak surroundings maintained a jaunty, cosmopolitan air. Each year the caravans marched through on their way from the frankincense groves of South Arabia and across the desert from the seaports of the Persian Gulf. The visitors would buy provisions – and perhaps fresh camels – and leave a good bit of silver in return. In addition, the Meccans staged an annual religious festival that attracted thousands of desert tribesmen.

The visitors would barter in Mecca's bustling bazaars, feast on roast lamb and pilaf and exchange news with clansmen returning from distant pastures or trading ventures. Invariably, they would stop at the Kaba to worship Hubal, the chief resident deity, and the 360 lesser idols the shrine housed. (The people had long since strayed from exclusive allegiance to the single god of Abraham, for whom the shrine had originally been built.) At nearby Zamzam, the well found by Ishmael, visitors would sip the blessed waters and then hike to the summit of Mount Arafat, site of another shrine. Invariably, they would depart with their money belts lighter.

The annual mingling of tribesmen and the festive hubbub of voices from all parts of Arabia imposed a fleeting sense of Arab cultural unity. The city was controlled by the Quraysh, a powerful Hijaz tribe that worshipped a variety of gods. Other beliefs filtered in from the world beyond the peninsula, including the monotheism of both the Christians and the Jews. Converts to both religions had long been established on Arabia's perimeter, in Syria, and in the ancient kingdoms of South Arabia. At festival time the visitors would relate the biblical tales of Abraham, Moses and Jesus, along with their native tribal sagas. With its culture enriched by these ideas and its coffers swollen by the influx of visitors, Mecca at the turn of the seventh century was one of the leading cities of Arabia. Its position was only enhanced as political strife beyond the desert disrupted the traditional avenues of commerce.

South Arabia, however, had been experiencing a period of decline. As Christianity spread through the Western world, it brought a change in funerary customs. Christians favoured burial rather than cremation, and the result was a drop in the demand for frankincense. The resin was still used for ritual and cosmetic purposes, but it was no longer needed to mask the odour of smouldering funeral pyres.

South Arabia had also found itself caught up in the larger struggle for power between Byzantium and Sassanian Persia. Here religion played a key role. Christian churches had sprung up in the area over the years, and most of their members and clergy owed spiritual allegiance to Constantinople. (There were also Nestorian Christians, who were at odds with the Byzantine church.) Many Jews had taken up residence as farmers or traders, and some Arabs had been converted to Judaism. Such a hold had Judaism gained, in fact, that the ruling Yemenite prince, a handsome young man named Dhu Nuwas, converted to the faith. Concerned about the growing power of Christian Byzantium, Dhu Nuwas allied himself with Persia. Byzantium responded by urging one of its client states, the neighbouring Christian kingdom of Ethiopia, to invade. Dhu Nuwas drove back the first Ethiopian attempt, but the second, in 525, proved too strong for him. As the Prince's army crumbled round him, the chronicles recorded, he mounted his charger, "plunged into the waves of the sea, and was never seen again".

The Ethiopian onslaught brought down the economy of South Arabia. The invaders attempted to colonize, but with limited success. During their stay, the great Marib dam, linchpin of the region's irrigation network, burst open; local agriculture never recovered. Around 570, an Ethiopian army with a baggage train of elephants trudged north to attack Mecca. It was defeated, according to Islamic tradition, by birds that pelted it with hot stones from the fires of hell. (Other sources credited a smallpox epidemic.) Future Muslims would view the Year of the Elephant as a symbol of Allah's triumphant intervention.

Five years later came another invasion – this time from Persia. The Ethiopians, weakened and demoralized, quickly gave in. For the next half century, South Arabia remained a Persian satrapy, until liberated by the armies of Islam.

Similar tensions gripped the broad arc of desert north of the Arabian Peninsula, where the two great empires had each set up Arab buffer states. The Banu Ghassan, who hailed from the South Arabian desert, were Byzantine vassals who occupied the hinterlands of Jordan and Syria, including the ancient cities and territories of Petra and Palmyra. In return for a subsidy from Constantinople, they defended Byzantium's southern border from the increasingly ferocious assaults of Bedouin war parties. They also served as frontline troops against the forces of Persia.

Directly east of the Ghassanids, the Banu Laikhm performed a similar border-defence role for the Persians. The two tribes were constantly at war, and their battles progressed with all the nastiness of a family feud. They were also at odds over religion. Both tribes had converted to Christianity, but they belonged to sects whose doctrines were bitterly opposed. Although the issues might seem obscure to later Christians, they were considered fundamental at the time: the Ghassanids were Monophysites, who believed Christ was wholly divine, while the Laikhmids were Nestorians, who said Christ had a dual nature, both human and divine.

Even so, the two tribes had much in common: in the eyes of their overlords, both were difficult and restless. Early in the seventh century the Byzantine emperor Heraclius earned the Ghassanids' enmity by cutting their government subsidies. And Persia, alarmed by the Laikhmids' independent ways, installed its own governor in their territory. The result, in 604, was an invasion of Laikhmid country by other Bedouins, who pushed back the borders of the Persian empire in that region.

While the kingdoms along Arabia's northern borders slid into decline, the tribes farther south began to prosper. In the relatively stable Hijaz region, the enterprising merchants of Mecca flourished. The city's Quraysh leaders, astute in both barter and diplomacy, secured trade agreements at every quarter of the compass — with Persia, Byzantium, Ethiopia and Yemen. A caravan merchant could count on netting as much as 100 per cent from each venture. And so the money poured in, along with the attitudes and amenities of the outside world. It was in the midst of this climate of growing prosperity and social change that the prophet Muhammad began to preach submission to a single god.

Few sure details about Muhammad's early life would be passed on to later generations, but its general outline was to be reverently preserved in legends and in oral tradition. He was

The Delights of Music

Music flourished as never before during the period of Islam's rise, as the figures on this and the following pages attest. Some of it was solemnly liturgical, such as the Gregorian chants of the Christian Church. But much more, especially in the Islamic world, was secular and joyful — lively tunes played at weddings and feasts or by tumblers and clowns as part of their street-corner acts. The music of Islam was enriched by the spread of a variety of new instruments, most of them originating in Persia, Arabia and other Eastern countries. From these lands emerged no fewer than 32 variants of the lute, 28 of the recorder and 22 of the oboe. Music was a passion in far-off China, too; Tang dynasty rulers imported tunes and musicians from India, Burma and Korea. So popular was the art in China that imperial orchestras of the age included as many as 800 musicians.

Syrian flautist in an eighth-century fresco.

A Chinese drummer of the Tang dynasty.

born in Mecca around 570 — in the Year of the Elephant, the traditions say, when Ethiopia's troops marched against the city. His family belonged to the Hashemite clan, a branch of the ruling Quraysh tribe, and though respectable it was not among the wealthiest families. Abdulla, his father, died shortly before Muhammad's birth. His mother was left with a small estate consisting of one slave, five camels and a flock of sheep. As was the custom, she sent the orphaned infant to live with a Bedouin family in the desert, where the hard, simple life was thought to promote health and character. When Muhammad was five years old, she brought him home but died soon afterwards, and the child's grandfather took over his upbringing. Within two years, however, the grandfather also died.

Luckily, Muhammad had an almost endless supply of relatives. He was taken in by an uncle, Abu Talib, who managed to support a large family by his work in the caravan trade. Abu Talib assumed responsibility for the lad's upbringing, teaching him the delicate arts of buying and selling and the rudiments of tending livestock. According to one traditional story, Muhammad, at the age of 12, rode with his uncle on a trading venture to Syria, where he fell in with a Christian monk who soon discerned his messianic potential. In fact, there was little to distinguish the boy from any other bright Arab youth. There was nothing in particular to mark him as the prophet whose message would lead to the growth of a great world religion.

As Muhammad grew to manhood he began to display a number of rather distinguishing — even if simple — virtues. Intelligent and hardworking, he quickly earned a reputation for unusually sound judgment and total reliability in his dealings, and inspired loyalty and trust. In appearance he was handsome, of medium height and build, with

An animal-horn trumpeter of ninth-century Europe.

The Hebrew king David playing a harp.

a somewhat ruddy complexion, large, heavy-lashed eyes, slightly curly black hair and a luxuriant black beard. He walked with a firm and steady stride. However, at 25 years of age he was still unmarried.

Muhammad's uncle Abu Talib introduced the young man to a rich, 40-year-old Quraysh widow named Khadija. Khadija, an astute businesswoman who equipped caravans for the trek to Syria, hired Muhammad as her agent to lead one of her camel trains. Shortly afterwards, the couple married. By all indications, their union was a happy one. Khadija had plucked Muhammad from relatively humble status and elevated him to a position of wealth and responsibility. She bore him six children – four healthy daughters and two sons who died in infancy. While she lived he took no other wife, although custom would have applauded it. Yet Muhammad was not entirely content. Underneath his solid, judicious air ran currents of passionate sensitivity. Each year he would retire to a cave on Mount Hira in the nearby desert to meditate and pray for days on end.

There was much that troubled Muhammad. His early life had been filled with tragedy, and now the death of his sons had left him without an heir to succeed him. But beyond these purely personal concerns, much wider issues absorbed him. All round the city, in the bazaars and shrines of Mecca, the ancient tribal virtues of honour and generosity seemed to be eroding. Ties of family loyalty were gradually giving way to the grasping standards of the marketplace. Greed was replacing bravery as the password of the day. The influx of great wealth into Mecca's coffers was causing wide disparities between rich and poor; the old ideals of freedom and equality were no longer applicable. Muhammad, in his years of struggle as an orphaned, impoverished cousin to a powerful tribe, was only too familiar with the indignities of second-class citizenship.

Equally disturbing was the arrogant manner in which Mecca's rulers were using the Kaba and its annual hordes of free-spending pilgrims as a source of profit. With its 360 idols, the shrine had become a mockery of true religious feeling; more often

Chinese mixed orchestra playing panpipes and shepherd's flutes.

than not, its precincts were congested by pedlars hawking trinkets and talismans. Against this tainted backdrop, filtering in from across the desert, came the strains of monotheism from Christians and Jews, with its avowed compassion for the humble and downtrodden. A group of local Arabs, the Hanifs, also embraced the concept of a single deity and led quiet lives of worthy self-denial. Perhaps in the example of these enlightened faiths might be found a remedy for Mecca's social ills.

So Muhammad lingered in his desert cave, mulling over these solemn issues. Then one night in 610, during the month of Ramadan, he heard a tinkling of bells. A disembodied voice cried out in majestic tones – later tradition would assign it to the archangel Gabriel. "Recite!" it commanded. Muhammad felt as if he were being gripped by great unseen hands and then released. He was terror-stricken. "What shall I recite?" he asked. The voice repeated its injunction. "In the name of thy Lord the Creator, who created mankind from a clot of blood, recite!" As the voice went on to speak of the nature of Allah, Muhammad memorized and recited everything that was said. Finally, the angel withdrew.

Deeply distressed, Muhammad hastened home to confide his strange story to Khadija. Had he gone mad? Was he possessed by an evil jinn? Khadija comforted him and then called in her cousin, an elderly convert to Christianity who was wise in religious matters. No, the Christian declared, Muhammad had not gone insane; he had experienced a true revelation similar to those God had allowed Moses and the prophets, and Muhammad must submit to it.

Obediently, Muhammad awaited further visitations. Time and again over many months the angel reappeared, as he had on that initial Night of Power and Excellence. (Future Muslims would commemorate that first night on its anniversary by staying awake and praying until first light.) Gabriel said Muhammad was "a messenger to instruct mankind" and on each visit delivered new insights and teachings. The divine messages flooded Muhammad's being "like the breaking of the dawn", he later said, and left him shaken. "Never once did I receive a revelation," he reported, "without thinking that my soul had been torn away from me."

The angel's message followed much the same lines taken centuries earlier by the biblical prophets. There were dire warnings against idolatry and the affirmation of a single god – in this case, called Allah. Moral reform played an essential role, with added emphasis on charity to the poor. Allah was portrayed as justly vengeful but compassionate, quick to punish injustice but generously forgiving to anyone who abandoned evil and submitted to his commands. "Give glory to your Lord and seek his pardon," the angel declared, "He is ever disposed to mercy." Beyond this came a powerful vision of life after death, to be spent in either a garden-like paradise or a fiery hell, as the case demanded – and an announcement of Judgment Day, on which it would be decided who went where: *When Earth is rocked in her last convulsion . . . then whoever has done an atom's weight of good shall see it, and whoever has done an atom's weight of evil shall see it also.*

Thus was revealed one of the basic principles of Islam – Arabic for "submitting to God's will". For the 40-year-old businessman charged with delivering those principles, the task must have seemed formidable. Yet with the voice of the angel ringing in his ears, he began to spread God's word – secretly at first, addressing small gatherings on remote hillsides and in private homes, out of sight of the city's powers. His earliest converts were drawn, understandably, from his own immediate household – his wife, a favourite slave whom he had freed and his cousin Ali, who was the son of his former guardian Abu Talib. A wealthy merchant and close friend, Abu Bakr, became an early supporter. Muhammad also attracted some discontented members of lesser clans and even some ambitious young men from Mecca's most influential families who were ready for social change. There was Uthman, a quiet youth from a leading Quraysh family, who would play a vital role in the spread of Islam. So would the strong-willed Umar ibn al-Khattab, recruited from a minor Quraysh branch. Islam's message also appealed directly to Mecca's lowest strata – the enslaved, the impoverished, the dispossessed. In 613, three

"Three things make the heart live long: looking at water, at greenery and at a beautiful face."

years after receiving his first revelation, Muhammad began preaching to the public.

As Muhammad gained adherents, called Muslims (literally, those who surrender), Islam's nascent but growing power began to alarm the city's aristocratic governors. The Prophet's decrees against idolatry struck hard at the system of Kaba pilgrimages, a prime source of municipal wealth. His espousal of the poor discomforted the rich. One Islamic proposal that they found particularly obnoxious was *zakat*, a mandatory annual contribution to charity of 2.5 per cent of a family's excess wealth – that is, of any money or possessions not actually needed for the family's own support. *Zakat* literally meant "to purify", and this yearly contribution to the poor was intended to help a Muslim striving for purity. The city fathers, led by the powerful Umayyad branch of the Quraysh tribe, first launched a campaign of ridicule, then one of violent harassment. An elder of Muhammad's own Hashemite clan turned against him, and some of his followers fled to Ethiopia. But Muhammad remained, continuing to preach and awaiting his opportunity.

The opportunity came from the oasis town of Yathrib, some 400 kilometres to the north, where two mutually hostile resident Arab tribes – the Aws and the Khazraj – were frequently fighting with each other or with the several Jewish clans that also lived there. On pilgrimages to Mecca, Arabs from both tribes heard Muhammad's message and were converted to Islam. Over the next couple of years, these new Muslims urged Muhammad to take up residence in their town, because in Mecca his liberty and life were threatened. His followers were already being persecuted. In 622, he journeyed to Yathrib, accompanied by his friend Abu Bakr. This exodus from Mecca became known as the *hijra* – literally, the flight – usually spelt hegira in English. The event would be indelibly etched on the Islamic faith and calendar. Thereafter, Muslims would number each passing year from that time with the notation AH, which represented After Hegira. And the oasis itself would acquire a new name — Medina, city of the Prophet.

Muhammad was armed with considerable moral authority. He continued to preach and make converts, but he also worked to sort out Medina's political tangles. In fact, his words began to deal increasingly with worldly matters. In Islam, there would be no differentiation between religious and secular concerns. All aspects of life were governed by the doctrines of the faith. Muhammad's preachings focused on such down-to-earth matters as marriage and divorce, inheritance,

"A man without a brother is like a left hand without a right hand."

Like the Chinese, the Arabs placed great value on beautiful calligraphy. In the world of Islam, writing was thought to have been invented by Allah, and the artful use of the pen was therefore a divine skill. So exalted was writing that panels of enlarged script were used along with geometric designs to decorate many buildings; the great Islamic palace, the Alhambra in Grenada, Spain, abounds with inscriptions. The classic form of writing was Kufic; here two ancient Arabic sayings — one by the prophet Muhammad *(left)* and the other *(right)* by the fourth caliph, Ali ibn abi Talib — are shown rendered in Kufic with translations.

punishments for theft and other crimes, and even questions of diet and personal hygiene. He prescribed rules for domestic behaviour and carefully spelt out the relationships between his followers and nonbelievers. All of his precepts were presented as revelations from the Almighty, although some seemed to be derived from tribal custom. As both seer and statesman, Muhammad now bore responsibility for a sizable Islamic community, and he adroitly sought to blend both roles.

His seat of operations was a mud-brick compound in the oasis' centre, with a row of domestic cabins facing a large walled courtyard. The cabins housed his growing family, for during the last dark years in Mecca Khadija had died, and the Prophet had taken several other wives. The courtyard was the site where Muhammad, in typical Arab fashion, conducted his business — judging disputes, receiving town delegates and addressing his followers. It also served as a place of worship.

Here Muhammad would preach the message revealed by God, while his followers memorized his words or inscribed them on scraps of parchment, palm leaves or leather — whatever came to hand. (Later, Islamic scholars would gather these oral and written fragments to compile the Koran, Islam's sacred book.) Here also, at sunrise, sunset and other fixed times, the community would perform rites of devotion, intoning: "Praise be to Allah, Lord of Creation, the Compassionate, the Merciful, Thee alone we worship, and to Thee alone we pray for help." Then they would prostrate themselves, in the manner of the Jews, with their heads towards Jerusalem, a city of significance in the lives of Abraham and other prophets, including Jesus. Later, Muhammad conveyed a command from Allah that Muslims should instead pray in the direction of Abraham's shrine in Mecca, the Kaba.

Muhammad had little means of material support. The main business of the oasis was date farming, and for this the émigrés from Mecca, former traders and caravan

These beautifully detailed and delicately coloured mosaics from the interior of the Great Mosque in Damascus offer a virtual catalogue of Muslim architecture: from ornate palaces *(right)* and many-pillared public buildings *(far right)* to clusters of modest village houses *(above)* with their characteristic narrow windows high under the eaves. Executed around 706, the Damascus mosaics show how swiftly and thoroughly Islamic craftsmen absorbed the artistic techniques of conquered lands, especially those of the Byzantine Empire, where mosaic work had long flourished.

drivers, had virtually no aptitude. They were living, for the most part, on hand-outs from their Arab hosts. Self-sufficiency was essential if Islam was to grow and flourish. It was in the time-honoured tradition of the desert for a people in need to attain their material requirements by raiding. And in this instance, the Muslims had a natural enemy in the Quraysh from Mecca, who had been persecuting them. So Muhammad's men began raiding Quraysh caravans on the road to Syria.

The first forays were failures. The Muslims, always outnumbered, either missed intercepting the caravans or were easily rebuffed by superior force. No blood was shed and no booty seized. Then early in 624, a Muslim raiding party attacked a camel train near Mecca, killing one of the escorts. The next scheduled shipment, a larger caravan of some 70 merchants carrying 50,000 dinars' worth of goods, was due to pass by soon on its return trip from Gaza to Mecca. All the leading Quraysh families had invested in it. To ensure the safe arrival of the valuable caravan they mustered a force comprising some 950 armed warriors, which quickly made its way north from the city to provide an escort.

Muhammad's band, perhaps 300 strong, lay hidden in ambush round a well at Badr, a village near Medina. The site was cleverly chosen. As the force from Mecca approached the well, the Muslims struck, unleashing a hail of arrows. Earlier, the Prophet had issued a decree: "Not one who fights this day and bears himself with steadfast courage . . . shall meet his death without Allah bringing him to paradise!" Spurred on by this promise, the followers of Islam hurled themselves at the Meccans, putting them to rout. As the victors soon discovered, unfortunately, the trading caravan they coveted had escaped by taking a different route, but defeating the Quraysh warriors was a momentous feat in itself, and it provided some spoils: 150 camels, 10 horses, a quantity of arms and armour, and numerous captives to be held for ransom. Muhammad kept part of the booty to distribute to the needy and gave the rest in equal portions to his soldiers. The Battle of Badr gave an enormous boost to the morale and prestige of Muhammad and his followers. It was seen as a tangible sign of God's favour, a divine endorsement of Islam. The Prophet became a widely admired figure, even among the Bedouin tribesmen who patrolled the desert trade routes, for whom there was no success like success in battle.

Although a defeat the following year by a Quraysh force on the slopes of Mount Uhud cost the Muslims prestige in the eyes of the Bedouins, the Quraysh establishment still viewed Muhammad's growing power as a dangerous challenge. The attacks on its caravans could not be allowed to continue. So in the spring of 627, a Meccan army of 10,000 men set out for Medina, trekking north through the desert wastes, confident of a swift and overwhelming triumph. But when they reached Medina they were quickly disillusioned. Muhammad, on learning of the enemy's move, had ordered his followers to dig an enormous ditch across the approaches to Medina that were vulnerable to cavalry attack – a stratagem that tradition said was suggested by a convert from imperial Persia. The Meccans drew up their ranks and tried several abortive assaults over the next two weeks. Finally, with their water and provisions running out, they turned round and marched home.

The Battle of the Ditch may have been no great military triumph, but it confirmed Muhammad's status as a leader to be reckoned with. It also aroused his ill will towards Medina's last group of Jewish residents. After both previous battles, at Badr and Uhud, one of the local Jewish clans had been accused of conspiring with the enemy. Muhammad, believing the charges, had run those families out of town. Now he learnt that the last Jewish clan, named Banu Qurayza, had collaborated with the Meccans. The Muslim response was ruthless. The Jewish men were put to the sword, and the women and children were sold into slavery. Muslim and Jew were now fixed in an attitude of intense mutual animosity that would be a recurring debilitating feature of Middle Eastern life and politics.

With their army's fiasco at Medina, the Meccans saw all of their worst fears realized. The Bedouin tribes of the Hijaz started breaking their ties of fealty to Mecca's leaders, preferring to deal with Muhammad. The Muslims gained control of more and more trade routes. Playing from strength, Muhammad negotiated a truce with the Quraysh that allowed him to travel to Mecca for the pilgrimage.

This was the chance he had been waiting for. Once again in the city of his birth, Muhammad began to gather fresh converts, including at least one of the city's military leaders. Finally, in 630, he felt powerful enough to return in force. Leading an army of 10,000 men, he advanced on the city gates. The Quraysh leaders, overawed, quickly submitted. Little blood was shed, and no reprisals were taken. En masse, the Meccans embraced the new religion.

Submission to Allah was remarkably painless, in fact. Muhammad dedicated the Kaba to the one true god, Allah, and cleansed the shrine of its numerous idols. But to the relief of the merchants of Mecca, the pilgrimages would continue under Islam. Indeed, the hajj, or pilgrimage to Mecca, was made obligatory for all believers. The caravan traders resumed their journeys under the protective shield of Islam. Their single new financial burden was *zakat,* the contribution to the poor.

Muhammad returned in triumph to Medina, his adopted capital. The early trickle of delegates from the desert tribes now swelled to a flood. In return for guarantees of independence and the right to continue their nomadic life, the Bedouins agreed to be loyal to Muhammad and to pay *zakat*. Most apparently also accepted Islam. Fragile as this pact would prove to be, it was an extraordinary achievement. For the first time, most of Arabia was united under one banner, that of Islam and its charismatic leader. In a final exhortation, Muhammad stated: "Know that every Muslim is a brother to every other Muslim and that you are now one brotherhood."

The mission of the Prophet had come to an end. At more than 60 years of age, he was stricken by a sudden illness. He retired to the cabin of his favourite wife, Aisha, and appointed Aisha's father, his old friend Abu Bakr, to lead the public worship in his place. Then on June 8, 632, Allah took his soul. Muhammad's death threw the Muslim community into crisis. While no one had regarded him as immortal, neither had anyone foreseen his immediate loss or thought to face its consequences. Islam may have cast a broad net, but one man had held the strands. All edicts of law, all acts of government, all strategic decisions had been Muhammad's alone. And according to the orthodox version of events, that accepted by most Muslims, no provision had been made for a successor.

In traditional Arab society, tribal leaders were chosen by consensus. A clan's elders met and hammered out an agreement whereby one of them would be named sheikh. But Islam, in theory at least, superseded clan loyalties. In the confusion of the moment, a number of rival groups claimed pre-eminence. The native Medinans formed one party and the early converts from Mecca another; each asserted its authority to select the Prophet's successor. Finally, a compromise candidate was elected: Abu Bakr – gentle, pious, wise with the understanding of his 60 years, and Muhammad's earliest supporter outside his immediate family. It seemed a perfect choice, but one faction was not completely satisfied. Muhammad's closest male relative was his young cousin Ali, who had grown up in the Prophet's household, married Muhammad's daughter Fatima, and fathered the only two surviving grandsons of the great man. Some Muslims felt that Ali, as Muhammad's natural heir, should have been made the new chief of state.

Abu Bakr took the title caliph – successor. His first task was to deal with mass defections by many Arab tribes. The tribes maintained that they had pledged their loyalty to a leader, not to an ideology, and at the Prophet's death they considered themselves released from further obligation. But any shrinking of Islam's influence at this crucial moment would have been disastrous for Muhammad's successors. So the new caliph sent his best generals to bring the defectors back into the fold. By 634, after two years of bloody conflict, the banners of Islam fluttered triumphantly across Arabia and beyond, to the border lands of Syria and Iraq.

In that period, Abu Bakr had succumbed to his advancing years, and another caliph now assumed command: Umar ibn al-Khattab. The strongest and most decisive of Muhammad's close companions, Umar felt his mission to be the vigorous expansion of Islam's realm. Besides spreading the faith, an expansionist policy perhaps also promised an outlet for the warlike instincts of the Bedouins. Instead of harassing Medina or feuding among themselves, they could ride against the infidel to uphold the Islamic principle of jihad, or "struggle in the way of God". Jihad implied, at first, a battle of conscience against the temptations of Satan. But it quickly took on a heroic, military resonance – a holy war against nonbelievers.

And so the march began. Led by Quraysh generals – in particular the masterful Khalid ibn al-Walid, "the Sword of Allah" – the Arabs swept east into Mesopotamia, then north through Palestine and Syria. In 635, they took Damascus after a six-month-long siege. This was Byzantine territory, and when the armies of Constantinople marched south to meet them, the Muslims faded into the desert to await their chance. It came the next year at Yarmak, a river in Jordan; 25,000 strong, they galloped out of the haze of a desert sandstorm to defeat a Byzantine force twice that size. The emperor's brother Theodorus died in the battle. Then the Syrian cities of Antioch and Aleppo fell. The Muslims seized Jerusalem in 637.

Once again they turned east, marching through southern Iraq into the heartland of Sassanian Persia. They met the Persian armies at al-Qadisiya in 637, in another dust storm, and put them to rout. Crossing the Tigris, they reached Ctesiphon, the Sassanian capital, and took it easily. At Ctesiphon, the desert warriors paused to gaze at the wonders of the Middle East's most sumptuous city, its lavish palaces filled with shimmering tapestries and furniture, its storerooms brimming with gold. Some of the Arabs had never seen gold before, did not know its value, and traded their shares of it for equal volumes of silver. Mistaking camphor for salt, they flavoured their cooking with the medicinal crystals. In time, they moved on. Ahead of them lay the ancient strongholds of the Iranian plateau: Isfahan; Nihavand and Ecbatana in the land of the Medes; and Istakhr, birthplace of the Sassanian empire. Each fell. In little more than a decade, the Muslims swept east to India.

The fierce efficiency of the desert warriors and their fervour under Islam contributed to this explosive campaign of conquest. Small in numbers and nimble in tactics, they campaigned in a manner that confounded their opponents. They lived off the land and thus depended on no vulnerable lines of supply. Using the desert as their sanctuary, they could pick the time and place for battle, darting out to attack at opportune moments, then retreating into the sandy wastes that discouraged pursuit. The small, tough Arab horse was their mount in battle. But their camels gave them staying power, providing both sustenance and transport over the long arid distances of their far-reaching campaigns.

Another advantage was the weakened condition of the two great empires opposing them. Byzantium and Persia had exhausted their powers over centuries of antagonism and war with each other, depleting their economies and taxing the loyalty of their subjects. Internal political problems troubled both of them. Each relied on Arab buffer states to protect its desert borders – not a strategically sound position in the face of Islam's Pan-Arabic crusade.

Then there was the tremendous appeal of the religion itself. Islam's basic demands were simple. There were only five requirements, called the Five Pillars: acknowledging that there was no god but Allah and that Muhammad was his messenger; praying five times a day while facing Mecca; fasting during the month of Ramadan; paying *zakat*; and, if possible, making at least one hajj, or pilgrimage to Mecca. Islam's rewards were also enticing, particularly for Arabs. Not only would they join their ethnic brothers in a unifying movement of great spiritual force, but they would also share in the rewards of victory. Islam's simple codes also offered relief from the burdens of Byzantine or Persian imperial rule. As a result, Islam's expansion came as much by conversion as by conquest. Consider the Ghassanids, Byzantium's Arab vassals

Abstract plant fronds decorate this plate of lustreware made in Muslim-ruled Mesopotamia in the ninth century. Arabian craftsmen learnt the technique of making lustreware in conquered Egypt – and improved on it. The Egyptians had long made glass objects with shiny surfaces by applying pigments that contained metallic compounds, then firing them in a kiln in such a way that the metals were turned into glossy oxides. Islamic artisans used the process to decorate pottery. The Arabic writing round the plate's border repeats the phrase "good fortune to the owner".

in Syria. As a cost-cutting measure, the emperor had suspended his subsidy for their border-patrol duties, earning their immediate rancour. Furthermore, they belonged to a Christian sect, the Monophysites, that Constantinople had strongly censured on grounds of doctrine. So as Muslim troops charged north into Syria, the Ghassanids knew what to do: they simply switched loyalties, embracing Islam.

A similar dissatisfaction prevailed in Egypt, where taxes were heavy and the populace restive, and where a theological dispute had broken out between Constantinople and the local Coptic patriarch. When a Muslim general marched his army across the border in 639, many people greeted the newcomers as liberators. Many difficult battles had to be fought against Byzantine garrisons, including a year-long siege of Alexandria, the capital, but by 642, all Egypt was in Arab hands.

The changeover to Muslim rule was in most cases remarkably smooth and painless. Umar the caliph, holding court from a simple mud-brick compound in Medina, proved to be a wise and highly effective administrator. The conquered peoples were allowed to keep their own laws and follow their own religious beliefs. No one was forced to convert to Islam. Local administrators continued at their posts under the supervision of a senior Arab official. Taxes were generally lighter than under the imperial regimes, and justice was strictly enforced. As a native of Syria remarked: "We like your rule and justice far better than the state of oppression and tyranny under which we have been living."

In 644, Umar was struck down at the zenith of his powers. As he was preparing to lead the morning prayers in the Medina mosque, Umar was assassinated by a Persian slave, who stabbed him with a poisoned dagger. Umar would be held in reverence as the greatest of the early caliphs.

On his deathbed, Umar made arrangements for choosing his successor. The man selected was Uthman, another early convert known for his piety and good nature. Uthman was also a member of the Umayyad clan, the most powerful and aristocratic branch of the powerful Quraysh, and thus had the backing of Mecca's mercantile establishment. Under Uthman the Muslim domain expanded even farther — into Armenia and Asia Minor and into Bactria and other central Asian territories — but the decade of major conquest was now over. And a subtle transformation gradually started to reshape the character of the Islamic regime. Vast wealth began pouring in from the recently acquired territories, and with it came all the vices of corruption and easy living. The garrison towns were expanding from clusters of soldiers' tents into thriving brick communities with mosques, bazaars and artisans' workshops. Both Mecca and Medina grew prosperous. The simple austerity of early Islam began to slide away.

A few years earlier, Umar had dismissed his best general — Khalid, the Sword of Allah — for bathing in wine and hiring poets to sing his praises. Umar himself had slept on a bed of palm leaves and worn the same woollen tunic until it came apart in tatters. Uthman, on the other hand, despite his devout and mild

Favours were dispensed and mandates announced to the people of conquered Palestine from this magnificent diwan, or throne room, part of the Islamic palace of Khirbat al-Mafjar in the Jordan River valley. The local ruler, or caliph, held court from the partially domed alcove on the right, while those awaiting his decisions sat on benches along the walls of the main room, which was brightly lit by the windows in the dome above. Much of the plaster was painted to look like marble; the floor of the caliph's alcove *(inset)* was decorated with a mosaic of a tree and animals; the lion which is shown attacking a gazelle may have symbolized imperial Islam's power.

temperament, increased his already considerable personal wealth during his rule. He also favoured Umayyad relatives when making appointments to important posts – a policy that rankled other Muslims from lesser tribes.

Dissatisfaction simmered in the garrison towns. The tribal warriors, their swords now sheathed, were growing restless, and Uthman lacked the decisiveness to control them. The first revolt broke out in 655 at Kufa, near Ctesiphon in present-day Iraq. Other mutinies followed. A delegation arrived from Egypt demanding that Uthman abdicate. When the Caliph refused, the Egyptian emissaries stormed the palace, where they found him reading the Koran. They cut him down on the spot.

This regicidal sword thrust opened a wound in Islam that would never heal. The next caliph to be chosen was the Prophet's cousin Ali, who had lost in the first election so many years earlier. His accession now was a triumph for the anti-Umayyad opposition and for a faction of "legitimists" who believed that rule over Islam should descend by inheritance to Muhammad's closest male heir. But there were many who disagreed. The loudest outcry came from Aisha, the Prophet's widow, who had long been at odds with Ali over an old family squabble. She joined forces with two elders from Mecca, named Talha and Zubayr, who had their own designs on the caliphate, and the three proceeded to Basra in Iraq. There they raised an army and delivered their challenge.

Ali was hardly a skilful politician, but he was no coward. Marching at the head of his own force of warriors, he hurried to Iraq. At Kufa, site of the first revolt and a stronghold of pious fervour, he picked up more supporters. The two sides met outside Basra, with Aisha riding on to the field on a camel to witness the fray. Any hopes she harboured were quickly dashed. Ali's men won in a particularly bloody engagement. The two rebel elders died fighting, along with 13,000 others, and Aisha was sent back home to Medina in disgrace. The Battle of the Camel was the first major clash between Muslim and Muslim, and it set an ominous precedent.

A more serious challenge arose in Damascus, which was ruled by the assassinated caliph's Umayyad cousin Muawiya. Muawiya believed that Ali had not attempted to bring Uthman's assassins to justice. Crying vengeance, he raised as his banner Uthman's bloodied shirt. When Ali called upon him to resign, he refused.

An armed confrontation was inevitable, and it occurred in 657 near the ruined Roman town of Siffin on the Euphrates. At first, the tide of battle ran in Ali's favour. But Muawiya, a wily and resourceful campaigner, countered with an ingenious ploy: he ordered his men to stick pages of the Koran on their spear tips. They then advanced, crying, "Let God decide." No devout Muslim could strike down God's book. There was a call for arbitration and Ali, against his better judgment, was forced to comply. Muawiya returned to Damascus, satisfied with his day's work. Ali marched back to Kufa, his adopted capital, having suffered a moral defeat. Slowly, his prestige declined. A group of former supporters, the Kharijites, staged a revolt that he barely quelled. Then in 661, he fell to a Kharijite's dagger.

Ali's death marked the end of an era. Muhammad's first four successors, known to Arab chroniclers as the "rightly guided" caliphs, were men of deep piety and commitment. All four were related to the Prophet, and were among his first converts. They had reigned at a time of exuberant change and expansion, when Islam was in its first, purest flower, when zeal for Allah seemed the highest good, and before the joys of conquest had hardened into the ponderous structures of imperial rule. But Islam now was an empire, the largest on earth, and it needed a governor

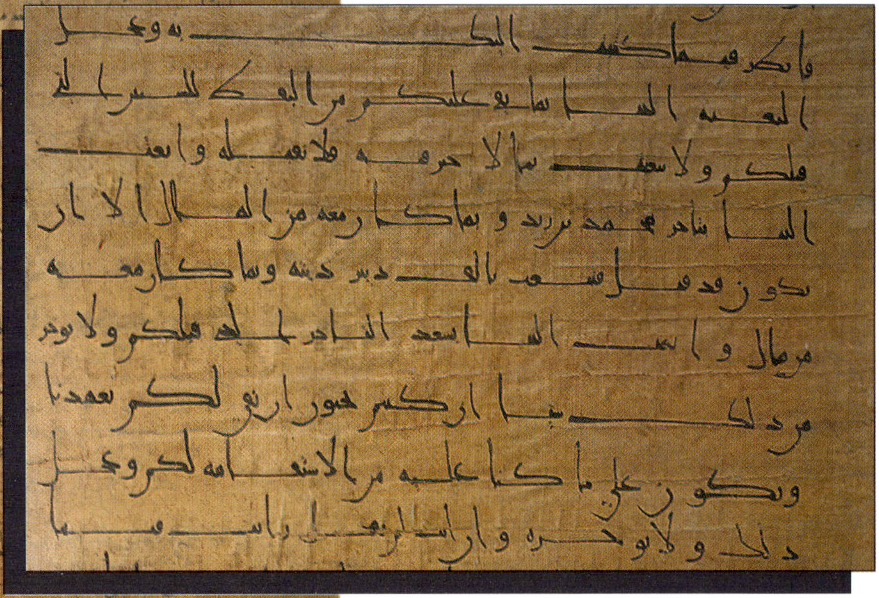

who could gather the reins of power and play them with skill and determination. Muawiya believed there was no better candidate than himself.

First Syria, then, gradually, the rest of the empire hailed Muawiya as caliph. When the partisans at Kufa proposed Ali's eldest son, Hasan, Muawiya knew just how to deal with them. Upon the offer of a generous, life-long income, Hasan renounced his claim; he retired to a harem in Medina where, by one account, he married – and divorced – some 90 Arab beauties before he died at the age of 45.

Muawiya made his capital at Damascus, where the groundwork for his administration was already firmly in place. The apparatus of government, inherited from Roman times, retained much of its former imperial structure. Christian scribes filled many key posts and conducted their business in Greek or in Aramaic. The Caliph's chief secretary was a Christian. In dealing with his fellow Arabs – whose sense of racial superiority he took care to flatter – the Caliph represented himself as a tribal sheikh, as the first among equals. But his control over the empire was never in doubt – he was a masterly politician. "Let a single hair bind me to my people, and I will not let it snap," the Caliph said; "when they pull, I loosen, and if they loosen, I pull."

A firmer hand was needed in Iraq, where rebellious groups still caused trouble. Here the Caliph appointed a series of Arab governors who were ruthless in stamping out dissent. In Basra, the governor, speaking from the main mosque, announced a dusk-to-dawn curfew: "Beware of prowling at night; I will kill everyone who is found in the streets at night." But order did prevail in the region, along with a rough but even-handed justice.

Muawiya was the first in a line of Umayyad caliphs that would govern the empire for nearly a century. All of his Umayyad successors were his direct descendants – a transition to dynastic rule that he achieved simply by naming his eldest son to succeed him. In a bow to desert tradition, he obtained the consensus of his Arab advisers and tribal chieftains, but precedent was already set. Elective theocracy was replaced by the hereditary process of imperial regimes the world over.

Under the Umayyads, the government of Islam continued to follow the increasingly secular path laid out by Muawiya, its dynastic founder. Mecca and Medina remained as religious centres, the twin hubs of piety and theological concern. But the power had moved irrevocably to

The long arm of Muslim authority stretched beyond the conquered lands, as shown by this letter *(left)* written on papyrus in 758 by Moussa ibn Kab, Arab prefect of Egypt. In it, he demands that Nubia's king honour certain agreements – including safe passage for Egyptians – and asks about a merchant who had been held there and possibly murdered. Part of the Kufic writing in the inset reads: "Send to us the merchant of Muhammad ibn Zayd and the wealth that was with him, unless he has been killed, in which case send the thousand dinars, his blood money."

worldly, cosmopolitan Damascus. At the same time, the swirling forces of political and cultural upheaval, set in motion with the conquest of highly civilized lands by a tribal people, began to settle into a stable social order.The Arab conquerors, as the ruling warrior caste, presided at the top of the social pyramid. A government stipend supplied part of their material needs. Many acquired large landed estates, despite an early ban against owning property outside Arabia. Many still profited from the caravan trade. Their only financial obligation was payment of *zakat.*

But a problem arose with the increasing number of foreign subjects who converted to Islam. So many non-Arabs embraced the new faith that they soon outnumbered their Arab rulers, who thus found themselves in an embarrassing double bind. Muhammad had directed his message to his fellow Arabs; yet he also had decreed that all believers should be treated as brothers. How could an Arab have a non-Arab brother? And how could an Arab Muslim retain his lofty status if he had to share it with everyone else? There was also a financial complication: while Muslims paid *zakat,* non-Muslims were subject to heavier taxes, including a head tax and levies on property, that provided most of the state's funding. Many conversions were prompted by the hope of escaping these fees. But without them, the state would go bankrupt. So new land taxes were imposed without any regard to who owned the property, Arab or non-Arab, Muslim or nonbeliever. In other respects, the *mawalis,* or non-Arab Muslims, remained second-class citizens.

Farther down the social pyramid were the Jews and Christians – the "People of the Book", as the Koran called them. They were given full religious freedom and, on payment of the head tax, exemption from military service – a benefit later extended to the monotheistic Zoroastrians of Persia. The people from the desert could only marvel at the cultural sophistication of these three groups, who tended to fill the ranks of government officialdom but were the Arabs' inferiors socially. At the bottom of the pyramid were the slaves – Greeks, Turks, Armenians, Berbers and black Africans who were taken in conquest and generally sold for profit.

As time went on, the rulers in Damascus and their deputies in the eastern capitals began to acquire the urban polish of their subjects. In 696, the caliph Abd al-Malik decreed that Arabic would be the official language of the empire, and he replaced the old Byzantine and Sassanian currencies with new Arabic coins stamped with Islamic inscriptions. A distinctive new culture began to take shape, one that blended the august heritage of Rome and Persia with the lessons of the Prophet and the resonant cadences of the Arabic tongue. For all their racial pride, the Arabs had a great respect for the achievements of past civilizations, for scholarship, and particularly for the written word. Scribes began to study works of the ancients, including the science and mathematics of the Greeks. The translation into Arabic of these half-forgotten texts led to an intellectual awakening that would mould Arabic thought down the centuries – and preserve a heritage in danger of vanishing.

Under the Umayyads a new wave of conquests was launched, extending the empire to its utmost dimension. Muawiya had set it going with advances in North Africa and in eastern Persia. But his true objective was Byzantium. Mobilizing a navy, Islam's first, he swept the Mediterranean clear of Byzantine warships and twice besieged Constantinople. His successors, after some years of consolidation, resumed the campaign. They thrust east into Turkestan, capturing Bukhara and Samarkand, and moved through Afghanistan to the border of China and on through India's Indus Valley. Other armies rolled across North Africa to the Straits of

Among the finest mathematicians of their day, the Muslims delighted in geometric patterns such as the window grate on the left. These patterns, found on many Islamic buildings, symbolized the perfect, logical order of the universe, as created by Allah.

Gibraltar. In 711, they spilt across to Spain and fought their way north over the Pyrenees and into France. They came to within 160 kilometres of Paris before the Frankish ruler Charles Martel defeated them at the Battle of Tours in 732.

Despite these foreign triumphs, the Umayyads were troubled by uprisings within the realm. The old factions of dissent and rival claims to the caliphate were never stilled. One of the most serious challenges to Umayyad rule came from Mecca. It was raised by one Abdulla ibn al-Zubayr – son of the Zubayr who had joined forces with the widow Aisha and subsequently died in the Battle of the Camel. During a brief interregnum at Damascus in 683, Abdulla claimed the caliphate. By combining force and diplomacy, he won the backing of key Muslim leaders and began setting off brush fires of revolt throughout the empire.

Finally, an Umayyad came to power who was strong enough to deal with Abdulla. He was Abd al-Malik, the caliph who would build the Dome of the Rock in Jerusalem and issue new Islamic coinage. His solution was an assault on Mecca. He sent his fiercest general, who ravaged the holy city. Stone missiles crashed into the religious quarter, and a fire broke out in the Kaba; the sacred meteorite cracked. But the rebellion was put down, and no one heard from Abdulla again.

Yet the cauldron of resentments continued to bubble, fuelled by social and economic inequities and the increasingly high-handed methods of the Umayyad rulers. One perpetual centre of discontent was Iraq, where sympathy still ran strong for the claims of Ali, last of the "rightly guided" caliphs. In 680, Ali's second son, Husayn, the Prophet's only living grandson, had been trekking through the desert with a small band of partisans, en route to join rebels in Iraq, when they were waylaid at Karbala by a much larger government force. Refusing to surrender, they were cut down to the last man. Husayn's severed head was sent as a trophy to Damascus. As dissatisfaction with the ruling regime mounted, the incident became a symbol of heroic opposition. A political movement took shape, calling itself Shiat Ali – the Party of Ali – and dedicated to restoring the Alid line. Shiite cells sprang up throughout the Islamic empire, particularly in the eastern provinces, and the site of the massacre became a shrine. (Shiites would eventually become one of the two primary sects of Islam, second in numbers only to the Sunnis, the name that was later given to those mainstream, orthodox Muslims who regarded the first four caliphs as Muhammad's rightful successors.)

Other opposition groups added to the revolutionary fires. The Kharijites, Ali's turnabout followers, continued to spread anarchy and confusion. Large numbers of non-Arab converts, the *mawalis*, sought ways to protest their inferior status; many joined forces with one or another of the proliferating Shiite sects. Native Arabs from lesser tribes, who were missing out on the wealth and power that flowed to their better-placed brethren, muttered their discontent. And pious Muslims everywhere looked up from their Korans to cry out for change. As it happened, change came from an alliance of convenience among all these dissidents. In the far east of the empire, in the Persian province of Khurasan, an Arab family descended from the Prophet's uncle Abu al-Abbas began to weld together the forces of revolt.

Eastern Persia, like Iraq, had always been particularly restless under Umayyad rule. Its Arab conquerors had intermarried with the local Sassanian aristocracy and adapted most comfortably to Persian manners and traditions. Local *mawalis* had unusually strong influence in both government and intellectual circles. The region was a hotbed of Shiism. Therefore, when the Abbasids, in the honoured tradition of the "rightly guided" caliphs, posed as Islam's true champions and raised their black banner of revolution, the entire eastern Muslim world fell in behind it.

The Abbasids deposed Khurasan's loyalist governor in 747 and quickly gained control of the Iranian plateau. Then, led by their commanding general, former Persian slave Abu Muslim, they began their triumphal progress west. In 749, they entered Kufa in Iraq to popular acclaim. Abu al-Abbas, called al-Saffah, the Bloodspiller, became the first Abbasid caliph and claimed victory after victory. The last loyalist resistance crumpled at the Battle of the Great Zab, a tributary of the Tigris, in 750. Al-Saffah celebrated by beheading the living Umayyads and scourging the corpses of their dead. Only one Umayyad escaped, Abd al-Rahman, who fled to Spain and set up a court at Cordoba that would shine over the next few centuries.

The Abbasids now commanded the giant's portion of the Muslim world, and they began to construct a royal Islamic state that would surpass all predecessors in its extravagance and autocratic power. The dynasty made its capital at Baghdad, a tiny Sassanian village just upstream from the ruined splendours of Ctesiphon. Al-Saffah's successor, Abu Jafar al-Mansur, began building in 762 with an eye to military defence. Baghdad's three concentric walls rose 27 metres above the surrounding plain and were pierced by four majestic gateways. The palace stood at the centre, the shimmering green dome of its audience chamber soaring to a height of 40 metres. A great mosque stood beside it. Round the palace and mosque were army barracks, government offices and the dwellings of high-ranking officials.

Within this glittering enclave the Abbasid caliphs held court in a manner more reminiscent of imperial Persia than of tribal Arabia. They took extravagant titles, such as the Shadow of God upon Earth. Some Abbasid officials built lavish villas along the Tigris, where they drank Persian wines, kept Persian mistresses, and entertained themselves with the gentle charms of perfumed slave girls singing Persian songs. Yet the Abbasids also showed energetic support for the institutions of Islam. They built mosques throughout the empire, schools for studying the Koran, and hospitals. Government grants expanded the courtyard surrounding the Kaba and established guard posts and wells along the pilgrimage routes.

Under the Abbasids the empire prospered as never before. Baghdad became the centre of a vast commercial enterprise. Caravans and sailing ships fanned out to bring gold from Nubia, linens from Egypt, carpets from Armenia, rubies from India and spices from the East Indies. From China came peacocks and horses; felt, silk and brocades; rhubarb and drugs; slave girls, hydraulic engineers and eunuchs. Scandinavia and Russia supplied wax, amber and pelts of fox, beaver and ermine.

The intellectual awakening that had begun in Damascus now blossomed, aided by the introduction of paper and ink from China. A medical school was founded in Baghdad. Scholars pored over the Koran, compiling from extracts a body of laws called the Sharia. Some poets began to write new lyrics, blending the sensuous themes of Eastern verse with the vibrant nuances of Arabic, while others returned to the stately rhymed prose of the heroic tribal tradition.

Abbasid power and creative energy reached its loftiest summit during the reign of Harun al-Rashid, which began in 786 and continued through the turn of the century. But by then new troubles were beginning, and new voices of dissent demanded attention. Soon rival leaders would come to power in distant provinces, and the edges of the empire would begin to flake away. Harun's successors would be hard put to maintain their supremacy under the flag of Islam.

THE STRUCTURES OF ISLAM

The striking architectural accomplishments of the Islamic world arose from humble foundations. The first Muslims lived in the simplest of dwellings – tents of woven camel's hair, or mud-brick huts with partitions of palm branches arrayed at the edge of walled courtyards. Muhammad's own courtyard in Medina was frequented by dogs and camels as well as countless pilgrims, whose protracted visits sometimes inconvenienced the Prophet and his wives. On one occasion, two of Muhammad's followers became embroiled late at night in a dispute over a debt, prompting their master to lift the curtain of his room and call out for quiet. The proximity of the dwellings to the courtyard reportedly drove one of Muhammad's wives, while he was away, to build an addition to her hut that enabled her to retreat behind a brick wall. She explained to her husband on his return that she was only attempting to "shut out the glances of men thereby", but he disapproved of the expense. "The most unprofitable thing that eateth up the wealth of a Believer," he told her, "is building."

In one regard, at least, Muhammad's austere approach had a lasting impact on Islamic architecture: the dusty courtyard where his followers gathered to attend his words became the model for the mosque cloister, shielded from the outside world yet open to the heavens. In other respects, however, Muhammad's successors soon departed from his strictures, devoting the profits of their conquests to magnificent buildings that owed more to the alluring examples of Persia and Byzantium than to the rugged traditions of Arabia. Indeed, one of the first great Muslim structures the Dome of the Rock in Jerusalem *(pages 50-51)* – invoked not only the style but the substance of the rival cultures that had long dominated that holy city. Built at a site sacred both to Jews and to Christians, it symbolized the assurance of the Muslims that their faith was the fulfilment of the promises of Abraham and Christ.

But other feats of Islamic architecture stemmed from more worldly impulses. Wealthy caliphs and their heirs built palatial retreats such as Khirbat al-Mafjar *(pages 52-53),* full of aqueducts, fountains and baths that recalled the marvels of Rome. And shifts of power within Islam led to the laying out of new administrative centres, chief among them the walled city of the Abbasid caliphs at Baghdad *(pages 54-55).* Such lavish, self-contained realms were a far cry from Muhammad's simple square at Medina, yet they expressed a similar impulse – the search of the elect for sanctuary in a hostile world.

A Splendid Sanctum

In 687, 50 years after Jerusalem fell to the Muslims, Umayyad caliph Abd al-Malik commissioned a shrine to stand as a symbol of Islamic ascendancy there. Its mighty dome – built to enclose the rock on top of Mount Moriah where Abraham was said to have offered his son Isaac to God – was meant primarily to rival Jewish and Christian sanctuaries, but it may have also been intended to compete with the Kaba in Mecca, then in the hands of hostile Muslims. By one account, Abd al-Malik claimed that the rock was the place where Muhammad had begun a night journey to heaven – a belief that became widespread. In contrast to the plain Kaba, the new holy place was built along the opulent lines of Byzantine churches. The dome, whose frame rose from an octagonal base *(below)*, was gilded on the outside. The interior mosaics *(right)* delighted the eye with scrolls and floral motifs but depicted no living creatures, as this was idolatrous. The dome attracted the faithful, who came to the rock where prophets had been touched by God.

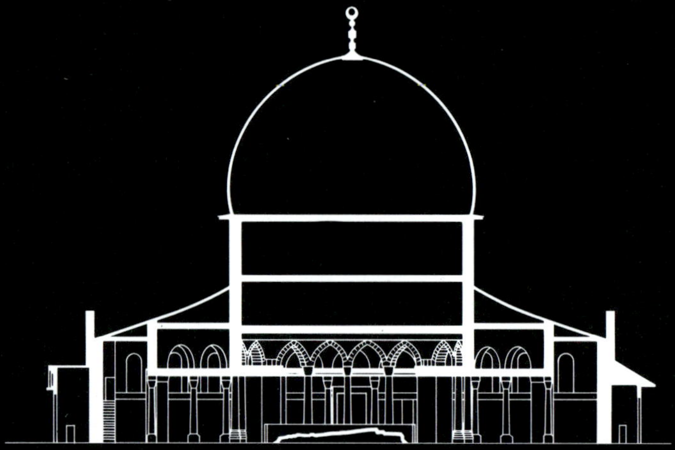

A Courtly Refuge

In the late days of the Umayyad dynasty, caliphs and their kinsfolk shunned populous places as breeding grounds of disease and discontent. Instead, the elite frequented fortified retreats at the desert's fringes. Khirbat al-Mafjar, one of the most ambitious compounds, was begun in the Jordan River valley around 740. Its plan *(diagram, right)* reflected the increasingly cosmopolitan tastes of Muslim leaders. Like Persia's royal estates, it included a park with game, while its bath hall *(above, right)* followed Roman precedents, featuring hot and cold chambers and a lavatory with three rows of toilet seats facing a fountain. Before the complex was completed, however, an earthquake ravaged the site in 748, even as stresses were building within Islam that would topple the dynasty itself.

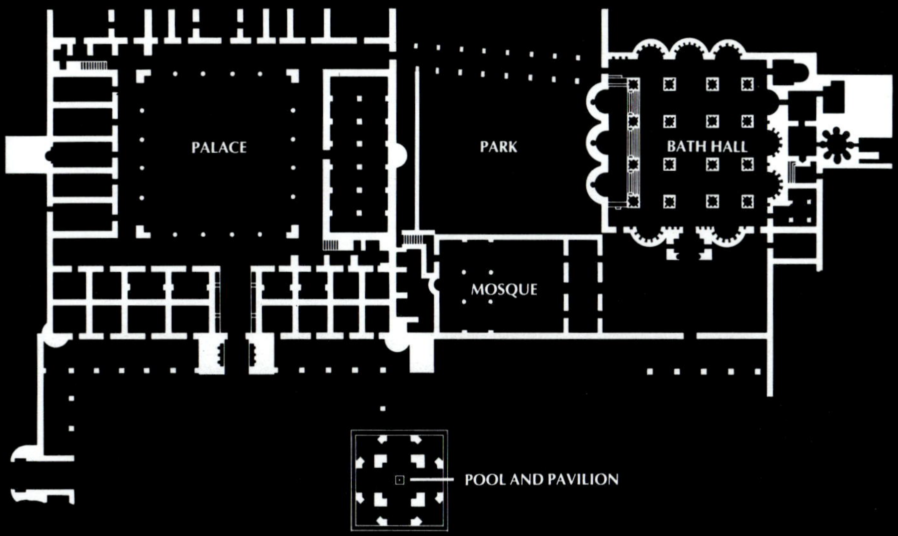

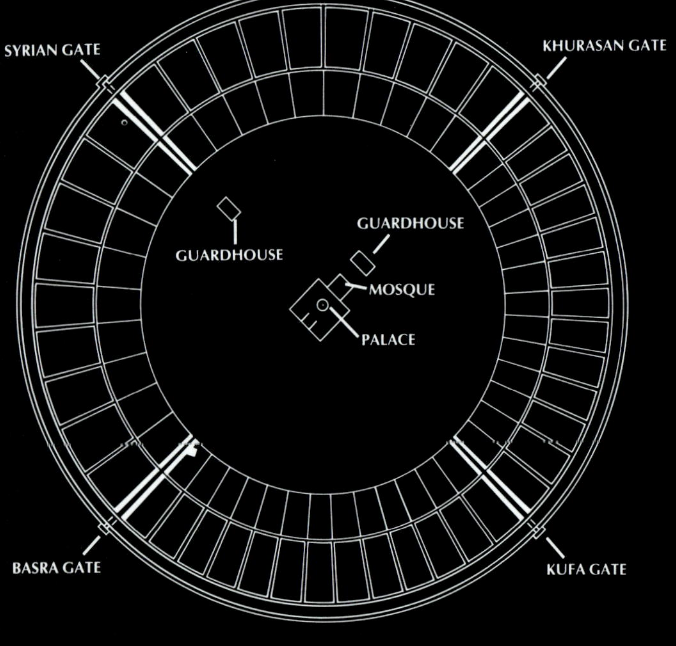

The Citadel in the Round

In 762, the Abbasid caliph Abu Jafar al-Mansur laid the first brick of his new capital at Baghdad. The circular plan of this citadel *(left)* harked back to the armed camps of the ancient Assyrians, befitting a dynasty that had established itself by force only recently and still had enemies within Islam. The caliph's residence, with its broad dome *(top)*, was insulated from surrounding settlements. Ringing the guarded palace were two walled districts; the one closer to the palace was probably reserved for the royal household and high officials. Girding the entire complex was a massive bulwark whose gate towers offered entry only at the side *(above, right)* to deter a frontal assault. But within 50 years the proud bastion was humbled, as a struggle for succession led to a bitter siege.

THE CHANGING FACE OF EUROPE

2

In 610, a 35-year-old warrior called Heraclius nailed an icon of the Virgin Mary to his masthead and, with that sacred emblem protecting his fleet, set sail from Carthage on the coast of North Africa. His destination was Constantinople, capital of what remained of the Roman Empire. Although Heraclius and other citizens continued to refer to themselves as Romans, later historians would call them Byzantines and their empire Byzantium, after the ancient Greek town upon whose site Constantinople had been founded two centuries before.

Heraclius was on a mission of surpassing importance to all Byzantines. He was a pivotal figure in a revolt against the inept emperor Phocas, a minor military officer who had usurped the throne eight years earlier, in 602. On the success of Heraclius' mission rested the fate of Byzantium itself, now menaced on its own territory by invading Persians and other enemies.

The uprising against Phocas had been under way for two years. A prominent general named Priskus, who also happened to be the Emperor's son-in-law, had brought matters to a head by sending a secret letter to Heraclius' father and namesake, the exarch, or governor, of the prosperous Byzantine province centred in Carthage. Priskus invited rebellion by the elder Heraclius, a hero of the wars against Persia and a patriot of power and rectitude.

The old governor responded by ordering his minions to hold back the fleet that normally carried African grain from Carthage to Constantinople. Next, he dispatched an army under the command of his nephew Niketas to occupy Byzantine coastal regions east of Carthage, including Tripoli and Egypt. And then the exarch sent his son across the Mediterranean to depose the Emperor in Constantinople.

With skilled Moorish seafarers manning the vessels, Heraclius reached the Aegean Sea without major incident. His insurgent fleet slipped through the Dardanelles, the slender strait dividing Europe and Asia and linking the Aegean to the Sea of Marmara, and then dropped anchor in a harbour located a little downhill from Constantinople's magnificent palace complex.

Heraclius stepped ashore to the cheers of the city's hungry, rebellious citizens, who hailed him as their saviour. Phocas had won public acclaim eight years earlier when he assassinated the emperor Maurice, who had been much disliked. But Phocas' popularity had dwindled, and by now even the imperial army had abandoned him. After learning of Heraclius' arrival, Phocas fled into one of the palace churches, where two senators discovered him cowering and proceeded to place him under arrest. Heraclius, who was quickly proclaimed emperor, exacted the ultimate penalty: Phocas — who was believed to have been responsible not only for the death of Maurice but for the murders of Maurice's wife and their eight children — was hacked to pieces. It was said that when the newly installed emperor

In the seventh century, the centres of power in Europe were inexorably shifting. Byzantium, with its capital at Constantinople, was embattled on all its frontiers: in the west by the Avars, Lombards and Bulgars and in the east by Persians and Arabs. In central Europe, the Franks – the mounted warrior on the sixth-century plaque on the right is symbolic of their emerging power – were absorbing their barbarian neighbours and building a foundation for the establishment in the eighth century of Charlemagne's empire and the birth of the Carolingian dynasty.

confronted Phocas just prior to the execution, the condemned man gathered his courage and spat out a taunting challenge: "You do better!"

Heraclius' task was daunting indeed. He now presided over an empire whose problems — an empty treasury, a demoralized army, enemies at every turn — matched its size. Byzantium embraced millions of people, a diversity of ethnic groups held together by three common bonds: Roman political heritage, Greek culture and the Christian religion. The core areas of the empire were Asia Minor, Syria, Egypt and Europe south of the Danube River, including the old Greek lands of Thrace and Macedonia. But Byzantine provinces also reached west along the North African coast and included parts of the Italian and Iberian peninsulas.

Even so, Byzantium was greatly diminished from the maximum extent of the old Roman Empire. Rome's Latin culture and Christian religion still thrived in western Europe, but over the previous two centuries former barbarians had removed most of that half of the old Roman domain from imperial control. Visigoths now ruled much of Spain — a sophisticated Christian realm, which no longer answered to Constantinople. Angles and Saxons, relative newcomers to Britain, vied with the longer-established Celts for control of the island. Franks held the vast area that later became France, the Low Countries, and much of Germany, and Lombards occupied northern Italy; both peoples were Christians who had Roman-created governmental and social structures but were politically independent of Byzantium.

And now, its enemies were encroaching further upon the Roman inheritance, threatening the very existence of the empire. Heraclius took charge of a government desperately fighting a two-front war on Byzantine soil. In eastern Europe the Avars — a warlike Turkic people of central Asian origin — and their Slavic allies had crossed the Danube and penetrated deep into the Balkan Peninsula. To the southeast the Persians — who had been warring against the empire on and off for many centuries — had recently overrun much of Byzantium's territory in Syria and Mesopotamia and were advancing across Asia Minor towards Constantinople. And the Byzantines were unaware of an even greater threat that before long would materialize out of the flaming visions of an Arab prophet named Muhammad.

As the new emperor set out to save his beleaguered empire, he might have found a useful ally and adviser in Priskus, the general who had instigated the plot to unseat Phocas. But Heraclius suspected Priskus of having designs on the imperial throne, so he sent the general off to fight the Persians and later stripped him of his wealth and titles and forced him to enter a monastery. Heraclius lost much popular support when his wife died and he insisted on marrying his own niece, Martina, in a union condemned as immoral both by the Church and by the citizenry at large. Not long afterwards, he came close to losing his life. When the Avars, in one of their raids from the north, suddenly galloped to within a few leagues of Constantinople, the Emperor rushed outside the city walls in the hope of negotiating with the invaders. He neglected to take along a strong enough bodyguard and barely avoided capture and death at the hands of the barbarians.

Heraclius' problems over the next decade must have seemed practically overwhelming. Constantinople suffered from a shortage of food — a situation that could prove disastrous should the city come under siege — and the imperial treasury did not have adequate funds to finance the administration, much less support armies in the field. Nor did Heraclius have enough troops to meet the threats at hand. To solve his financial problems, the Emperor let it be known that he was considering transferring the Byzantine government across the Mediterranean to the security of Carthage. As he expected, church officials wanted neither to be left without protection in Constantinople nor to abandon their exceedingly valuable property, so they opened their treasuries to help meet imperial needs.

Of all the serious concerns weighing on the new ruler, the heaviest by far was the aggression of the Persians and their ambitious monarch, King Chosroes II. A Persian force was rampaging through Asia Minor, destroying revered cities of antiquity and devastating the agricultural economy of the region. But more importantly, the Persians were also invading Syria, the wealthy commercial crossroads of the eastern Mediterranean. They seized the bustling Syrian metropolis of Antioch in the year 613, and then they descended on Palestine.

In May of 614, they swarmed into the holy city of Jerusalem, slaughtering, looting, and razing Christian monuments. By the account of a survivor who was forced to help bury the dead, an appalling 66,509 men, women and children perished. Perhaps as many as 35,000 Byzantine survivors were marched away in chains to Ctesiphon on the Tigris River, the capital city of Persia's Sassanian dynasty. Even worse, the Persians – fire-worshipping Zoroastrians who were viewed as heathens by Byzantine Christians – pried from the Church of the Holy Sepulchre the most treasured relic in all of Christendom, the True Cross on which Christ was said to have died, and carried it off as booty.

From Palestine, the Persians were in a position to pounce upon Egypt, essential to Byzantium for its grain and tax revenues, which provided a quarter of the imperial budget. Egypt fell to the Persian sword in 619, and the flow of grain from Alexandria to Constantinople was choked off. To his sorrow, Heraclius was forced to end the long-established practice of distributing free bread to the citizens of Constantinople. Meanwhile, the Persians pushed westwards through Asia Minor. By 620, they had advanced so far that watchers on the walls of Constantinople could see enemy campfires flickering in the night across the Bosporus, the narrow strait leading from the Sea of Marmara to the Black Sea.

Belatedly but with fierce resolve, Heraclius built up his armies for a counter-offensive. He recruited fresh soldiers, paying them and suppliers with coins minted by melting down all the metal the government could collect, not only church treasures but even bronze statues taken from homes and public places.

As he had demonstrated in sailing to Constantinople under the icon of the Virgin, the Emperor was a master at harnessing the imagery and psychology of religion. The Byzantines believed that their emperor was not merely a secular ruler but God's representative on earth. They saw themselves as chosen people surrounded by pagans – those alien folk an old imperial edict had declared "demented and insane". Heraclius meant to lead his army into battle personally, something no Byzantine emperor had done for two centuries. In preparation, he pored over books of military tactics and stoked the fires of religious fervour. He couched his coming campaign in the rhetoric of a holy war – to drive a Christian sword into the heart of Zoroastrian Persia and recover the True Cross.

In 622, with the blessing of Sergius, the patriarch of Constantinople, and with icons of the Virgin and Christ, Heraclius led his army eastwards into Asia Minor. He defeated a large Persian force in Armenia during the winter of 622-623, but after four years of bloody fighting, he was unable to achieve decisive victory. In 626, he was with his troops in Armenia, some 1,300 kilometres from the Bosporus, when alarming news reached him from Constantinople: the Byzantine capital was under siege. The Avars and Slavs had seized control of the city's northern approaches. Worse, a collaborating Persian force had manoeuvred through Asia Minor to Chalcedon, across the Bosporus from Constantinople, and was waiting to be ferried to the European side by the Slavs in their large wooden canoes.

Heraclius had entrusted the defence of the capital to the patriarch Sergius and a general named Bonus. They proved to be a remarkably formidable pair. While the General led a series of sharp sorties against the Avars and laid plans to destroy the Slav canoes, the Patriarch went about the Lord's work. He lifted the spirits of the faithful by painting images of Christ and the Virgin on the city gates to bring down God's wrath upon the Avars. Day after day, night after night, Constantinople throbbed with prayerful processions, as throngs of citizens, carrying church relics and chanting hymns, paraded round the city's 21-kilometre walled perimeter.

Many said that Constantinople was saved by divine deliverance. At the height of the crisis, it was related, the Virgin herself was seen on the parapets standing next to Byzantine defenders. In any case, after only 11 days, the Avars and Slavs gave up and turned for home, their forces punished and their canoes destroyed by the troops of General Bonus. On the far side of the Bosporus, the Persians clung to their camps until the following winter. Then they, too, withdrew.

At his field headquarters, Heraclius now prepared to resume his offensive. Firstly, he concluded an alliance with the Persian-hating Khazars, a fierce Turkic people from north of the Caucasus. Then he struck south into the vitals of Chosroes' empire. In a brilliant march in 627, he led his small, well-disciplined army across the Armenian highlands and on to the plain of the Tigris.

In December of that year, the Byzantines confronted the Persians near the ruins of the ancient city of Nineveh. Heraclius heroically charged into battle at the head of his men and was credited with personally slaying three Persian generals. The Persians fled with the Byzantines raging after them. Within a few months, Heraclius reached the gates of the Persian city of Dastagird, which he swiftly captured and put to the torch, destroying among other structures an ancient palace sacred to all Persians. Humiliated by this bold strike at the Persian empire's heart, Chosroes II's ministers deposed and murdered their failed monarch in 628.

The peace settlement that followed restored to Byzantium all the eastern provinces lost to the Persians and returned the True Cross to Christendom. In 630, the victorious Heraclius himself carried the relic into Jerusalem, entering the city barefoot and shouldering his holy burden. The gesture symbolized both the re-establishment of Byzantine authority in the lands of the eastern Mediterranean and the conviction that, in time of war, God favoured his most ardent followers.

After the triumph in Persia, Heraclius confronted a long-standing theological issue that deeply affected the unity of the empire. The official, imperial church and a sizable sect of Christians known as Monophysites strongly disagreed about the nature of Christ. The official position, affirmed at the Council of Chalcedon in 451, held that Christ had two natures, human and divine. Monophysites insisted that he had one nature, a unity of the human and the divine. The dispute had burdened Byzantine emperors since the fourth-century reign of Constantine the Great, and all efforts to resolve differences between the two sides had ultimately failed.

Persecution by the official church had alienated dissident worshippers in Syria and Egypt, where Monophysites constituted a majority of the Christian population.

People in those areas developed ties of loyalty to local religious leaders instead of to imperial authorities. Although Monophysites in Syria and Egypt had not actually welcomed the Persian invaders during the war, they did experience greater religious freedom during Persian occupation than under Byzantium's rule. Their churches had thrived under the Persians, and they could hardly be expected to give their loyalties to the Emperor when his troops returned.

Hoping to heal the schism and reassert imperial authority, Heraclius asked Patriarch Sergius to shape a compromise between the official and Monophysite positions. The result of this request was a doctrine called Monothelitism, which held that Christ had two natures but only one will.

The new doctrine won the approval of Pope Honorius in Rome but found no favour with the Monophysites. Among those who rejected it were Egypt's Coptic Christians – so called for the Coptic language, derived from ancient Egyptian, that they used in their liturgy. Heraclius ordered the new patriarch of Alexandria, Cyrus, to persuade the Coptic church to accept the idea of one will. Cyrus, who also acted as civil governor, was less interested in reason than in force. He launched a full-scale persecution of those who failed to accept the Emperor's compromise, dispatching soldiers to monasteries to flog and torture recalcitrant abbots and their monks. The prisons began to fill with holy men. Cyrus reserved special treatment for Menas, brother of the Coptic patriarch; torturers seared Menas with torches, pulled his teeth from his jaws, and finally stuffed him into a weighted sack and rowed him out to sea. When Menas refused a third and final command to refute Monophysitism, they cold-bloodedly dumped him overboard.

The increasingly bitter disunity added to the exhaustion from the lengthy war with Persia and rendered the empire ever more vulnerable. Disaster struck in 634, only six years after the victory over Chosroes. Swarming out of the Arabian deserts, shouting declarations of unwavering faith in Allah and his prophet Muhammad, Muslim warriors intent on conquest swept northwards into southern Palestine. Neither the Byzantines nor their ageing leader were prepared for the onslaught.

Heraclius, by now a weary old warhorse, took up a forward command post in Syria. About 60 years old, struggling with ill health, and scarred by a lifetime of battle, the great emperor was not able to assume personal command of the army, but was forced to leave it to lesser leaders. Nevertheless, the Byzantine armies appeared formidable. Divided into 400-man regiments of light and heavy cavalry, along with infantry, the Byzantines were mobile, well armed, well trained, and organized. Each infantry section of 16 men, for example, was accompanied by a cart containing entrenching tools and other useful implements, including a hand mill for grinding the daily maize. And in contrast to many armies of the time, which were not equipped to care for their wounded, a medical corps of stretcher-bearers and surgeons followed the Byzantines into battle.

By comparison, Arab armies appeared to the Byzantines to be a disorderly rabble, without any unit organization,

A reliquary in the shape of an early Irish church *(left)* held the remains of Saint Columba, who in 563 established a monastery at Iona, an island off Scotland's west coast. In the following years, Irish missionaries spread Celtic Christianity from Scotland to Northumbria in England. They were opposed in the early seventh century by Pope Gregory's emissaries, who arrived in Northumbria preaching the Roman version of Christianity and bearing such treasures as the silver and gilt reliquary on the right; the receptacle was said to hold a piece of Jesus' cross.

formal tactical training, pay or doctors, and wielding largely inferior weapons. Yet after the first skirmishes, the Arabs never lost a land battle to the forces of the empire. Wild and warlike, superb horsemen from childhood, they flowed like a terrible tide round the Byzantine troops. In attack they were fearless, in defence unyielding – for had not the prophet Muhammad promised them that to die in battle was to gain immediate admission to the realm of Paradise? This fervent belief imbued the Arabs with a zeal that outweighed any superiority that the Byzantine armies had in arms and in discipline.

Bit by bit the empire surrendered; one by one the eastern strongholds fell. At Antioch in 636, Heraclius learnt of a crushing defeat suffered by the Byzantines at the Yarmak River in southern Palestine and probably witnessed the disheartening panorama of some of his units fleeing northwards with the Muslims in close pursuit. Jerusalem was captured in 637, after its patriarch surrendered in order to avoid a repetition of the ghastly slaughter that had occurred when Persians took the city 23 years before. Syria was overrun by 639. Byzantines there suffered further indignity when their local commander was captured by the Arabs and sewn up inside a dead camel. And in December of that year, 3,500 ragged Bedouins invaded Egypt, following the same age-old caravan track from Palestine that Persian troops had taken earlier. The Arab invaders were soon joined by 12,000 reinforcements. They faced little resistance from the Coptic Christians, who had heard that their Monophysite brethren in Syria were in fact faring better under the Muslim Arabs than they had under the Christian Byzantines.

As news of his losses reached him on his journey homewards, Heraclius became increasingly feeble and broken in spirit. On the Asiatic side of the Bosporus, he was seized by a sudden irrational terror of crossing the water, and consequently, he advanced no farther. The fear-stricken emperor remained at Chalcedon for a full year. He crossed over to Constantinople and resumed control of his faltering empire only when a pontoon bridge was constructed and covered with foliage to hide the water, thus enabling him to control his terror. Heraclius died on February 11, 641, after vowing in a final eruption of will to sail for Egypt and take command of his battered army there. Nine months later, one of the brightest jewels of the Byzantine Empire, Alexandria – the largest city in Egypt, a commercial centre perhaps even richer than Constantinople itself, a major repository of Greek culture, and a capital of Christendom – capitulated to the Muslim forces.

During a time when the Byzantines desperately needed to be able to present a united front against the Arabs, the empire continued to be dogged by religious controversy. The dispute that had weakened the eastern provinces now infected the western reaches of the empire. Prelates and politicians in Rome and Carthage had long been bitterly opposed to the eastern Monophysites, who insisted that Christ had only one nature. Westerners clung fiercely to the official position that Christ had two natures. But like the Monophysites, they equally opposed the temporizing Monothelites of Constantinople.

The potential for calamity, apparent to everyone, was realized in 647 in Carthage, where the exarch Gregory proclaimed independence from Constantinople, ostensibly on the grounds of religious disagreement. Ironically, the Arabs crushed the North African revolt: they invaded Carthage from Libya, executed the Exarch, took advantage of the confusion to plunder, and then withdrew from the area, thereby enabling the Byzantines to reassert dominion.

Emperor Constans II, Heraclius' grandson, in 648 attempted to stop the religious strife. On the advice of the patriarch of Constantinople, Constans issued a decree called the Typos, or Statement, which forbade discussion of the natures and wills of Christ. Those who defied the decree could be flogged, imprisoned, or exiled.

The ban satisfied neither the Monophysites nor many of those who opposed them. And it exacerbated an old and growing tension between Constantinople and Rome. Rome, long ago displaced by Constantinople as the political and economic capital of the empire, had so far managed to retain its position as the spiritual capital. Now, as shown by the Typos and other imperial edicts, Constantinople seemed intent on supplanting Rome as the empire's religious centre. But the pope and other Roman church officials were determined to resist such encroachments on their authority. For their opposition, some of them were beaten and imprisoned.

The far-reaching accomplishments of Pope Gregory I, shown here in a ninth-century ivory panel, earned him the epithet "the great". Born to a wealthy Italian family, at the age of 33 Gregory resigned his position as prefect of Rome to enter the priesthood. As pope from 590 to 604, Gregory's strict enforcement of religious doctrine and his notable political acumen immeasurably strengthened the power of the papacy, while his missionary zeal spread the Christian faith to the very farthest borders of Western civilization.

The city whose role they defended was a shrunken relic of its glorious past. Rome's population, once counted in the millions, now numbered in the tens of thousands. Decay was everywhere. The great aqueducts, damaged in wars and only poorly maintained in peace, leaked so badly that stagnant malarial swamps formed round them. The complex system of drainage canals and embankments along the Tiber had fallen into disrepair and no longer contained the flood. Sometimes the river burst through, inundating the piazzas with water 2.5 metres deep. The floods undermined the tall apartment blocks called *insulae* that once housed multitudes, causing the buildings to crash into rubble. As civic administration broke down, many old temples and civic structures were abandoned, and gutted by looters seeking marble and other items of value. Some of the buildings that survived owed their preservation to the Church. The Pantheon and the Senate House in the Forum, among others, escaped ruin only by their conversion into churches.

Rome was governed by the provincial exarch based at Ravenna, the old Ostrogothic capital to the northeast. The two cities were connected by a narrow, 240-kilometre-long corridor that ran through territory controlled by the Lombards, who occasionally threatened Rome. Because no help was provided by the east, the pope himself sometimes had to raise the funds needed to pay soldiers and bribe the Lombards. It was the pope and the growth of the Vatican, with its monasteries and shrines on the edge of the city, that ensured Rome's continued prestige.

Roman antagonism towards Constans II's ban on discussion of Christ's natures and wills was so strong that after Pope Theodore died in May 649, the city's clergy and others responsible for electing the pope violated an old practice of deference to imperial authority. They installed Theodore's successor, Martin, without waiting for the traditional confirmation from the emperor in Constantinople.

Three months later, Pope Martin convened a synod of 105 bishops from Italy, Sicily, Africa and Sardinia. The synod flouted the discussion ban, condemned Monothelitism, and denounced the four eastern patriarchs who had backed the one-will doctrine. Martin publicized these conclusions by ordering frescoes of the synod to be painted in a church in the Forum and by circulating copies of the decisions across the empire. He sent Constans a copy together with an encyclical letter inviting the Emperor to join him in denouncing Monothelitism.

Although the synod scrupulously avoided any criticism of the Emperor – the Pope, in fact, took pains to reassert his loyalty to the throne – Constans reacted

A Roman fresco of a monk carrying a church symbolizes the great Christian missionary movement that swept through Europe in the seventh and eighth centuries. The Church achieved its greatest success in pagan Britain and Ireland, regions that Pope Gregory was especially keen to convert. Augustine, the Pope's emissary to Britain, is said to have baptized some 10,000 people on Christmas Day of 597.

with white-faced fury. Only 19 years of age and filled with youthful conceit, he perceived the events in Rome as attacks on his imperial person. Even before the synod he had dispatched his current exarch, Olympius, to Italy with the express purpose of bringing the new pope to heel.

Olympius arrived in Rome shortly after the end of the synod. Bearing instructions to arrest Martin, Olympius ended up attempting to have the Pope assassinated while he officiated at high mass. When the attempt failed, Olympius in sudden contrition confessed his involvement to the Pope and then marched off south to help defend Sicily against an Arab attack. There, according to enemies whose desire it was to tar both the Exarch and Martin with the brush of treason, Olympius proclaimed himself emperor and prepared to overthrow the local government – but instead he succumbed to a fever that was ravaging his army.

Back in Constantinople, Emperor Constans was undeterred by this tragicomedy. He reappointed a former exarch, Theodore Calliopas, to succeed Olympius and told him to arrest the Pope. Calliopas and his troops marched into Rome from the provincial capital at Ravenna in June 653. He and his soldiers burst into the Lateran basilica, where Martin had taken refuge, and found the sickly pontiff lying on a bed in front of the altar, surrounded by his clergy. The troops began to vandalize the opulent basilica, hacking at its fitments and smashing vessels and candlesticks. Scuffles broke out between the soldiers and priests, and citizens rushed in from the street to hurl insults at the Exarch and his men. The ill pope finally ended the fracas by agreeing to appear before the Emperor at Constantinople.

So many clergy and laymen clamoured to accompany Martin on the journey that the Exarch spirited him away under cover of darkness to prevent public demonstration. The voyage was a nightmare. Martin was allowed ashore only once. At other ports of call, bishops and congregations who tried to bring him gifts were assaulted and robbed by the Exarch's men. When the ship docked at Constantinople after a voyage lasting four months, Martin – weakened by gout, dysentery and seasickness – was carried to the palace guardroom on a litter. After three months of solitary confinement, the Pope came to trial before the Senate on trumped-up charges of treason. Instead of referring to Martin's theological transgressions, the prosecutors falsely accused him of sending money to the Arabs and of conspiring with his own would-be assassin, Olympius. Though denied the right to discuss theological matters and forced to remain standing throughout the proceedings, Martin retained his spirit and sense of irony. He complimented the prosecution for rehearsing its witnesses so thoroughly and suggested they be spared from testifying under oath so that their lies would not further imperil their immortal souls.

Afterwards the Pope was escorted to the palace courtyard. While the Emperor watched from a balcony, Martin was stripped of his vestments and flogged, then led away in chains to prison. His death sentence was later commuted to exile, and he was sent to the Crimea north of the Black Sea, where he spent the remaining months of his life suffering great physical hardship. But his most painful punishment was that of neglect; his supporters acted as though he had disappeared from the face of the earth. "I am surprised at the indifference and hardheartedness of my former associates," he wrote before his death in September 655. "They have so completely forgotten me that they do not even want to know whether I am alive." The behaviour of his old friends in Rome showed that, although prepared to argue with Constantinople about religious issues, they would not generally defy imperial authority.

Martin was venerated as a martyr, but because he had been ordained without imperial confirmation and was deposed by the Emperor, he was now a source of embarrassment to the Roman church. Rome's clergy elected a successor, Eugenius I, a compliant soul properly conciliatory to Constantinople. The Emperor declared his approval of the new pope in 654, and in a letter to one of Martin's former associates he made matters absolutely clear to those who might still harbour notions of independence: "Know that when we get a rest from the heathen, we will treat you like the pope who is now lifted up, and we will roast all of you, each in his own place, as Pope Martin has been roasted." The recipient, a monk who would be remembered as one of the most distinguished theologians of the era, Maximus the Confessor, remained defiant until 662, when a Constantinople court – to prevent his speaking or writing against the Emperor – ordered him deprived of his tongue and right hand and sent him into exile at the age of 82.

During this period, the papacy was having more success propagating its beliefs beyond the borders of Byzantium than within the empire. Success was particularly noticeable in the British Isles, which had once represented the northwest extremities of the old Roman Empire. Christianity had come to the Britons from nearby Gaul during the fourth century and had later taken root among the Celtic people of Ireland, owing at least in part to the efforts of a proselytizer who would be remembered as Saint Patrick. But subsequent invasions from the Continent by the Angles and Saxons had snuffed out the influence of the papacy in Britain. What Christianity there was was guided by the Irish church, which was always threatened by the pagan newcomers. To remedy this problem and convert the pagan patchwork of Anglo-Saxon kingdoms in England, Pope Gregory sent a mission composed of 40 monks to Kent in 597. The Pope wisely instructed his missionaries to adapt some of the heathen institutions to Christian use instead of attacking them head on. Pagan temples, for instance, were ritually cleansed and dedicated as churches, thereby providing new converts with a familiar setting for worship. Pagan idols were destroyed, but animal sacrifices were transformed into feasts given in honour of various Christian saints. The Pope's mission converted the heathen in such great numbers that Gregory soon exulted: "Behold, the tongue of Britain which before could utter only barbarous sounds has lately learnt to make the Alleluia of the Hebrews resound in praise of God."

But Gregory's monks found themselves in conflict with Saint Patrick's Celtic church, which had been saving British souls for more than a hundred years. Evolving in relative isolation far from the reach of Rome, the Celts developed distinctive regional traditions, such as their strong emphasis on monasticism. Many of the Irish monasteries were built on islands, the most remarkable of which was Skellig Michael, a 200-metre pyramid of rock towering above the Atlantic off the southwest coast of Ireland. Monks there lived and worshipped in a beehive of cells carved into the precipice. Missionaries from the Celtic church travelled afar, establishing footholds in Scotland, Wales and England.

Symbolic of the differences between the Celtic and Roman churches were their methods for calculating the date of the movable feast of Easter. This issue crystallized in the kingdom of Northumbria, in northeast England. A seventh-century Northumbrian king by the name of Oswy, reared in the Celtic church that was long

Legacy of the Pagan Kings

In the seventh century, when the first Christian missionaries arrived in Britain, they encountered proud Anglo-Saxon warriors, descendants of the Germanic tribes that had invaded in the fifth century. The Anglo-Saxons were pagans whose cultural and religious life was as complex as that of the missionaries who so zealously converted them to Christianity.

The Anglo-Saxons were loosely organized into seven kingdoms, each with a ruler who had battled for his royal status. Each king had a retinue of fighting men, whose loyalty, battle prowess and ability to accumulate treasure and territory were crucial to his power. The rough-and-ready lives of these warrior-kings were celebrated in songs and epic poetry. *Beowulf,* the saga of a mythical dragon-slaying warrior, is the most renowned of these ballads.

After their death, Anglo-Saxon rulers were buried with the trappings of royalty. One tomb, near the modern-day estate of Sutton Hoo, contained the remains of royalty – probably a king named Redwald. Some of his treasure appears here, along with excerpts from *Beowulf.*

"A man bold with his spear was held in honour far and wide both for his acts of goodness and his acts of war. In wisdom he ruled his domain."

The royal sceptre from Sutton Hoo is surmounted by a bronze stag on a rotating ring formed from intertwined wires. These pagan symbols may have represented the forces of nature that formed the basis for Anglo-Saxon religious belief.

A massive shield testifies to the king's warrior status and the military prowess that Anglo-Saxons valued above all other human attributes. The shield is constructed of limewood, covered with hide, and elaborately embossed with iron and bronze cast in the shape of dragons and birds of prey. The shield's ornamental handgrip *(right)* – made from gilt bronze and iron wrapped in gold foil – is in the shape of a dragon, a mythical creature that figured prominently in period epics, including *Beowulf.*

"They set their braced shields at their heads, their beautiful shields. There on the bench above each prince were displayed the helmet that towers in battle, the shirt of meshed rings and the majestic spear. That was their custom, so that they were usually ready for battle both at home and in the field."

"Then they saw many sorts of serpents swimming about the water, uncanny sea-dragons making trial of the pool, water-monsters, besides, lying on the shelves of the ravine, the kind that in the forenoon often carry out some course full of grief on the sail-road, serpents and other wild beasts."

"Around what the fire left, they built a wall of the worthiest kind their most discerning men could devise. Golden arm-bands and jewels they put into that barrow, all such adornments as men bent on trouble had taken before. They let earth keep the treasure of heroes, left the gold in the ground, where it lives on still to this day, as useless to men as it earlier was."

The treasure entombed with the king included a large gold belt buckle *(top)* and gold shoulder-clasps inlaid with garnets and coloured glass *(left)*. Such finery was unusual among the Anglo-Saxons and was a mark of royal status. Much of a king's regalia was customarily buried with his remains.

established in his land, married a royal princess from Kent, who had been brought up in the Roman tradition as taught by Gregory's missionaries. The variance in the timing of Easter, for instance, produced a typical conflict. King Oswy sometimes found himself feasting to celebrate Christ's resurrection while his wife, Eanfled, was still fasting on her calendar's Palm Sunday.

To resolve the dilemma, the King's son arranged for a synod in 664 at a monastery in the town of Whitby on the North Sea. Celtic monks and clerics came to debate the matter with a number of Roman-oriented priests. After listening to the arguments pro and con, King Oswy finally agreed to adopt his wife's Roman Easter. His decision evidently turned less on the merits of the priests' arguments than on his fear of offending the spirit of the Roman apostle Peter. "Since he is the doorkeeper," said King Oswy, "I will not contradict him. Otherwise when I come to the gates of the Kingdom of Heaven, there may be no one to open them." On this frail thread hung the fate of Christendom in that part of England: after the Synod of Whitby, the Church in Northumbria continued to look to the Roman rather than Celtic tradition for spiritual leadership.

During that same period, Rome's relations with Constantinople also appeared to be improving, possibly in part because a new factor made the Muslim threat to the Byzantine Empire more ominous than ever, and that in turn made the Emperor acutely aware of the need for Christian unity.

The new element in the Byzantine-Muslim struggle was the development of Arab sea power. For centuries, the Mediterranean had been a Roman lake and then almost totally under the control of Byzantine naval forces. It was Byzantium's command of the sea, including the Black Sea, that had permitted Heraclius to continue his campaign in Armenia while a Persian army camped across the Bosporus from Constantinople. More recently, unchallenged Byzantine sea power had meant that the Muslims, despite their success in land battles, could not rest secure in the conquered coastal areas of Egypt and Syria; Arabs in any seacoast city unprotected by a sizable garrison might wake one day to find a Byzantine fleet offshore.

One of the first Arabs to recognize this was Muawiya, the governor of Syria who would become caliph some years later. He proposed to Caliph Umar ibn al-Khattab that the Muslims should build their own fleet. Umar asked an adviser what naval combat was like and was told that men on a ship were in much the same position as insects trying to hold on to a twig buffeted by the wind. The Caliph forbade Muawiya to send Arabs to sea. But Uthman, the next caliph, reversed this decision. Muawiya was permitted to organize a naval expedition against the Byzantine-held island of Cyprus if he recruited volunteers only and if his wife accompanied him — a provision apparently intended to ensure Muawiya's caution.

Muawiya's sailors joined another group assembled in Egypt and brought Cyprus to submission without a fight in 649. In 652, Byzantines in a large fleet approached Muslim-held Alexandria, apparently with intentions of retaking the city. They were surprised by an Arab naval force that fought them to a standstill, first ship to ship and then man to man in a grim and savage struggle of knives and swords. The Byzantines finally broke off and sailed away.

Neither the Byzantines nor the Arabs of this era would leave evidence providing future generations with clear-cut details about their ships, but it is possible that the Muslims were exploiting a technological advantage. For many centuries Arab

Irish Christianity blended Byzantine elements, showing its origins, with pagan motifs retained from the pre-Christian era. The arms of this stone Celtic cross, dating from the eighth century, are encompassed by a circle symbolizing the great wheel of the universe, while the interlocking ornamental figures of animals were inspired by pagan art. The stylized portraits of saints, apostles and biblical heroes exhibit certain Byzantine characteristics.

sailors, principally in the Red and Arabian seas, had been using the lateen sail, a fore-and-aft rig that enabled vessels to sail at an angle into oncoming winds. During much of that time, Romans and other Mediterranean seamen had depended mainly on the square sail, which was effective only when a following wind pushed the ship from behind. When they wished to move against the wind, they were compelled to row. Although the Byzantines are known to have employed some fore-and-aft sails earlier than the seventh century and were gradually using them more during this era, the Arabs, with their lateenrigged vessels, may have still been enjoying superior manoeuvrability in these early naval encounters.

Whatever the reason, in 655, the Arabs dealt another resounding defeat to the Byzantine fleet — which was accompanied this time by the Byzantine emperor himself — off the southwestern coast of Asia Minor, in an engagement the Muslims called the Battle of the Masts. By this point it was evident that the Byzantine command of the sea had been shattered.

The Battle of the Masts was still fresh in Byzantine memory in 662, when Emperor Constans II sailed for Italy on the first state visit to Rome by a reigning emperor since the fall of the western Roman Empire. His professed purpose was to find ways to prevent further losses of Byzantine territory to the Arabs. Constans also hoped that his absence would allow tempers to cool at home in Constantinople, where he had become distinctly unpopular, partly because of his disastrous naval defeat. Recently, Constans had earned more public disfavour by turning on his own brother Theodosius. Fearing, apparently without reason, that Theodosius coveted the throne, Constans had had him assassinated. Thereafter, wherever the Emperor went in Constantinople, crowds cried after him "Cain! Cain!"

Accompanied by 20,000 troops, Constans landed in Italy and launched a brief campaign against Benevento, the independent Lombard duchy to the southeast of Rome. After capturing a few towns, he made his state visit to Rome in July 664. Escorted by yet another new pope, Vitalian, Constans prayed at Saint Peter's and took part in a number of solemn ceremonies during his 12-day visit. But his efforts to improve relations with Rome were not helped by an orgy of imperial looting in the already ravaged city. On his orders, Byzantine troops hauled away all the metal they could find — statues, public ornaments and even metal roofing and any other copper or bronze structural elements that could be stripped from buildings — and shipped it to Syracuse on the island of Sicily. The booty was supposed to be forwarded to Constantinople for making armaments, but Arab sea raiders intercepted it off Syracuse and sold the seized cargo in Egypt.

The Emperor himself moved on to Syracuse. From a temporary court he established there he spent the next four years attempting to bolster the defences of Sicily and safeguard the sea-lanes between that island and Carthage. He paid for the build-up by levying heavy taxes on the West and expropriating the church plate.

In 668, Constans was bludgeoned to death, while in his bath, by conspiring officers. The revolt provided an occasion for Pope Vitalian to demonstrate his loyalty to the throne in the face of the dead emperor's deplorable behaviour. The Pope assumed a prominent role in mobilizing troops from Sardinia and from mainland Italy to put down the rebellion and ensure the succession of Constans' 14-year-old son and heir, who would rule as Constantine IV.

It was not long before the youthful Constantine was forced to contend with the ever-present and troublesome Arabs. In 670, the combined land and sea forces of the Muslims threatened the imperial capital itself. A large Arab fleet, having taken Rhodes as well as Cyprus, sailed unopposed through the Dardanelles into the Sea of Marmara. The Arabs landed 11 kilometres west of Constantinople and marched on the city. Now seen by the Byzantines as militarily sophisticated, not just as wild desert warriors, the Muslims reached the city walls and unlimbered their battering rams and other equipment, including gigantic mangonels — catapults capable of hurling huge stones against the ramparts. Like the Avars, Slavs and Persians before them, the Arabs were determined to pound the Byzantine capital into submission.

The desperate Byzantines managed to hold out all summer behind their massive walls. In the autumn, the Arabs — who much preferred mobile warfare to the prolonged tedium of siege and who feared the effects of winter storms on their ships — withdrew to Cyzicus, on the Sea of Marmara 130 kilometres from Constantinople. Summer after summer, they returned to the Byzantine capital, and each time the city withstood their assault.

The decisive instrument in the Byzantine defence was a new weapon called Greek fire. Probably made up primarily of naphtha, sulphur and saltpetre — the Byzantines guarded the formula for centuries — the liquid was so combustible it ignited spontaneously and burnt even on water. Constantinople's defenders used catapults to hurl clay pots filled with this terrifying incendiary, and Byzantine ships were rigged with air pumps that forced burning jets of Greek fire through bronze-lined wooden spouts called siphons. Finally, in 678, the Arabs lifted the siege and agreed to a truce, and the brash young Constantine exacted from them a ransom of men, money and horses. But the Muslims were not so easily denied. As the century ended, the promise engendered by Constantine's success was devastated by the drastic inroads of Islam. The Muslims seized Sardinia, and the last Byzantine stronghold in North Africa, Carthage, fell to an Arab fleet in 698, reducing the empire to a fraction of the size it had been 100 years earlier. Then, like a latter-day Heraclius, a capable Syrian-born soldier came to the throne in March 717. He was crowned Emperor Leo III, and his assumption of power was to be an act of deliverance, for the Arabs were again approaching the gates of Constantinople.

Determined to make the strategic city the centre of an Islamic empire, the great caliph Sulayman had mounted a three-pronged drive on the Byzantine capital. Two separate armies cut through Asia Minor from the east while a Muslim armada made

An early Christian Anglo-Saxon casket, carved from whale ivory, bears a curious mixture of Roman, pagan and Christian symbolism, signifying a complex interaction of cultures in early eighth-century Britain. The carvings include representations of Romulus and Remus, the mythological founders of ancient Rome; Wayland the Smith, a pagan hero of German origin; and the Christian Adoration of the Magi.

its way from the Aegean. The Arabs converged on Constantinople that winter and mounted their second siege in less than half a century. The city's defences were not yet fully prepared, and many Byzantines despaired. Their anxiety was reflected in a sudden spate of literature predicting the end of the world.

The new soldier-emperor met the peril with a judicious mixture of canny diplomacy, clever tactics and religious fervour. He enlisted the aid of his neighbours to the northwest, the Bulgars, a Slavic people who had been arriving in the Balkans during the previous two centuries. He combined the devastating effects of Greek fire with an old naval-warfare technique, the use of fireboats, sending a blazing flotilla of small craft into the crowded Arab anchorages. And he invoked help from on high by leading a great procession to the sea walls, where he smote the waters with a cross and called on God to repel the enemy. As it happened, a brutal winter dealt harshly with the Arabs, who were unprepared for the cold. They half-heartedly attacked again in the spring, but withdrew in dejection during the summer of 718.

Triumphant in his defence of the capital, Leo went on to secure his borders and restore internal order. But he ruled a battered domain that Muslim invaders had pushed to the verge of collapse twice in the last 50 years. Only a ruined vestige remained of the commerce that had characterized the wealthy Byzantium of earlier days. Impoverished squatters inhabited rubble where handsome and affluent cities once stood. It was only natural for a deeply religious people and emperor to wonder if they were doing something in particular to merit God's disfavour. Leo decided they were indeed, and his assessment of the cause of Byzantium's woes would soon plunge his reign into turmoil.

Early Christians had followed the Jews in strictly interpreting the commandment against graven images. No statues or pictures of divine or revered beings were involved in worship. But by the sixth century, Byzantines had begun to depart from this course. Many of the faithful now prayed before icons of Christ, the Virgin and various saints. And one of Leo's predecessors had the image of Christ stamped on imperial coins. Could these relatively recent developments be the spiritual transgressions that were causing the empire's troubles? The devout emperor knew that even those hated infidels, the Muslims, had eliminated graven images from the coins they minted in the former Byzantine provinces.

In 726, a great natural catastrophe convinced Leo that something had to be done and gave him the opportunity to do it. A tremendous volcanic eruption on the floor of the Aegean unleashed a cataclysmic tidal wave, darkened the sky with pumice and ash, and created a new island near the ancient isle of Thera. The Emperor blamed the event on divine wrath caused by the people's idolatry, and he ordered the removal and destruction of all icons in the churches of Byzantium. For a time, it seemed as though the Emperor would be able to achieve his aim: icons gradually disappeared from view, and they were replaced by officially sanctioned images such as the cross or floral patterns, birds, or other designs taken from nature – "a fruit shop and an aviary", as one chronicler wrote acidly.

But before long, it was clear that Iconoclasm – as Leo's anti-image movement came to be called – was tearing at the unity of the empire. A majority of Leo's subjects found themselves in the position of dissenters simply because they felt an icon helped to focus their prayers when they beseeched Christ or Mary or a saint for assistance. The patriarch of Constantinople resigned over the issue. There was an open religious revolt in Greece. In Italy, the growing reaction against Iconoclasm galvanized an already dangerous discontent with imperial authority – particularly since Leo had recently attempted to double property taxes. The armies of Ravenna and many other cities mutinied, and only the suasion of Pope Gregory II stopped them from electing their own imperial claimant and sailing against Constantinople.

It was not that Gregory approved of Iconoclasm; he denounced it as heresy and stood fast against the Emperor's attempt to define the faith. "Dogma is not the business of emperors but of priests," he is reported to have written to Leo. But Gregory doggedly adhered to his own careful distinction between ecclesiastical and political authority, and he remained loyal to the empire.

Leo answered the papal opposition by sending a naval armada to intimidate the Italians. It foundered in an Adriatic storm, but even that did not deter the stubborn emperor. He transferred dioceses in southern Italy and Sicily from papal jurisdiction to the jurisdiction of the patriarch of Constantinople, a position held by a loyal Iconoclast. And then Leo confiscated the papal estates in those regions, properties yielding large annual revenues essential to cover the expenses of the Church and clergy.

Faced with such treatment from Constantinople and, closer to home, confronted by a Lombard king named Liutprand who wanted to unify the entire Italian peninsula under his rule, the papacy underwent a fundamental change during this period. To defend Rome, successive popes assumed ever-greater secular power, functioning much like the rulers of a sovereign state. They became commanders-in-chief, mobilizing armies and navies while spending church treasure to repair the city walls. They became diplomats, cajoling and bribing, and forging local alliances for and against various Lombard factions. By the time a man named Zacharias became pontiff in 741, the pope was even appointing the duke of Rome – nominally its highest-ranking officer under Byzantine rule.

Short, slender and balding, Zacharias was nonetheless a figure of overpowering personal charisma, and he proved to be a highly successful pontiff. On three different occasions, he set out from Rome to meet face to face with the Lombard king. He went, recorded his scribes, "as a true pastor to recover the rest of his flocks and the things which they had lost". And at each of these meetings, Pope Zacharias charmed the Lombard ruler Liutprand, who was an adherent of the Roman church, into relinquishing the territory that his people had seized from the duchy of Rome or from the much more extensive Byzantine province centred in the city of Ravenna.

One of Liutprand's successors, a king named Aistulf, was less accommodating. He captured Ravenna in 751 and then attacked the duchy of Rome. Pope Stephen II, a Roman-born aristocrat who had been elected in 752, attempted to emulate his predecessor Zacharias' persuasiveness and dispatched gifts to his enemy

Aistulf. When that measure failed, Stephen beseeched the Byzantine emperor Constantine V, Leo's son, for military assistance, but to no avail.

Finally, the Pope — barefoot and bearing an icon of Christ outlawed by imperial edict — led processions of clergy and laity in an appeal for divine aid against the Lombards. When this failed, Stephen took the historic step that marked the beginning of the final separation of Rome from Byzantium: he asked the help of Pepin, king of the Franks, whose dominions covered a large section of western Europe.

The sturdy Franks, from whom France would derive its name, were a Germanic people who had conquered much of Roman-occupied Gaul late in the fifth century under their brilliant king, Clovis I. Following his reign, however, their kingdom shrank and fragmented into smaller states that were frequently at war with one another. By the close of the seventh century, the Merovingian royal house so auspiciously founded by Clovis was characterized by figurehead monarchs who would be tellingly remembered as the Do-Nothing Kings.

Real power resided with the landed and military aristocracy — and in particular with the personages known as mayors of the palace. The title stemmed from an earlier time when the man who held this office was chief of the royal bureaucratic household. As monarchs came and went, the palace bureaucracy developed into an enduring institution that was responsible for the detailed administration of the realm and provided continuity no matter who was on the throne — and during succession squabbles, when no one was. In time, the office of mayor of the palace became hereditary, and the mayors became kings in all but name.

The mayors supervised a largely agricultural realm. The land was divided into small plots cultivated mainly on a two or three-year crop rotation by slaves and free peasants, who also kept a few animals and fowl. Their huts were usually grouped round a manor built on the pattern of a Roman villa, where the land-owning seigneur resided. Most communities were self-sufficient; they wove their own cloth and forged their own implements and weapons from surface iron-ore deposits.

Set into this matrix of hamlets were the towns, many of them ancient Roman settlements, enclosed by walls and bristling with towers hastily erected against the barbarian menace in the third and fourth centuries. The houses, two and three storeys high, were packed tightly together along streets that might or might not be paved. The towns were more numerous in the south — in Provence, Narbonne and the Rhone Valley, where Roman settlement had been heaviest — and more widely scattered in the northern reaches of the realm. For many years, the Frankish cities remained small. The original walls of Reims encompassed only 20 to 30 hectares, those of Bordeaux and Marseilles about 30 hectares, Dijon less than 12, and Paris, future City of Light, scarcely eight hectares. The urban areas housed tiny populations: 10,000 people in Marseilles, 6,000 in Reims. And this at a time when Constantinople boasted a population of several hundred thousand.

With the increasing influence of the Christian church, the local bishops in these towns represented the highest moral authorities and frequently assumed political power. Energetic and far-sighted, these bishops were great builders. Numerous churches rose within each city. And outside the walls, the

By the eighth century, the veneration of religious icons — such as that of the Coptic bishop Abraham *(left)* — had spread throughout the Byzantine Empire. Although many Christians believed such images to be vested with miraculous powers, theologians considered the worship of icons to be a form of religious idolatry and encouraged the movement known as Iconoclasm — a term derived from the Greek words for image breaking. After Emperor Leo III issued an edict banning the adoration of icons, many images were whitewashed by zealous Iconoclasts *(below)*.

DE DONIS DI · OFFERIT
THEODE · LENDA REG
GLORIO · SISSEMA
SCO IOHA · NNI BAPT

In 603, Pope Gregory the Great presented the gem-studded gold gospel cover on the left as a peace offering to Theudelinda of Lombardy, whose warlike people occupied much of northern Italy. The Queen joined many of her subjects in converting to Christianity, but other Lombards remained pagan – among them her husband King Agiluf, shown receiving tribute from his warriors on the gilded helmet visor above.

bishops founded sanctuaries that became magnets for new settlers, travellers and pilgrims. In the course of time, new communities located outside the urban nucleus melded together, and the whole was yet again completely enclosed by fortified walls.

Though commerce and industry were much diminished since Roman days, manufacturing still continued. Artisans produced pottery, glassware and other handiworks for sale throughout the countryside. Silver coins replaced the old gold coinage used by the Romans, yet a modest trade in luxuries remained; silks, spices and ivory still travelled inland to the manors and churches from Mediterranean ports, but not in quantities that filled the ships, as had once been common. Olive oil was still used for illumination and for cooking, but locally made parchment had replaced Egyptian papyrus as the favoured writing medium for the monastery scribes. And new commerce developed as the Frisian people travelled south from their northern home carrying wool that was then woven into garments, among them a popular, short, striped tunic, or *pallum frisonica.*

It was in this unprepossessing rural soil that a leader named Pepin of Herstal, grandfather of the king Pepin to whom Pope Stephen would later appeal for help, seeded a new and vigorous Frankish dynasty. Pepin of Herstal displaced a legitimate hereditary claimant to make himself mayor of the palace of the Frankish splinter kingdom of Austrasia. Beginning in 687, he fought and won a series of battles against other Frankish states and rival contestants for the position.

His illegitimate son and successor, Charles, went on to fight and rule so forcefully that posterity awarded him the surname Martel – French for hammer. Charles Martel reunified the fragmented Frankish kingdom and as mayor of the palace re-established its authority over the Frisians and Saxons – Germanic peoples who had earlier asserted their independence. Above all, he won renown by confronting and halting the sweeping tide of Islam.

After crossing the Straits of Gibraltar from North Africa to Spain in 711, Muslim armies had conquered most of the Iberian Peninsula and brought an end to the Christian kingdom the Visigoths had established there. In 732, a century after the death of the Prophet, a great Arab host – some chroniclers reported 350,000 men – swarmed across the Pyrenees and advanced towards the Loire River.

Charles and his army met the enemy near Tours. The Hammer's force was built round indomitable infantrymen who may have fought with their shields overlapping to form a virtual wall, much like the barrier that centuries before had made a Greek phalanx so impenetrable. Wielding axes and barbed spears, the Frankish infantry withstood charge after charge by the lightly armed Muslim horsemen. The fighting raged for six days, the initiative surging back and forth, until in the end, the Arab commander was dead and the demoralized Muslim cavalry left the field. Contemporary chroniclers credited the triumph to Martel's inspiring leadership.

Yet Martel could not follow up his victory because of his own lack of horsemen, and he realized full well the need for a heavily armed cavalry. From then on, every landlord was required to provide at least one fully outfitted knight – wealthier seigneurs had to field more, the exact number depending on the size of their estates – in addition to the usual levy of infantry. Gradually, the mounted soldier became dominant in Frankish warfare. The introduction of the stirrup enabled a rider to maintain his balance while swinging a sword or couching a lance, the war saddle enhanced his stability, and the bit helped him to control his mount while the iron horseshoe prevented crippling injuries to the beast's hooves. All of these innovations made the knight an increasingly formidable figure in war – and a man of elevated status in peacetime. In the Frankish realms, he eventually became a member of the aristocracy.

But Martel was more than a warrior and tactician. Although at one point he confiscated church lands in order to build up his armies – particularly his force of knights – he was a devout Christian and generally demonstrated a benign and protective attitude towards the Church. From the year 722, he sponsored the great English missionary Boniface, who went to Germany to convert pagans conquered by Martel. Counting on Martel's piety as well as his battlefield prowess, the pope, Gregory III, asked the Frankish ruler to aid Rome against the Lombards in 739. Martel refused the request because the Lombards were supplying troops to help him to ward off the Arabs in southern Gaul.

But the way was soon paved for Pope Stephen's later plea. Charles the Hammer died in 741. In 751, his son Pepin decided he should be monarch in name as well as fact. With the help of the nobility, he seized the throne from its

On the western flank of Byzantium, the Frankish emperor Charlemagne – who is depicted in Roman garb on the coin above – built an empire that emerged as the dominant power in western Europe. Although Charlemagne displayed considerable talents as a diplomat and peacemaker, he never hesitated to use force when diplomacy failed, and waged many campaigns against neighbouring barbarian kingdoms. In 773, Charlemagne marched into northern Italy, ostensibly to relieve Lombard pressure on the papal domains to the south. He quickly vanquished Lombard warriors such as the cavalryman shown above. Saxony, on Charlemagne's northern border, proved more difficult to conquer, but that land eventually fell to Frankish forces after 25 years of warfare *(right)*. As a condition of their surrender, Charlemagne required the pagan Saxons to be baptized as Christians.

Merovingian puppet, Childeric III, and sought blessing for the deed from Pope Zacharias. The Pope gladly gave it and delegated his personal envoy Boniface to anoint the new Frankish sovereign. In the ancient biblical manner, Boniface poured the holy unguent on the head of King Pepin, founder of what would be known as the Carolingian dynasty. Thus, when Pope Stephen, Zacharias' successor, wrote to the King two years later requesting his help against the Lombards, Pepin sent his personal emissaries to escort the aged pontiff to a meeting on Frankish soil.

Starting this historic journey late in 753, Pope Stephen travelled first to the Lombard capital of Pavia, in a final, futile attempt to dissuade King Aistulf from further aggression. Then, in the snow and the November cold, the Pontiff and his entourage crossed over the Alps through the Great Saint Bernard Pass. His discussions with King Pepin resulted in the formation of an important new alliance. The Pope re-enacted the coronation of Pepin and bestowed on the Frank and his two sons the titles of Patricians of Rome. Pepin promised that they would live up to the title by protecting the Holy See, and in particular pledged himself to "restore" to the papacy lands that had been conquered by the Lombards. (The lands in question had actually belonged to the Byzantine Empire rather than the papacy, before they were seized by the Lombard invaders.)

Pepin made good his promise in 755, after trying without success to negotiate with the Lombards. He led an army across the Alps and laid a vicelike siege on Pavia until the Lombard ruler swore that he would return the conquered lands. When the bellicose Aistulf reneged on his oath and besieged Rome at the beginning of 756, threatening to kill the Pope with his own hands, Pepin marched south again and soundly thrashed the Lombards in the ensuing battle.

This time, the settlement was established. The terms may have distressed Constantinople, for the Byzantines still considered the region a part of their own empire and were far from certain that they could count on the future allegiance of the Pope – any more than the Pope could count on the support of Constantinople. The Lombards yielded to the papacy not only the captured towns in the duchy of Rome, but also the city and environs of Ravenna, hitherto the seat of Byzantine provincial government on the Italian peninsula. A wide swath extending across the peninsula from Rome to Ravenna now belonged to the newly constituted Papal States – the Republic of Saint Peter, as some chroniclers would style it. Constantinople, fully aware of the dangers of offending the papacy's new protector, could do very little but observe the situation from afar.

The Franks grew more powerful still under the leadership of Pepin's son Charles, who succeeded his father to the throne in 768 at the age of 26. (Charles was actually crowned in tandem with his older brother, Carloman, but Carloman died a short time afterwards.) A warrior-statesman of enormous physical strength and energy, Charles proved to be such an effective leader that the clerics of his court started referring to him in Latin as *Carolus Magnus* – Charles the Great, or in the language of the modern French, Charlemagne.

Charlemagne's success depended largely upon his remarkable ability to compel loyalty at all levels of Frankish society. He expanded the practice of vassalage begun by his forebears, the mayors of the palace, who exchanged grants of land for the fealty of soldiers and others sworn to serve them. Charlemagne broadened the principle by making personal vassals of all those in high authority – counts, dukes and church officials as well as ranking officers – and he encouraged them to follow

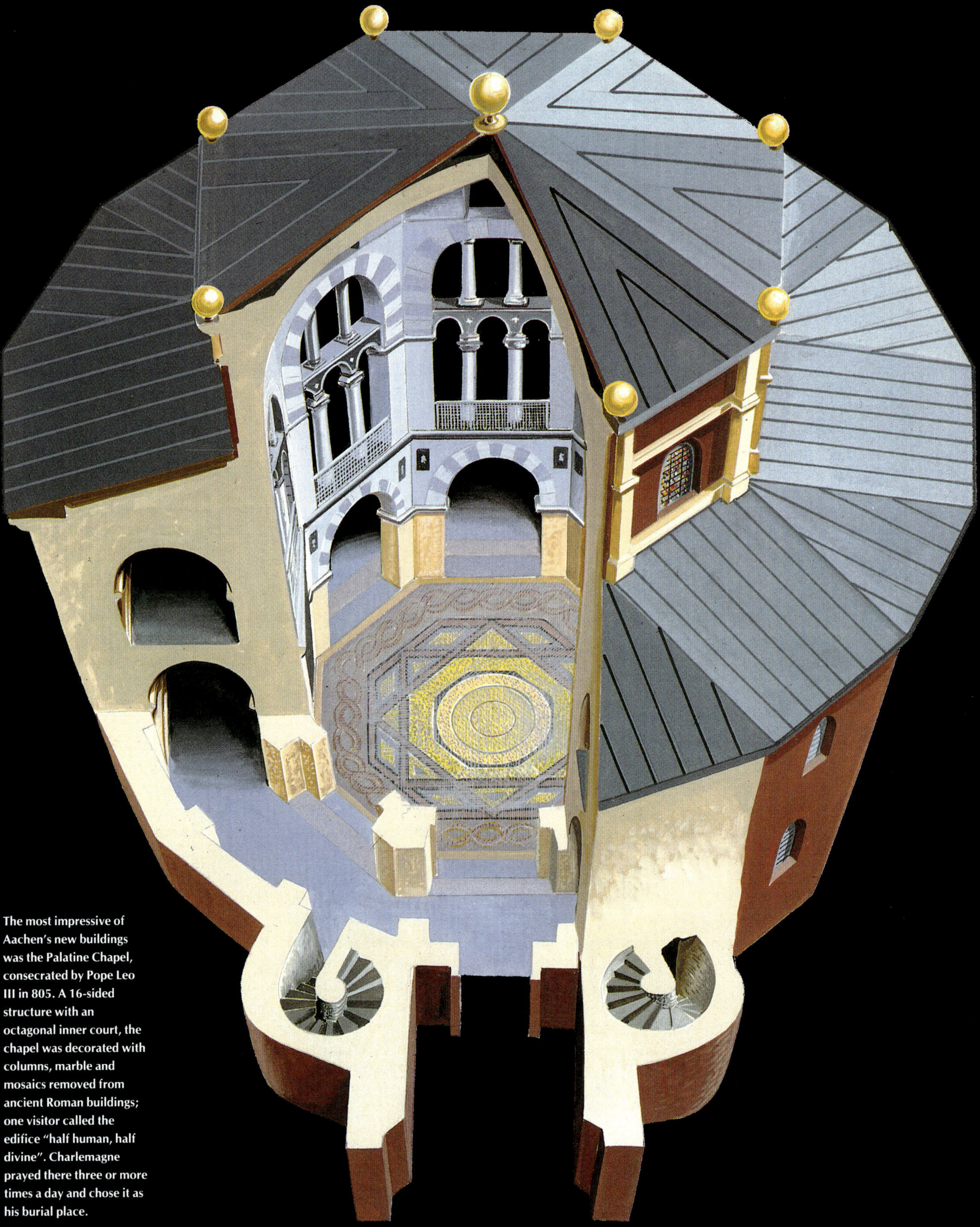

The most impressive of Aachen's new buildings was the Palatine Chapel, consecrated by Pope Leo III in 805. A 16-sided structure with an octagonal inner court, the chapel was decorated with columns, marble and mosaics removed from ancient Roman buildings; one visitor called the edifice "half human, half divine". Charlemagne prayed there three or more times a day and chose it as his burial place.

AN IMPERIAL CAPITAL

In 794, Charlemagne, wearied by years of travelling from place to place in his far-flung empire, determined to settle his imperial entourage at Aachen, in the rolling hills between the Rhine and Meuse rivers. Renowned for its mineral springs, Aachen had been a popular spa ever since Roman times, and its healthy climate and proximity to rich game preserves appealed to Charlemagne's love of the outdoors. More importantly, however, the town was strategically located on road and river arteries that provided access to much of the Frankish kingdom.

Summoning highly skilled artisans from throughout his vast domain, the King directed his chief architect, Odo of Metz, to design an imperial capital that would match Rome and Ravenna in grandeur. No expense was spared, and Odo made liberal use of multicoloured Italian marble and fixtures of gold, silver and brass. The new complex of Aachen matched Charlemagne's expectations and ranked among the very finest structures of the age.

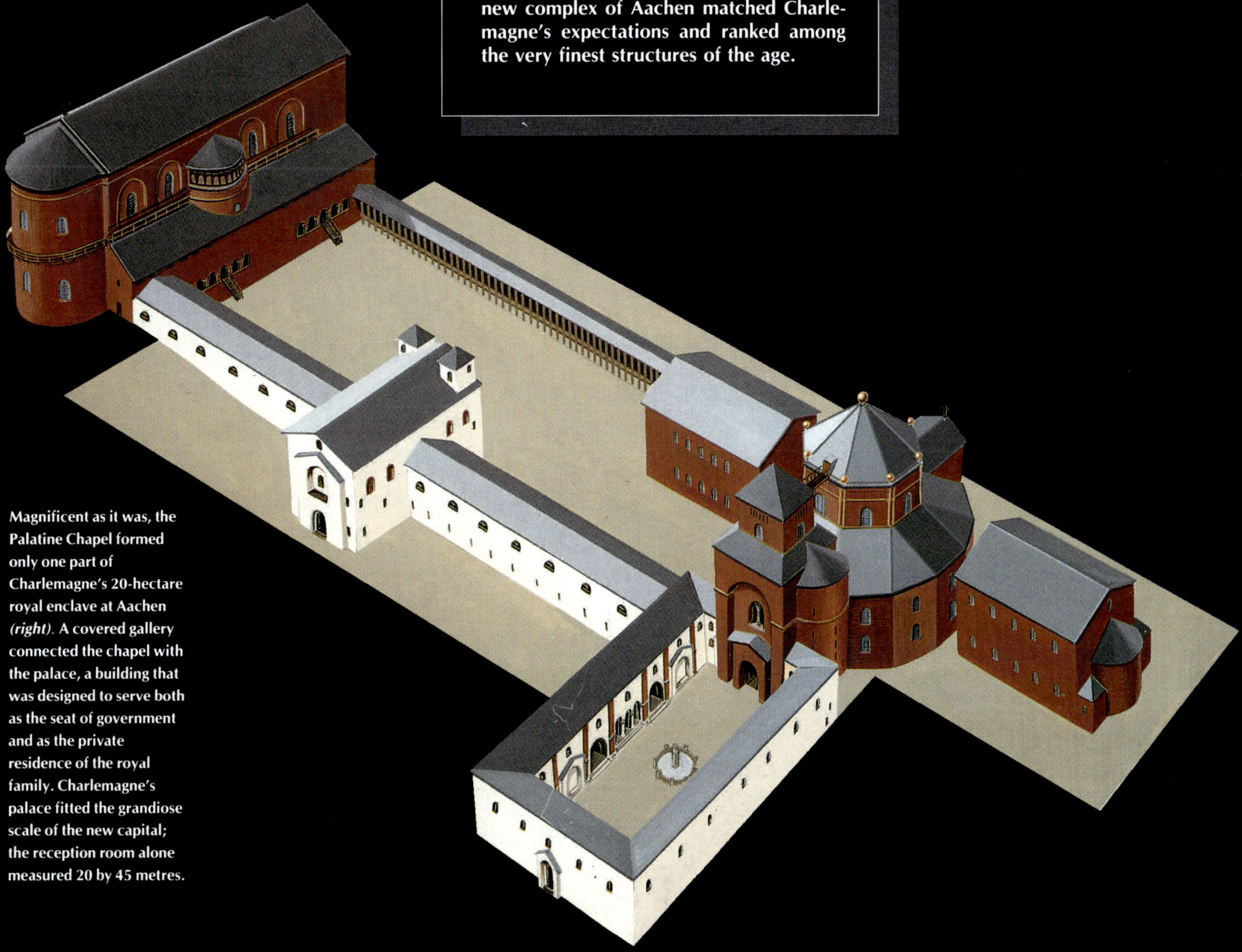

Magnificent as it was, the Palatine Chapel formed only one part of Charlemagne's 20-hectare royal enclave at Aachen *(right)*. A covered gallery connected the chapel with the palace, a building that was designed to serve both as the seat of government and as the private residence of the royal family. Charlemagne's palace fitted the grandiose scale of the new capital; the reception room alone measured 20 by 45 metres.

his example by developing their own network of vassals. He thus forged a chain of fealty that reached through every class of society.

Late in his life, Charlemagne established his capital at Aachen, a former Roman spa in what would later be western Germany. But until then he ruled through a court that travelled with him as he moved throughout his empire. His chief minister, called the count of the palace, sifted through matters that came up for royal attention, submitting to the King those involving great men or high policy and adjudicating minor cases himself. Administration of local territorial divisions, the *comitatus*, or counties, was usually the responsibility of lesser counts who served at the pleasure of the King. In Frankish Gaul, there were about 300 of these small counties. The count administered oaths of loyalty to freemen, published and enforced royal edicts and ordinances (with particular attention to those concerning justice), recruited royal army units, and levied fines and taxes, one-third of which he could keep for himself. The King commissioned a corps of inspectors, *missi dominici,* high-ranking representatives who went out in pairs – usually a noble layman and a bishop – to assess the honesty and efficiency of local administrators.

The King's own personal magnetism helped gather the notoriously balky aristocracy to his government and causes. He was jovial and approachable. When in residence at Aachen late in his life, he swam every day in the hot springs and would often invite friends and associates, even bodyguards and attendants, to join him. It was not unusual for a visitor to come upon 100 or more men, including Charlemagne himself, frolicking about with great hilarity in the hot waters.

Charlemagne imported scholars from England, Ireland and Italy to his palace to instruct him and his court in astronomy and mathematics, in Greek and Latin. The

A Cultural Reawakening

Anxious to establish Christian supremacy and promote the educational and spiritual enrichment of his subjects, Charlemagne sparked a cultural revival. The Carolingian Renaissance drew scholars from across Europe to Aachen's palace school, among them the English monk Alcuin *(right),* who espoused Charlemagne's ambition to create "a new Athens enriched by the sevenfold fullness of the Holy Spirit".

The new enlightenment was marked by a desire for unity and order based on Christian precepts. Monasteries, built to an ideal design *(far right)* and governed by rules of conduct set down by Saint Benedict, became self-sufficient communities and centres of learning. Among the cultural advances generated there was the standardization of written characters in an easily legible script that was called Carolingian minuscule *(overleaf)* and of liturgical chants in the Gregorian model.

The scholar Alcuin *(right)* and a fellow monk.

King encouraged the clergy to become teachers, and pressured the Church into opening schools in cathedrals, monasteries and even rural parishes. His palace school at Aachen was the cradle of the Carolingian Renaissance. Calling himself a "most devoted son of the Church", the King increasingly involved himself in religion. Scarcely any aspect of the spiritual sphere escaped his attention. He headed councils of bishops called to rule on ecclesiastical matters, lectured the clergy on how they ought to live, and enjoined his people to pray. He instituted a law requiring Christians to tithe by turning over to the Church one tenth of the products of their labours and even required that each new pope notify him immediately of his election – formerly a prerogative of the Byzantine emperor.

Although he demonstrated his genius for the arts of peace, it was Charlemagne's brilliance as a warrior that made all his other achievements possible. Rare was the year in which he did not embark on a campaign. To the southwest, his troops penetrated the Pyrenees and drove the Muslims back to Barcelona and beyond. To the north, they crossed upper Germany through Friesland to the North Sea and through Saxony to the Baltic. To the east, they took Bavaria and thrust into the central basin of the Danube, where they defeated Byzantium's old enemies, the Avars.

And to the southeast, the Franks intervened again in northern Italy at the request of the pope when the insistent Lombards assaulted the Papal States. As before, the Franks compelled Pavia to surrender. This time, however, Charlemagne decided to eliminate future problems by annexing the conquered land and, in 774, had himself crowned King of the Lombards.

Indisputably the colossus of the West, Charlemagne entertained overtures from the empire that still dominated eastern Europe – Byzantium. These overtures came in 781 not from the emperor, Constantine VI, who was only 11 years of age, but from his widowed mother, Irene, who governed as his regent. A woman of vaulting ambition, Irene proposed to Charlemagne a marriage alliance uniting her son and his daughter, Rotrud, who was then only six or seven years old. Such a union, she

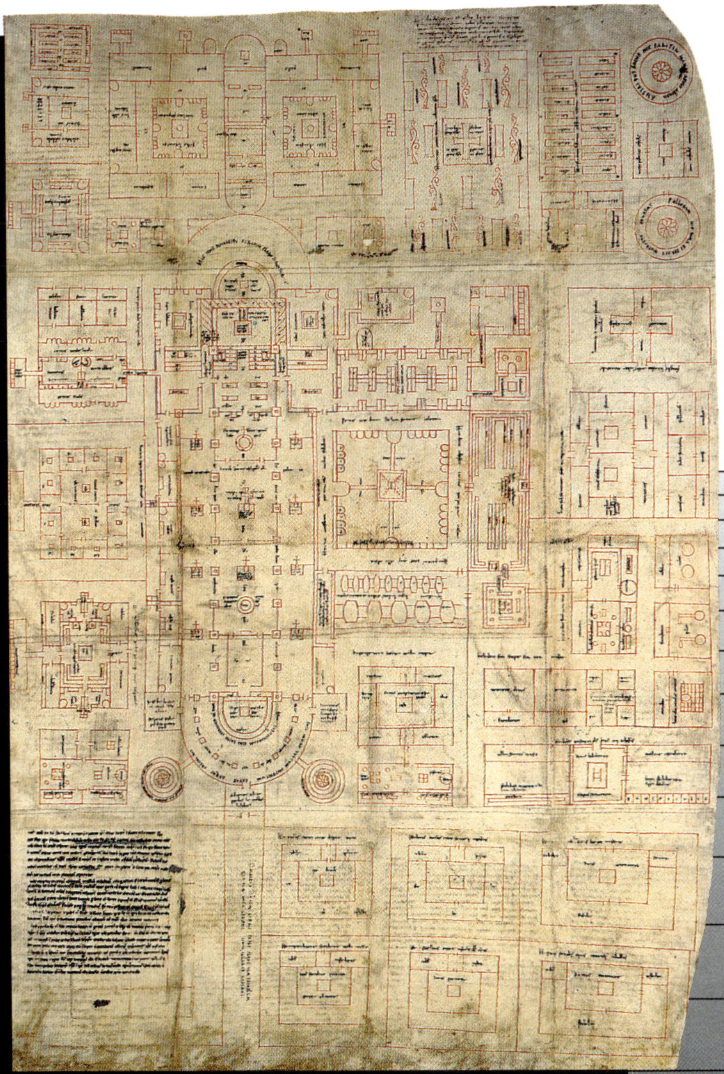

Plan of an ideal Carolingian monastery.

hoped, might dissuade the Franks from absorbing the remaining Byzantine holdings in southern Italy and Sicily. Charlemagne, for his part, welcomed the opportunity to link his royal house with the empire that still enjoyed enormous prestige.

The children were duly betrothed, and Charlemagne's daughter began learning Greek and Byzantine customs. But the arrangement collapsed before any marriage could take place. Charlemagne was displeased when Irene sent an army to invade Benevento, an independent duchy south of Rome. His soldiers helped Benevento's forces defeat the Byzantines. He was further annoyed by her sponsorship of an ecumenical council. The council's decision to rescind the 60-year-old ban on icons, thus removing a divisive issue between Byzantium and Rome, greatly disturbed Charlemagne, who was also annoyed that Irene had not invited him or any of his bishops to this august gathering of the church hierarchy in the first place.

And Irene had more grandiose plans still. In 797, after falling out with her son, the emperor, she plotted his overthrow, had the young man blinded in order to preclude his return, and then she took the throne in her own name, assuming the full title of emperor, rather than empress.

In Rome, Pope Leo III viewed the events with a growing sense of distaste. Like many others in the West, Leo considered the Byzantine throne vacant because no male occupied it. Leo, moreover, had made some important enemies in Rome and was anxious to ensure the favour and protection of Charlemagne. What better way to do so than to bestow the title of Roman emperor upon the man who now ruled over much of the West and who served as protector and patrician of its ancient seat?

Even though the title was *Roman* emperor, it belonged by historical provenance to Constantinople and was not Rome's to give. But this did not matter. In 800, during the services on Christmas Day at Saint Peter's in Rome, the Pope approached Charlemagne as the King knelt in prayer and placed a magnificent crown upon his head. Then, in a ceremonial chant that was copied from the imperial coronation ritual of the Byzantines, the Roman clergy and congregation

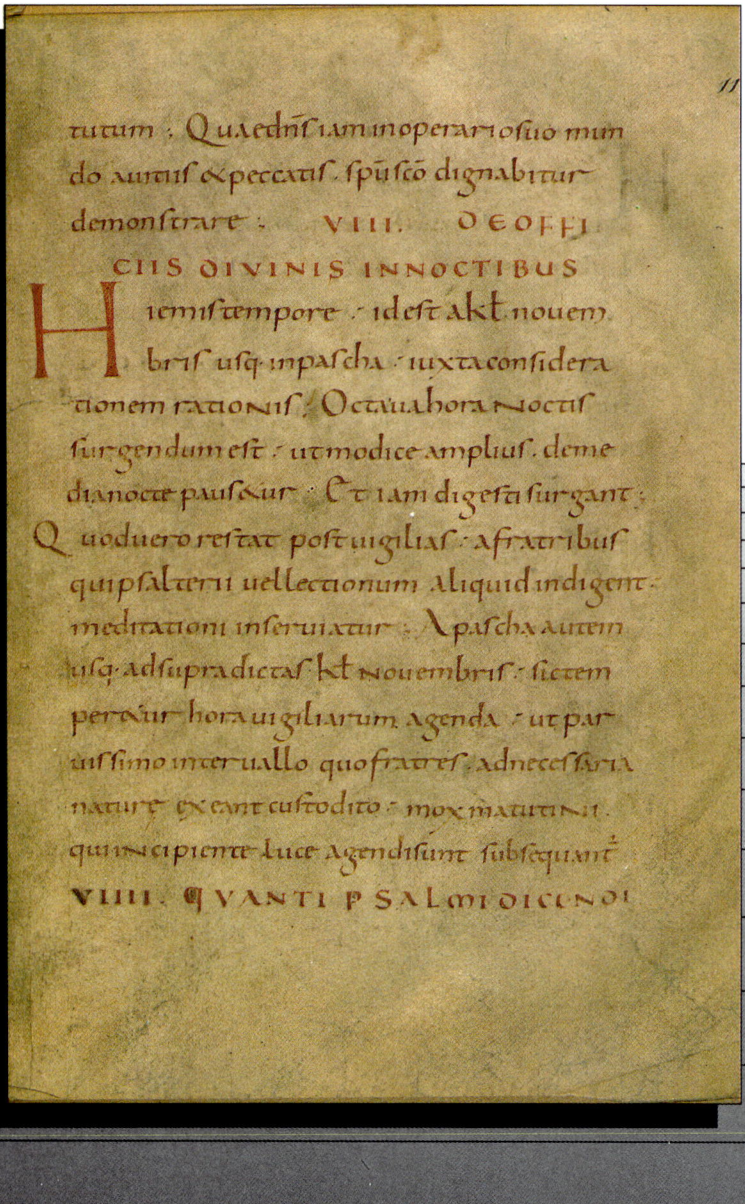

Page from the Rule of St. Benedict, in Caroline minuscule.

shouted their acclamation of Charlemagne: "To Charles the Augustus, crowned of God, the great and pacific emperor, life and victory!" This was an unequivocal declaration of the final shift of papal loyalty away from Byzantium and to the West.

Charlemagne appears not to have taken such a simplistic view of matters. There is some evidence that he was surprised and perhaps put off when the chorus of acclamation was intoned by only the Romans present, not the Franks, who had apparently not been apprised of the Pope's plans in advance. In any event, he was to spend most of the remaining years of his life and rule working to secure Byzantine recognition and heal the rift between East and West. It required a great deal of negotiation – and some fighting – but eventually, in 811, Charlemagne succeeded in making the Byzantines recognize his imperial title. The emperor Irene had long since been deposed, and her son Nicephorus had died in battle against the Bulgarians. It was Nicephorus' successor, Michael I Rangabe, who ratified the treaty accepting the idea of two coequal emperors, presiding side by side, over the West and East. To the Byzantines, it was an excruciatingly painful moment, for as one of their scribes wrote, "Barbarians and those who have arisen from among foreign peoples were not eligible for the imperial dignity."

The Byzantines, however, would go on from this low pass in their fortunes to triumphs hardly dreamt of in AD 800. The next four centuries were to glimmer so brilliantly for them that the era would be known as the Golden Age of Byzantium. Charlemagne's heirs, however, would not be so successful in their stewardship of the vast empire he had constructed. While it lasted, it was the largest and most stable political unit to have risen in the West since classical times. But it had been in large measure Charlemagne's personal creation, and his sons and grandsons lacked the great man's vision, supreme statesmanship, military prowess and vast energy. The empire of Charlemagne was to fall apart within 30 years of his death in 814, as the West entered a period marked by violence and upheaval.

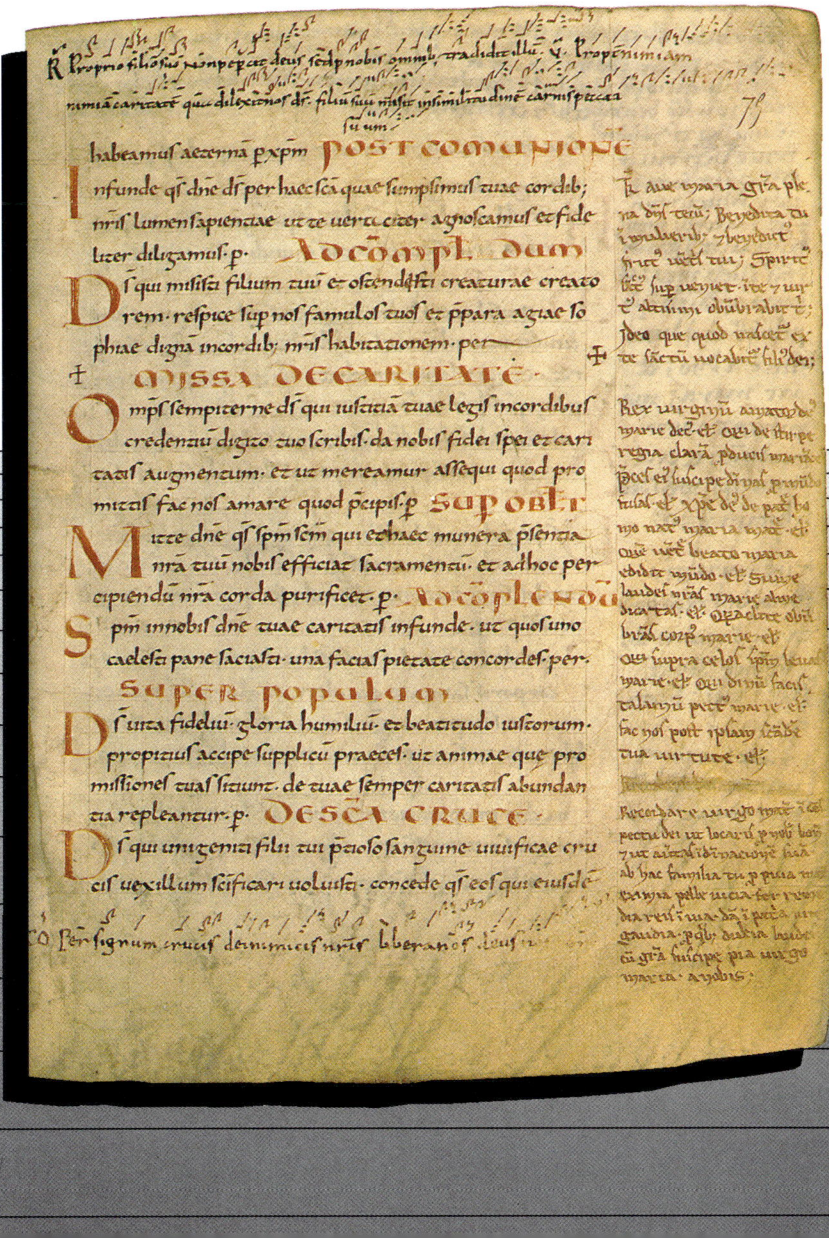

Page from a Gregorian chant of the Carolingian period.

EMPIRE-BUILDING IN THE EAST

3

Early in the seventh century, a Chinese Buddhist monk by the name of Xuanzang ignored – at no small risk to his head – an imperial ban on foreign travel and set out on a pilgrimage to India, the Buddhist holy land. He wished to see for himself the wondrous place of peace and plenty described by Faxian – another Buddhist monk who had visited India two centuries before, at the peak of the Gupta empire.

Following the ancient Silk Road, a series of oases strung like pearls along the edge of central Asia's wastelands, the venturesome monk eventually reached India, where he spent the next eight years travelling and learning. Parts of northern India had recently been reunited by the charismatic young ruler Harsha, after a century of desolation following the White Hun invasions. To the monk's eye, Harsha's land was blossoming with prosperity and culture; Xuanzang recorded what he saw and gathered a great store of Buddhist manuscripts to take back to China.

Upon his return home – fortunately to a forgiving emperor – the monk not only translated his treasured texts, but also produced, in 645, a lengthy account of his travels entitled *Record of the Western Regions.* Xuanzang wrote of lands that produced "abundant fruits and flowers", of cities with houses of "extraordinary height, sumptuous inside and economical outside, with floors strewn with flowers of the season", of a people "good-looking and fond of learning".

But the resemblance of this description to the past glories of the Gupta era was illusory, the merest of mirages. For all its glitter and apparent stability, Harsha's kingdom suffered insurmountable economic and religious problems. In 647, scarcely two years after Xuanzang's return to China, the emperor Harsha would be overthrown, after which India's petty kingdoms – numbering no fewer than 70 by Xuanzang's count – would revert to incessant internecine warfare. And India, once so dominant, would forfeit its position of power in Asia.

In India's stead, an increasingly powerful Islam would begin to assert its strength. The Muslim tide had already engulfed Persia. Now, spreading inexorably along the west coast of the Indian subcontinent, the Arabs would occupy the province of the Sind on the lower Indus River, advance to annex the central oases north of the Hindu Kush, and then wrest control of trade along the Indian Ocean.

With the waning of India, the entrepôt kingdoms of Southeast Asia, born centuries earlier of a marriage between Indian and local tradition, would shed much of their colonial heritage. Native art and enterprise would flourish from Borneo to Sumatra and from Burma to Siam. And ambitious local rulers would look with ever-growing fascination, not only upon Islam, but most importantly upon the might and majesty of the Chinese imperial courts.

Indeed, with the passage of time, China would assume India's erstwhile role as the dominant civilization in Asia. The days of Chinese disunion, when nomads

By the seventh century, China's expansionist Tang dynasty had extended its imperial control from the capital city of Changan to Manchuria and Korea in the north, to Vietnam in the south, and westwards through central Asia as far as Afghanistan and Persia. These subject states and protectorates were deeply influenced by their conqueror's religion and culture, as illustrated by the distinctively Chinese style of a bronze dragon's head *(left)*, which crowned a flagstaff in a Korean temple. Ultimately, administering this far-flung empire of 53 million subjects proved to be too demanding for the Tang dynasty's rulers; by the middle of the eighth century, a series of internal revolts and incursions by frontier tribes had begun to break up the Tang's empire into a mosaic of some 40 semi-independent military states.

from the steppes roamed the North China plain, were at an end. In the year 589, a vigorous dynasty – the Sui – had come to power and had forged a new empire, which under the Tang, the Sui's successors, would eclipse all earlier dominions, reaching from Tibet to Korea and from Mongolia to the South China Sea. Here, Buddhism would enjoy its zenith. Here, a vast and efficient bureaucracy would come into being. Here, great public works would take shape and enormous cities would grow – the biggest and most populous urban centres the world had ever known, thriving with commerce and industry and nurturing an exalted art and literature. At the Tang court, visitors from across the civilized world – Persian exiles, Sogdian mercenaries, Arab merchants, Nestorian missionaries – would mix with ministers, generals, historians, holy men and the greatest poets in China's history. Never before had Chinese society been so cosmopolitan, so open, so enthralled with the distant, the Western. And never would it be so again.

Harsha Vardhana, Xuanzang's remarkable young host in India, was a stripling of 16 in 606, when he succeeded to the throne of his native Thaneshwar – a kingdom strategically located at the entrance to the Ganges River plain. His father, like most petty kings, had spent his life slaying Huns and feuding with fellow monarchs. But the son was of finer stuff; despite his youth, he was a warrior of great skill, tenacity and vision. Within the space of six short years, Harsha Vardhana had conquered his squabbling neighbours and had welded them into a new North India kingdom.

Harsha's method of rule contrasted starkly with that of the Guptas. For example, he maintained tight control: while the Guptas had decentralized the administration of their empire, Harsha imposed strong central authority. He travelled continuously round his kingdom, inspecting local governments and redressing grievances. He opened his treasury to major public works and supported numerous charities.

And unlike the Guptas, who had fostered a rebirth of Hinduism, Harsha favoured Buddhism. Not only did he allow its practice, he proved to be a devoted patron of the faith, adding a large monastery to the university at Nalanda, which expanded to include no fewer than 4,000 students in his day.

By Harsha's time, however, Indian culture belonged at heart to the Hindus, not the Buddhists. Hinduism had matured in the fifth century under the Guptas, softening somewhat the harshness of its caste system, dominated by the priestly class of brahmans, by incorporating a number of popular cults. Harsha was said to have taken exception to some of the sterner aspects of Hindu law, including the practice of women immolating themselves on their husbands' funeral pyres as an act of piety. The Emperor even saved his own sister from committing this grisly act.

Nevertheless, Hinduism and caste were facts of Indian life that no ruler could ignore, and Harsha made sure that brahman ministers as well as Buddhist monks attended him at court. Under his benign patronage, Hinduism evolved its six schools of philosophy, and learning made enormous strides – particularly in the area of the sciences. Indian mathematicians calculated a more accurate value for pi than the Greeks; the physicist Brahmagupta promulgated teachings that anticipated gravitational theory; and the Vaisesika school invented an "atomic" theory of the universe, holding each element of nature to be unique.

Lenient, generous, widely admired, Harsha inspired historians to remember him as one of the best-known rulers in India's ancient past. Yet Harsha's kingdom held the seeds of its own destruction. With the fall of the Guptas, India had lost its land routes through Asia to the Western world, and trade with Rome had consequently collapsed – sharply reducing the amount of currency circulating throughout India. Harsha's failure to annex the Indus River Valley and India's western seaboard left him no alternative trade routes, and in time his treasury was all but depleted. To make matters even worse, Hindu tradition required Indian rulers to offer annual "gifts" – actually tribute – to the brahmans, and when the kings lacked sufficient currency they often substituted state lands. Harsha not only institutionalized the practice but also gave away state lands in the place of official salaries. Such policies were certain to aggravate the problems of a weakening economy, while enhancing the wealth and power of the brahmans at the expense of Harsha's own authority. Moreover, Hinduism was gaining steadily among the masses, while Buddhism was falling into disfavour.

Traditionally, India's wealthy and ruling classes had been attracted to Buddhism because they resented the brahman caste's claims of precedence over all others. A few Indian rulers had patronized Buddhism as an antidote to brahman arrogance and a check on brahman power. As the Hindu caste system strengthened its grip on Indian society, Buddhism seemed more and more to be the religion of the rich. And Indian leaders linked to the Buddhists became increasingly vulnerable.

Thus it came to pass that the brahmans felt powerful enough to plot against Harsha's life. According to one account, Harsha uncovered the conspiracy and ordered the arrest of 500 brahmans. Then, with typical leniency, he pardoned all but the ringleaders – which proved to be his undoing. The brahmans, led by one of the ministers Harsha had pardoned, quickly mounted a second conspiracy, and this time they succeeded. The Emperor was murdered by army officers in the year 647.

Following Harsha's death his empire disintegrated, and northern India became a bloody battleground on which various small kingdoms struggled for supremacy. Yet no ruler could reunite even part of the North India plain, and henceforth the more significant events in India's history would take place elsewhere – to the south on the vast Deccan Plateau and on the fertile plains of Tamil Nadu. The southern kingdoms were also addicted to warfare: one Deccan ruler boasted of fighting

108 battles in 12 years. Another, when he grew too old for combat, ceremonially drowned himself in a sacred river to the sound of appropriate music.

Commencing in the middle of the sixth century, and for 300 years thereafter, three major kingdoms were involved in the conflict – the Chalukyas, the Pallavas and the Pāndyas. Like their northern counterparts, these southern kingdoms appeared equally balanced in political and military strength, and the wars they fought created a seesawing of power in which no state proved supreme.

The Chalukyas controlled the Deccan, where they had established a kingdom strong enough to withstand even Harsha when he attempted to expand southwards. Their archenemies, the Pallavas, dominated much of the Indian peninsula. An aggressive people, seafarers as well as warriors, the Pallavas built urban fortresses in which they stored the wealth gained through commerce and conquest, and from which they set out to attack the Chalukyas. The third major dynasty, the Pāndyas, detested both of the others; their stronghold was in Madurai, south of Tamil Nadu, and they attacked either the Chalukyas or Pallavas at every opportunity.

Yet for all its warlike similarity to the north, the south was quite different in its manner of government. There was none of the centralized bureaucracy imposed upon northerners by Harsha. Southern villages and district administrations were largely autonomous, suffering little interference from the capitals. Most southerners were non-Aryan speakers of Dravidian, in contrast to the Aryan, Indo-European speakers of the north. Peasants in agricultural villages along the drainage basins of major rivers coexisted uneasily with the belligerent upland and forest tribes.

The families who asserted general authority over these areas turned to Hinduism for justification. Although the Chalukyas had probably originally migrated from central Asia, travelling with one of the White Hun tribes, they had their brahman scribes establish for them a respectably Aryan pedigree. And though the Pallavas clearly contained alien tribal strains, they enthusiastically adopted Hindu caste principles, even claiming as their ancestor the supreme deity Brahma himself.

As Harsha's kingdom collapsed and the dynasties of the south grew more influential, Dravidian beliefs and customs began to flow northwards. One sweeping

Priests and worshippers at a temple in Changan welcome a horse caravan bearing priceless Buddhist icons and manuscripts from India. This auspicious arrival, in 645, marked the end of an epic 16,000-kilometre pilgrimage by the Chinese monk Xuanzang *(right),* who had spent eight years studying at the feet of India's Buddhist masters. The monk's dedication and courage inspired Tang emperor Taizong to provide financial aid, enabling Xuanzang to translate sacred Sanskrit scriptures into Chinese and promote Buddhism throughout the empire.

effect of this cultural exchange was on religion: the faiths in the north that had traditionally been associated with the wealthy and powerful — Buddhism and Jainism — lost ground rapidly to Hinduism.

In fact, Hinduism, whose appeal lay in its variety, was ideally suited for a land of splintered domains and ephemeral powers. Its gods numbered in the millions, and devotees could worship all of them, or one of them, or none of them, with equal enthusiasm and propriety. No prophet, no religious leader like Muhammad, had yet appeared to codify and evangelize Hindu beliefs, and therefore Hinduism had not developed a rigid system of worship. Some Hindus prayed, others meditated, others made sacrifices, and still others participated in secret and sometimes orgiastic rituals. Springing from both primitive nature worship and the ancient, abstruse Sanskrit scriptures called the Vedas, Hinduism accommodated all classes, all intellects, all personalities. It tended to absorb rather than attack alien or hostile doctrines. And in the process it became more than a religion; it became an almost palpable framework for Indian society, one in which people of widely diverse backgrounds, beliefs, classes and education went their separate ways, yet were held together in a single culture by the caste system.

More and more, Hinduism organized its worship round temples, which in the south, particularly, became gigantic, the focal point of many a city. In the Deccan, eighth-century Hindu architects sculpted an immense structure at Ellora by excavating 30 metres downwards through solid rock, literally making a mountain into a freestanding house of worship. Inevitably, the temples became the focus of numerous and diverse social activities. Not only priests, architects and artists, but also dancers, singers, teachers and writers congregated inside their halls. Hindu colleges, generally attached to the temples, began to assert for the brahmans the control over education long exercised by Jains and Buddhists. At first open to any Hindu, the colleges — even those endowed by merchants — gradually developed into exclusively brahman institutions, devoted to advanced study. Extensive royal patronage eventually rendered these colleges hotbeds of political intrigue as the brahmans contrived to win favour and support.

With the rise of Hinduism, the Buddhist faith by the eighth century had become an empty shell of a religion. The Hindus had digested its doctrines and had relegated Buddha to a niche among its multitude of deities. Indian Buddhism retained its separate religious identity only on the fringes of the Indian world — in the lands of Sri Lanka, Burma and Tibet.

Yet for all its vitality, Hinduism could not restore India to its former greatness in the ancient world. The political landscape north and south remained fragmented and chaotic — and now the winds of Islam were starting to blow in from the west. Overrunning Persia in the seventh century, Arab armies and holy men had set about forcibly converting every man, woman and child to Islam. And in the eighth century, the Arabs invaded western India along the coast to the lower Indus River Valley. The Chalukyas in the Deccan managed to hold back the Muslim wave long enough for their southern neighbours to arm themselves, and the immediate danger from the Arabs passed. Checked for the moment from advancing farther into the Indian subcontinent, the Arabs took up settlement in the region of the Sind and themselves became traders and merchants.

By the ninth century, India had been reduced to impotence. Trade had shifted to foreigners, mostly Arabs, who operated along the coasts. Communication with the

While Buddhism flourished in seventh-century China under the imperial patronage of the Tang dynasty, India was forgoing Buddhism's increasingly exclusive and mystical practices for the eclectic and earthly teachings of Hinduism. Adding to its allure, Hinduism embraced the doctrines and deities of other religions, incorporating elements of Islam and Manichaeism and worshipping the Buddha as a reincarnation of Vishnu *(top)*, the Hindu god of regeneration and renewal. Even Vishnu's vengeful counterpart, Siva, the god of destruction *(bottom)*, presents no one-dimensional portrait of evil: Siva combines, in a contradictory mixture that has appeal for every adherent, creativity with destructiveness and compassion with cruelty.

Western world was indirect — via Arab intermediaries — and limited to commerce. India remained drifting, awaiting the day three centuries later when the Muslim whirlwind would whip over the weak, self-absorbed kingdoms of the subcontinent.

Across the Bay of Bengal, in Southeast Asia and on the islands of Indonesia, the Indian presence had transformed the cultural landscape. Indian traders had first braved the voyage across that treacherous bay some time in the first century AD. Those few daring souls who survived the monsoons and the pirates reported back that they had found a "land of gold", offering not only glittering metal but a great variety of other resources as well. Yet it was not until the third century that Indian merchants found themselves in a position to take advantage of their discoveries.

At that time, barbarian incursions into North China following the collapse of the Han dynasty provoked long-lasting disunity in China and severed the ancient trade routes through central Asia. Indian shippers exploited the situation, and by the fifth century, India was running Chinese trade through the Indonesian islands, where a number of small kingdoms began to prosper as international marketing centres. Laden with textiles, jewels, ivory, even elephants, Indian vessels sailed south to Sri Lanka, then beat southeast through the Malacca Straits to meet Chinese junks and exchange their wares for raw silk and amber. At the Southeast Asian ports of call, the Indians took aboard camphor, spices and rare woods and often unloaded Buddhist, Jain and Hindu missionaries.

From their guests, the rude courts of the little kingdoms learnt to appreciate the splendour and subtlety of Indian culture, then in flower under the Gupta dynasty. Soon, the local kings were calling themselves maharajahs and converting to Indian religions, imitating the royal houses of the subcontinent down to the smallest details. At first, these wealthy Hindu or Buddhist kingdoms seemed mere extensions of India. But after the demise of the imperial Guptas, they began to exercise their own creative energies and soon modified Indian traditions to suit their special needs and desires. And they also declared both their political and commercial independence by establishing trade relations directly with China.

Srivijaya, the first of the great maritime kingdoms, rose to power in the seventh century at Palembang in southeast Sumatra. Strategically situated midway between the Malacca and the Sunda straits, on the lower edge of the South China Sea, Palembang had long been the customary landing point for ships sailing from China with the northeast monsoon, and in time the port became a major distribution centre for goods from India, western Asia and China. Compelled by the logic of its own economy to command the straits, Srivijaya expanded northwestwards to the Malay Peninsula and southeastwards towards western Java. It took control not only of the straits but also of the islands dotting the approaches. From there, Srivijaya exercised commercial hegemony over Indonesia until the end of the 13th century.

Srivijaya owed its prosperity to China and understood that fact well. From the outset, Srivijayan monarchs had sent missions to the Chinese court, playing a masterful game of diplomacy. Chinese rulers called themselves Sons of Heaven; a foreigner approached such a divine personage as a supplicant or vassal and sought to engage in trade only under the guise of tribute. In order to curry favour, the Srivijayans acknowledged the Son of Heaven as their overlord. And they threw their island open to Chinese travellers as well as traders. Many Chinese holy men came to visit Srivijaya's centre for Buddhist studies; one monk, I-ching, found no fewer than 1,000 scholars there when he visited in 671 and recommended the centre to his fellow monks as an excellent place to research holy texts.

Yet China was not the sole source of Srivijayan strength. Unwilling to serve as mere middlemen in the China traffic, Palembang's ambitious merchants developed a thriving industry producing goods of their own for international markets – nipa mats, tortoiseshell, beeswax, aromatic woods and camphor. In this enterprise, they made allies of the Indonesian aborigines – the *orang asli,* or forest people, and the *orang laut,* or sea people. The forest people knew where to collect.aromatic woods, camphor, and other materials that fuelled local trade. Camphor, for example, took the form of small grains that developed inside the trunks of diseased trees, and the *orang asli* could detect its presence from a number of signs, including the smell of the wood when they chipped it. Commanding the loyalty of the sea people was more important still. Inhabiting the islands off Palembang and Jambi, the *orang laut* were intimately acquainted with every shoal and quirk of wind. Left to themselves, they engaged in piracy; treated well and properly supported, they guarded Srivijaya's sea approaches and guided traders to safe harbour.

The Srivijayans also shrewdly manipulated the petty fiefdoms along the coasts of Sumatra and the Malay Peninsula. The local lords shared in Srivijaya's remarkable trade, but the Srivijayans did not put their faith in economic rewards alone. Srivijayan monarchs propagated the belief in a special force that they, as gods or near gods, possessed. That force would strike down any vassal guilty of *derhaka,* or "treason to the ruler". The Malays believed that if one acted traitorously, the king's curse would strike one dead. The idea tended to produce extraordinarily devoted subjects and became so central to Srivijayan statesmanship that the personal followers of the monarch routinely committed suicide upon his death.

By 775, Srivijaya had extended its domain to the entire Malay Peninsula, swallowing up no fewer than 14 smaller city-kingdoms. But even as Srivijaya approached its apogee, there were other maritime powers rising in Southeast Asia to claim a share of the bounty. The Buddhist Chams, with roots in the region at least as deep as those of the Srivijayans, had established small coastal enclaves along the southern shores of Vietnam. To the west, the Hindu Khmers of Chen-la had swept southwards and deposed the last Buddhist king of Funan in the Mekong Delta. By the end of the seventh century, the Khmers had established a base for a powerful Cambodian empire with its capital at Angkor. Yet it was the envious and ambitious Javanese kings who became Srivijaya's strongest and most bellicose competitors.

Around the year 730, a piratical king named Sanjaya consolidated his hold on Java and relentlessly raided traffic throughout the area, striking at Sumatrans and Cambodians and possibly even the Chinese themselves. So exceedingly troublesome did the Javanese become that the Srivijayans were forced to come to terms with their aggressive neighbours. Ever cunning, the Srivijayans then bided their time until a new and more amenable dynasty – the Sailendras – came to power in Java. The Srivijayans may even have helped to overthrow their enemies. In any event, Srivijaya negotiated a peace with the Sailendras in 775 and cemented the relationship with a treaty and marriage alliance. By the mid-ninth century, the ruler of Srivijaya itself was a Sailendra, boasting of his Javanese ancestors.

The trade alliance with a major sea power and Java's own considerable agricultural wealth enabled the Sailendras to sustain vast religious undertakings. Like the Srivijayan kings, the Sailendra monarchs were ardent Buddhists, and towards the end of the eighth century they constructed a proper monument to their god on the Kedu Plain in the centre of the island. Immense by any measure, the building of the Borobudur temple required 56,600 cubic metres of stone and was adorned with 2,500 square metres of exquisite stone bas-relief.

Such devotion to Buddha was transitory, however. As in India, Hinduism was gaining favour among the Javanese people, and by the middle of the ninth century, even the Sailendra monarchs had converted to the rival religion, building temples at Prambanan as elaborate as those at Borobudur, 80 kilometres away. As went religion, so went politics. Before long, the alliance with the staunchly Buddhist Srivijayans crumbled, and the Javanese returned to their ancient ways, raiding their neighbour's shipping and attacking its coastal ports. So hostile did relations become that in 992 ambassadors from Palembang appeared at the Chinese court pleading for protection. The Chinese declined to intervene.

Throughout Southeast Asia, the kingdoms that now looked to China nevertheless retained much of their Indian heritage; it coloured their laws, their politics, their religion. But this was not the case with Vietnam. Almost alone among the kingdoms, it had always been Chinese in outlook. So close were the ties, in fact, that Chinese emperors tended to regard it as part of China, a pleasant, more or less peaceful province they called "the pacified south", or Annam. Vietnam had the trappings of a typical Chinese province — the classical studies, the civil service examination system, the orthodox Confucianism. But it also had something that most Chinese provinces did not: direct and constant, if uneasy, contact with outsiders. In the

Thundering down from the Asian steppes on spirited Mongolian ponies, bands of hard-riding nomads such as those on the left terrorized vulnerable Chinese frontier settlements and easily evaded the imperial foot soldiers who pursued them. Innovative Tang emperors eventually took a leaf from the raiders' own book, importing 700,000 horses to form a public stud and establishing an imperial cavalry force whose precision drills and manoeuvres elicited admiration, and fear, from their nomadic adversaries. Royal hunts and polo games – sports from Persia – lent riding skills high prestige among the Chinese aristocracy, encouraging the nobility to emulate the ease and grace of nomadic hunters like the one above, mounted with his dog.

southern part of Vietnam lived the distinctly unpacified Chams, who ruled the loosely knit kingdom of Champa. They lived both as pirates and as traders, with no particular preference, and touched the lives of the northerners at every turn.

In the first century AD, the Chinese warlord Ma Yuan, who had overseen the pacification of Annam, erected two bronze pillars on the lower border of the land, and there, it was assumed, the civilized world came to an end. Beyond the pillars lived only demons, ghosts and subhuman savages – and the Chams. Ruled by a king clad in cotton, adorned with gold necklaces and wearing flowers in his hair, the Chams brought up pearls from the South China Sea, produced amazingly potent drugs, and distilled incenses so rich, it was said, that they enticed the gods down to their altars. The Chams protected their rulers and their often ill-gotten gains with warriors dressed in rattan armour who rode elephants into battle. The Chinese in Annam called them those "malignant and tyrannical" Chams and constantly tried to push their way into Champa territory. The Chams for their part raided Chinese settlements without cease. The fighting would consume 800 years before the Vietnamese were finally able to absorb the Chams. But in the meantime, the Vietnamese lived in a cultural buffer zone.

The imperial China that asserted such power over Asia had itself only come into being during the seventh and eighth centuries. Before then, only one dynasty, the Han, had succeeded in creating a truly united and enduring empire. But the Han

In canopied ox-drawn carts filled with trade goods, merchants of a dozen countries journeyed along hazardous, bandit-infested trails that stretched from Persia to China, bringing precious stones and metals, glass, medicines and cotton textiles to the bustling bazaars of Changan, the Tang capital at the eastern terminus of the Silk Road. These hardy hagglers, such as the Near Eastern trader hefting a wineskin on the right, also served as efficient propagators of Chinese culture. In addition to Chinese silk, tea and ceramics, the traders carried back to their own lands numerous Tang innovations in art, science and technology.

royal house had fallen in the third century, toppled by discord at court and the destructive ambition of military commanders. Subsequent nomadic invaders from the northern steppes helped keep the country unstable and fragmented. As tribes of Huns, Turks, Mongols and even Tibetans roamed the north, establishing a bewildering series of petty and short-lived monarchies, many of the North China aristocracy fled south, where they learnt to eat rice instead of millet cakes and married into the established families they had once haughtily considered provincial. Meanwhile in the north, the nomad invaders, too, had – in the time-honoured tradition of barbarian conquerors – intermingled with the local population and adopted the civilization of the vanquished. In the resulting mosaic of races and cultures on the North China plain, there arose a military-minded, mixed-blood aristocracy that saw itself as the legitimate heir to China's proud traditions – despite the fact that many of its members spoke Turkish as well as Chinese. Throughout the sixth century, a succession of such dynasties sought to assume hegemony over China. All failed and went to their destruction in the bitter regional wars that racked the land. At last, in 589, one dynasty – the Sui – stronger and more effective than the others, beat down its rivals, and a new Chinese empire was born.

The founder of the Sui, General Yang Jian, was a veteran of the battles between the kingdoms of northwestern and northeastern China, then called the Northern Zhou and the Northern Chi. Yang was the leader of a group of powerful families responsible for establishing the Northern Zhou dynasty, whose Emperor Wu he served as a military commander. Yang Jian had led the army that overwhelmed the Northern Chi in 577 and made Wu master of all North China. The Emperor in turn heaped honours on his general and made him commandant of a key prefecture. There, Yang Jian gathered a core of ruthless men, skilled in battle and government.

When Emperor Wu died after a sudden illness in 578, he was succeeded by the crown prince Yu-wen Bin, son-in-law of Yang Jian, who turned out to be a pathological despot. Coarse and vicious, Bin raped the wife of a kinsman, terrorized the court, and threatened his own wife with the extermination of her entire clan. In 581 Bin ordered his father-in-law to court and instructed his attendants to kill the General if his demeanour should change even slightly. Bin then proceeded to hurl inflammatory insults at Yang Jian. But the General had been warned by friends; not a flicker of emotion crossed his features, and he survived.

There was obviously only one course of action to be taken – Bin's dynasty would have to be overthrown. Fate played a hand in the first step. Shortly after the humiliating episode, Bin providentially died of natural causes, and Yang Jian's friends at court forged an order giving him authority over the military. Yang promptly executed Bin's eight-year-old son and 59 of the imperial relatives; then he declared his own dynasty. Naming his house Sui after family lands in the Wei Valley, Yang Jian became Wendi, Emperor Wen.

As successor to the Northern Zhou, the Sui dynasty controlled North China, Hupei and the central Yangtze, plus the province of Sichuan in the west. It was a vast domain, yet within two years Wendi was looking south, where a weak and dissolute emperor of the Chen dynasty presided haphazardly over the south Yangtze Valley. But before Wendi could make his move, he had to deal with a threat to the north from a confederation of nomadic tribes led by the Turks.

To the Chinese, the Turks were an even more formidable enemy than the Huns, whose steppe empire the Turks had vanquished in 552. For some years, an uneasy truce had existed between the Turks and the North Chinese. But now, in the unsettled days immediately following Yang Jian's coup, a group of Turkish tribes saw an opportunity. Gathering their horsemen, the Turks smashed through the Great Wall, slaughtering and pillaging, bringing fire and ruin wherever they rode.

Fierce as they were, they were no fiercer than the old general Yang Jian, now Emperor Wen. Mobilizing his own forces, he halted the Turks in their tracks and then in 584 shrewdly negotiated a peace treaty sealed by a marriage alliance. The Turkish khan would not get his Chinese princess for 10 more years, but the truce held and gave Wendi time to repair the Great Wall and extend it westwards, to reform the military and garrison the frontier – and to conquer the south.

His attack, in 588, came like lightning from a clear blue sky, and within a year the whole of southern and eastern China from the Yangtze River to the South China Sea belonged to the Sui. Coldly, Wendi razed the city of Jiankang, the 300-year-old capital and cultural heart of China's southern dynasties. Its records and literature went up in flames together with its palaces, temples and houses; even the ground where it had stood was ploughed and divided into farms. Wendi meant to create one China, not only united politically, but integrated socially and culturally.

The task was immense. Four hundred years of acrid hatred – not to mention the savagery of the conquest – were not easily forgotten. The people of the south thought all northerners uncivilized barbarians – and particularly scorned Wendi's northwesterners. The northerners in turn regarded southerners as lazy and effete.

The customs of the people were different. Southern aristocrats kept their women secluded and enjoyed the company of concubines, while northern nobles often practised a stern monogamy and gave their women a certain independence, even power. Northern mothers decried the southern practice of female infanticide in noble families housing many concubines. Southerners sniffed that the northerners' speech sounded like the "braying of donkeys and the barking of dogs".

Wendi and his ministers had a strong sense of history, and they made the ancient Han dynasty their model for rebuilding China. They commissioned China's greatest architect and engineer, Yu-wen Kai, to plan a splendid new capital located in the northwest at Changan. Massive land reforms were decreed, based on the *juntian,* or "equal field" system, which called for land allotments to be distributed among and maintained by the common people. Plans took shape for a vast canal network, linking north and south, by which grain collected in taxes could be taken to huge new granaries near Changan. Provincial and local governments were reconfigured; legal codes revised; and a national bureaucracy reinstituted to centralize administration.

The Department of State Affairs administered the courts, supervised the routine workings of the government, took censuses, kept financial records, oversaw the army, raised a labour force and collected taxes. The Imperial Chancellery, which transmitted the emperor's official decrees, and the Grand Secretariat, which drafted and recorded imperial edicts, were ostensibly responsible for China's policy-making. But real power lay with the Council of State, consisting of the emperor, the dignitaries he appointed as ministers, and important civil servants, usually the chiefs of the six ministries forming the Department of State Affairs. Watching over all was the Censorate, or Court of Censors, assigned to note abuses of every sort – corruption, fraud, extortion – and to hear complaints from the public. It was a massive and well thought-out restructuring. Yet from the beginning, the bureaucracy tended to produce a relatively autonomous corps whose ideas and interests inevitably came into conflict with the factions that grew up at the imperial court – and with the designs of the emperor.

The old Han dynasty had for the most part relied on the recommendations of its nobles for appropriate appointments to public office, but it supplemented this patronage with a rudimentary form of public examination. Wendi, in need of good people regardless of their birth, tentatively reintroduced the examination system. Elaborated and gradually perfected, it would become the imperial selection system that lasted in one form or another until the 20th century.

In personality, the old warrior-emperor was complex, difficult and autocratic, often irascible and moody, capable of great violence one moment and deep contrition the next. Born in a monastery and devoutly Buddhist, Wendi was forever haunted by his murder of Yu-wen Bin's family and may well have established his second capital at Luoyang to escape their ghosts. Typical of his northwestern heritage, he remained faithful to his jealous and scheming empress, whose penchant for intrigue often disrupted his court and hampered the work of his ministers, many of whom were old friends and comrades-in-arms. He loved direct action, hated cant, and despised intellectuals, never feeling entirely comfortable with the Confucianist scholars produced by the examination system. He died in 604, having left a legacy such as no ruler had accomplished in more than 400 years.

The Emperor's son and successor, Yangdi, was a far more sophisticated man. He had spent many years in the south, had married into a family of impeccable ancestry, and felt altogether at home with scholars and poets. Yangdi came to the throne in 604 determined to complete the unification of China. He set up court at Luoyang, perhaps to avoid the northwesterners at Changan, and soon afterwards built a new southern capital at Yangzhou. He constructed the previously planned Grand Canal system between Beijing and Hangzhou, linking the North China plain and the Yangtze Valley with waterways 40 metres wide or more. Like his father, he fortified his northern borders by building up the Great Wall and distributed vast sums to the nomadic tribes in order to secure the trans-Asian trade routes.

The cost of Yangdi's public works was enormous. On any given day, the Emperor might have a million peasants at work on the canals under the harshest conditions of forced labour. When provincial officials complained about the waste of manpower or failed to meet quotas, the Emperor had them executed. Millions, too, were drafted to repair the Great Wall, where, in the summer of 607, five or six out of every 10 were reported to have perished from exhaustion and overwork.

Yangdi felt he had reason to hurry. The canal system was to play a vital logistical role in a military operation that he had in mind. The powerful kingdom of Koguryŏ, consisting of North Korea and South Manchuria, sat menacingly on China's northeastern border. Part of the region had once been incorporated into the Han empire, then lost. Yangdi was determined that it would again belong to China. In 611, when the canals were completed, he used them to provision his army and to transport troops to staging areas in the north. The following year, the Emperor launched, from the region surrounding the city of Beijing, the first of three campaigns against Koguryŏ – every one of which ended in disaster.

The military debacle only sparked widespread discontent with the government. As defeat followed defeat in Koguryŏ, rebellions broke out all over China, some of them spontaneous peasant revolts, many of them plots led or backed by the northwestern aristocrats. In seven years, China was rocked by more than 200 uprisings.

From the fourth deck of his royal barge, a dragon-shaped riverboat measuring 60 metres from mouth to tail, Emperor Yangdi would survey his domain as he cruised China's Grand Canal. The 1,500-kilometre waterway, built by conscript labour between 605 and 610, provided the perfect setting to display the Emperor's power.

Behind the imperial craft followed thousands of smaller boats, carrying attendants, concubines and retainers in a flotilla sometimes up to 100 kilometres long.

Extravagant spectacles such as these undoubtedly impressed Yangdi's subjects and also served to confirm the Emperor's foresight. The Grand Canal, constructed under his orders, was a strategic artery that linked China's two great rivers, the Yangtze in the south and the Yellow in the north. The waterway was used at times to provision troops and transport them to staging areas for campaigns on the northern frontier. But its longstanding role was commercial: a trading fleet of as many as 40,000 craft plied the canal, carrying rice from the south to the north.

A WATERBORNE SPECTACLE

Yangdi grimly clung to power in the north, and then in 616, he abandoned his bastions there and moved permanently south to his capital, Yangzhou. Two years later, he was assassinated. After scarcely 30 years, the Sui dynasty had come to a bloody end. Yet in that brief span, it had changed forever the face of China.

In 617, the year after Yangdi fled south, Li Yuan, Duke of Tang, one of the most powerful Sui generals, seized the Sui capital at Changan and there proclaimed himself ruler. Taking the name Gaozu, the new emperor immediately set about ending the rebellions devastating China. It took him until 624 to pacify the country, and he acted with remarkable restraint, earning a reputation as a generous and forgiving monarch. In one particularly shrewd move, Gaozu made certain to appoint high government officials from all the major regions of China, and he virtually doubled the number of prefectures and counties, offering administrative posts as incentives to rebel leaders to lay down their arms.

Yet it was Gaozu's son Taizong who set the Tang dynasty on the path to greatness. His name meant "Great Ancestor", and contemporary Chinese historians considered him, not his father, the founder of the dynasty. A dashing and successful commander, who at 16 had led his father's army in the attack on Changan, Taizong believed that people, not heaven, shaped human destiny. And he wasted little time in acting on his belief. At 25, barely two years after his father had pacified China, he accosted two of his brothers – one the Crown Prince – at the palace gate. He killed them both and then forced his ageing father to abdicate.

It was a cautionary beginning, but Taizong proved to be a just and wise ruler, as well as a deft politician and a military genius. He was blessed with an imperial bearing that made him not only a splendid figure in court but also an intimidating one. Nonetheless, he managed to develop a deep personal rapport with his advisers, many of whom he retained from his father's regime. He made them feel that they shared fully in the forming of policy and the governing of the state. So closely did his conduct approach the Confucian ideal that later Chinese historians made the name of his reign, True Vision, a byword for good government.

Considering how the Tangs themselves had forced their way to power, Taizong saw clearly the need to reorganize the army. The problem was to curb the power of the great military aristocrats while still protecting the frontiers. Taizong began by appointing generals of relatively humble birth to lead numerous small commands and sent them to garrison the northern borders. He then demobilized the huge armies of his father's day and created a frontier militia. Soldiers on active duty in the regular armies were given pensions and land in the border regions and made liable for call-up in emergencies. The militia trained during the cold months and conducted formal manoeuvres at the close of each winter. This system kept the army from becoming overly ambitious and yet maintained adequate reserves to deal with the frequent Turkish raids. As Taizong intended, military careers lost their appeal for the northern grandees, who came to prefer appointment to high civil office at court, where the only soldiers they ever saw were the imperial guards.

Taizong tried to streamline the burgeoning bureaucracy created by his father by reducing the number of official posts. He also placed provincial officials under the supervision of imperial inspectors, each operating in one of 10 circuits covering the empire. In time, Taizong replaced the prominent local clan members who held prefectural and county posts with career civil servants. To recruit the most capable men, he became the first ruler to exploit a Chinese institution, the civil service

The Leisurely Years

The inauguration of Emperor Taizong *(right)* in 626 ushered in an era of unprecedented peace and prosperity throughout Tang China. With agricultural bounty assured by the Emperor's innovative land reforms, and the frontiers and trade routes secured by his army, aristocrats and courtiers found time for frivolity. And merchants who prospered on flourishing foreign commerce could indulge newly acquired tastes.

At the imperial court, princes and princesses imported expensive Persian mounts to play the fashionable sport of polo. Gold and silver, previously used only in currency, were now in demand for jewellery. Fads in fashion and food captivated the elite. Some sought distinction in the exotic – sleeping in sky-blue Turkish tents, for example, or showing off rare pets such as lapdogs from Samarkand in central Asia.

New standards of personal comfort were attained. Bathrooms and water fountains became common, and mechanical fans circulated warm air in winter and ice-cooled breezes in summer. Amid this comfort and security, the sons and daughters of Tang amused themselves with all-day parties, entertained by troupes of dancers, musicians, acrobats and wrestlers.

After donning the yellow silk robes of the emperor, Taizong emerged as the most civic-minded ruler of the age.

The women of the Tang court enjoyed exceptional freedom. Princesses wrote poetry and played polo and politics – often besting men. Status also entailed hours of primping before ornate mirrors *(left)* and rewards – golden tiaras dripping with rubies and pearls *(below)*. Some noblewomen rejected luxury to be Buddhist nuns, shedding their locks *(above)* in a rite of passage.

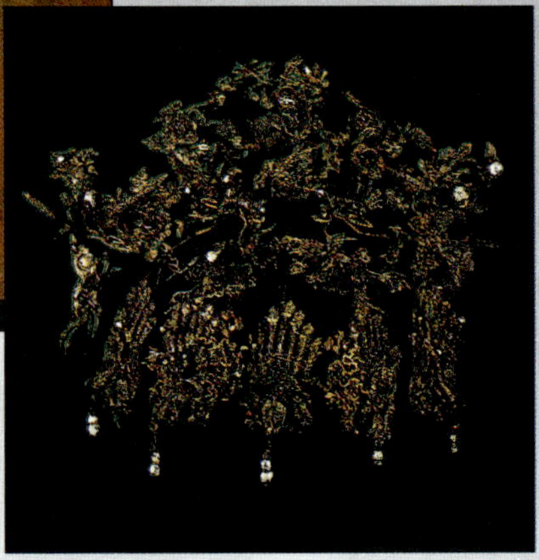

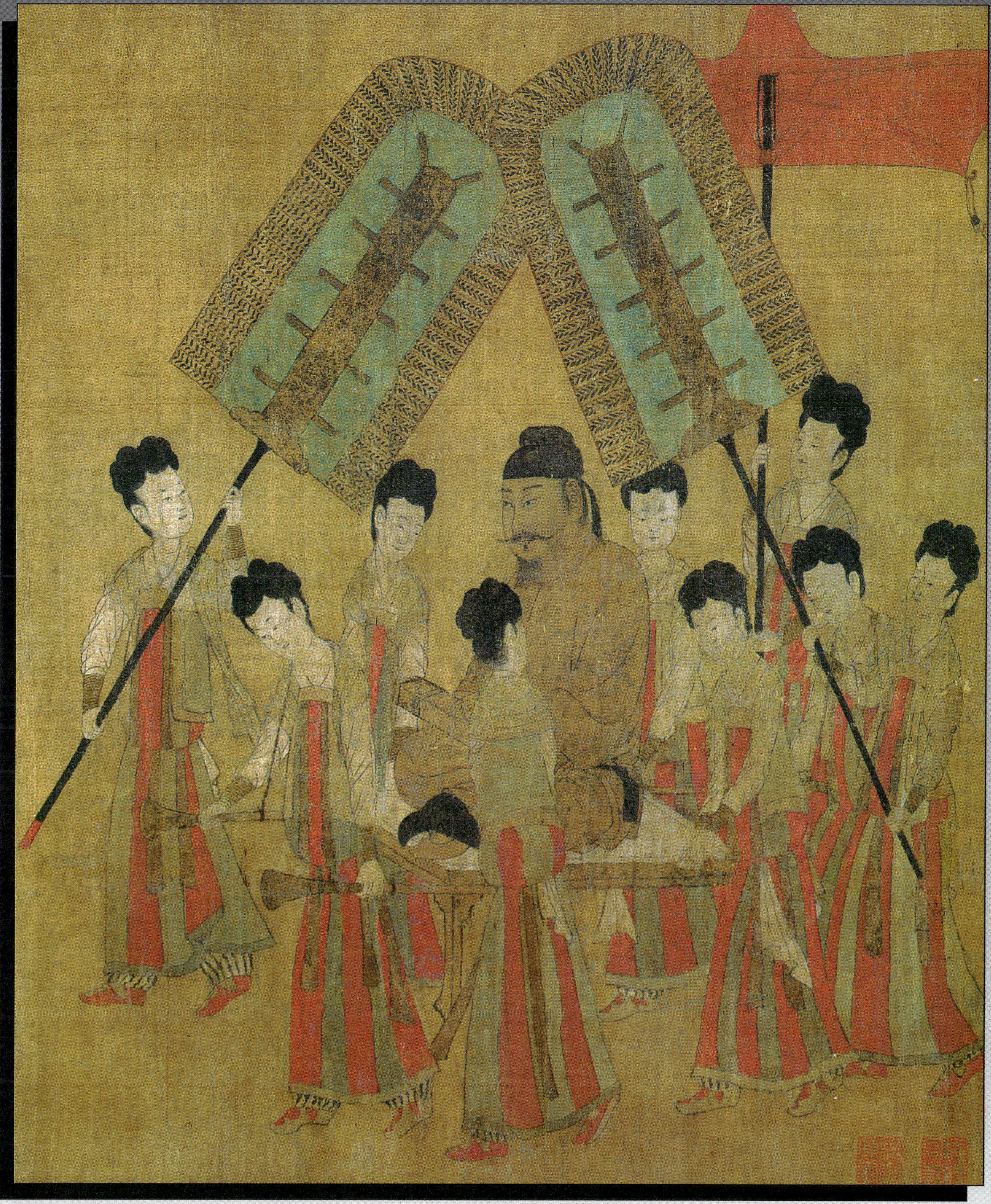

Shown here with his royal entourage, Taizong was a devoted and unstinting administrator, who often spent sleepless nights reviewing governmental policies and appointments.

examination system. The Board of Civil Office in Changan held the examinations annually and opened them to virtually all literate candidates. The subjects included history, the Confucian classics, poetry, administration and government.

The examinations encouraged the dreams of the common folk, but the tests were exceedingly difficult; only between two and 10 per cent of the thousands of aspirants each year achieved a passing grade. Even then, a satisfactory mark merely put a person's name on the "roll of officials", from which appointees could be chosen. Money, family, land, the right connections still played a role, and in practice, it was the sons of the established families who won the highest government posts. But nothing was automatic; they had to work for their positions, and the system served to produce an effective government, in which 13,465 officials exercised control down to county level over a population already in excess of 50 million.

Once Taizong was secure at home, he eagerly searched for opportunities to expand his empire. The moment came in 628 when rebellion broke out among the Eastern Turks. Taizong immediately raised an army of 100,000 men and the next year surged across the border and slaughtered thousands upon thousands of Turks – after which the survivors were only too willing to declare him khan. Firmly in control of Ordos and Inner Mongolia, Taizong used the same tactics on the Western Turks, and soon held all the oasis kingdoms of the Tarim basin. The ancient Silk Road thus fell into Tang hands. Within a few years, the Changan capital had become a great international metropolis, inundated with exotic goods and host to strange peoples, among them refugees from the conquest of Persia by the Arabs.

The refugees brought their religions with them, and the Emperor accepted the foreign faiths with tolerance, allowing sects as diverse as Persian Zoroastrians and Nestorian Christians to erect temples and churches in Changan. But Taizong was less relaxed about Buddhism. Five hundred years after it had first appeared from India, Buddhism permeated every level of Chinese society and each aspect of Chinese life. Its stupas and monasteries dotted the landscape, and the roofs of its

Tea, brewed in southern China since the third century AD, became a truly national beverage after northern Chinese aristocrats developed a taste for it during the Tang dynasty. Sipping from fine porcelain cups that enhanced the brew's green colour, Tang connoisseurs turned tea-making into an elaborate ritual that spread throughout China and as far away as Japan. But the popularity of tea among commoners may have had more far-reaching consequences: the hygienic benefits that resulted from boiling water for tea are believed to have played a major role in longevity and hence in China's rapid increase in population – from 41 to 53 million – during the first half of the eighth century.

temples and pagodas, curling elegantly heavenwards at the eaves, commanded the city skylines. The aristocracies of north and south alike had been ardent patrons of Buddhism long before the empire had come into being, and under the Tang they continued to turn their money and their land over to the monasteries, often giving up their elegant mansions and their best sons and daughters to the faith.

The Sui emperor Wen had seen Buddhism as a potent weapon in his ideological armoury and had elevated the faith to a status approaching state religion. But Taizong saw in Buddhism an alarming potential for subversion. In Buddhism's nirvana, there was no room for the Sons of Heaven, as Chinese emperors had styled themselves. A Buddhist had no reason, necessarily, to worship his ancestors and a solid doctrinal basis for not doing so. The religion thus threatened to undermine both the emperor's authority and his role as head of the traditional faith based on the cult of family. Confucianists, concerned with self-fulfilment in public office, disliked Buddhism's otherworldliness, and Daoists, whose doctrines were in some ways quite similar to Buddhism, condemned it as a "foreign" rival.

Although Taizong's clan was steeped in Buddhist tradition, the Emperor himself found Buddhism "not to his taste", and he withheld the lavish patronage it had enjoyed under the Suis. Taizong was also irritated by numerous abuses, particularly on the part of those wearing saffron-coloured robes simply to escape taxes and state labour requirements, and he occasionally took stern action against them. But Taizong was equally aware of the dangers of total alienation, and he welcomed the Buddhist scholar Xuanzang back from India with much fanfare and generosity. The Emperor spent many hours with the monk discussing religion and Xuanzang's travels, perhaps seeking intelligence useful to his foreign campaigns.

Or possibly the monk served as a welcome distraction from Taizong's growing vexation with his own advisers – precisely on the question of his aggressive foreign policy. The drive into central Asia, while successful, had caused heated debate among the ministers. And the discord swelled when the Emperor announced his intention to invade Koguryŏ. Many of his advisers were certain he would fail as his father had. He nevertheless tried – and his invasion failed dismally. The ministers never forgave him. His adventurism shattered the political equilibrium he had so carefully created. When he died in 649, an isolated ruler in his own government, he still had not launched his last planned campaign against Koguryŏ.

As the seventh century drew to a close, there came to the throne one of the most astonishing figures in Chinese history. Her name was Wu Zhao – better known as the empress Wu. The only woman ever to rule China, she started her career as a common concubine in the harem of Taizong. Wu Zhao first appeared at court in 640, when she was still in her early teens. Shortly thereafter, she is said to have seduced the Emperor's son, the teenage prince of Jin, who became heir to the throne in 643. When the old emperor passed away in 649, Wu Zhao, like other widowed concubines, shaved her head and entered a Buddhist nunnery, while her lover, now 21 years old, became the third Tang Son of Heaven, Gaozong. Under ordinary circumstances, Wu Zhao would have remained cloistered for the rest of her days. But a year after his father's death, Gaozong paid a visit to the convent and again fell prey to the beautiful young woman's charms. Restored to the court harem, she soon dominated the new emperor. Ever bold, she urged Gaozong to abandon his childless empress; when he refused, Wu Zhao smothered her own infant daughter and implicated the empress in the murder. Intrigue followed intrigue until in 655, six years after assuming power, the bewitched emperor Gaozong made her his principal consort, the empress Wu.

The new empress manipulated her weak and sickly husband from that day forwards until his death in 683, exerting a tremendous impact on political affairs. Under her influence, Gaozong's regime performed phenomenal feats of expansion, continuing the Tang march across central Asia and eventually subduing even the resilient Koguryŏ in the northeast. By 668, the Emperor and his empress Wu controlled more territory than any Chinese ruler before or after. Tang China reached from southern Manchuria to Kashmir and from Inner Mongolia to Vietnam.

Governing such a vast stretch demanded a monumental military and administrative effort. Kashgar, the westernmost oasis in the Tarim basin, lay 5,000 kilometres from Changan. Logistics and communications were daunting, to say nothing of the costs, and it soon became obvious that the empire was severely over-extended – so much so that a powerful new state, founded by barbarians in Tibet, was able to annex many of the new Chinese holdings in the west.

When Gaozong died in 683, the empress Wu quickly disposed of his successor, her own son, and replaced him with a more compliant younger son, through whom she continued to control court and country. She brooked no dissent. Sensing a plot by the Li clan of northwesterners, she brought down a reign of terror, summarily executing several hundred aristocrats, many of whom held posts in the Imperial Chancellery. But opposition to her rule persisted and in 684 she moved the capital from Changan to Luoyang. There, six years later, the former concubine forced her son to abdicate, assumed sovereign power, and declared a new dynasty, the Zhou.

Behind Wu Zhao's rise, and certainly her coronation, lay the enormous and continuing influence of the Buddhist church. The presumed coming of Bodhisattva Maitreya, a proclaimed Buddhist messiah, had spawned a number of millennial-minded sects. Now, a politically powerful monk named Xue Huai-ye, the lover of Wu Zhao, found an obscure text – or concocted one – suggesting that the Maitreya was a woman. From this text, the clergy calculated that the saviour would arrive soon and implied that Wu Zhao was she. The one-time concubine presumed to declare herself not only emperor, but also the Buddhist version of Christ. In 691, the year after she took the throne, she made Buddhism the official state religion.

The empress Wu's government was a model of tyranny. She turned the Censorate into an army of secret agents, conducted relentless purges, and continued to liquidate the aristocratic clans of the northwest. As capricious as she was cold-blooded, she appointed her young lovers to high office. And incessant intrigues produced an aura of fear and insecurity among her most important advisers. Yet she was a capable ruler. For the most part she maintained the stability of the empire and seems to have enjoyed considerable popular support, except from the old elite.

Empress Wu held the throne until she reached her mid-70s and grew very ill. She was deposed by a coup led by the Wei family, whose corrupt scion would head a short-lived, arbitrary and nepotic regime. Wu Zhao had spent half a century at the centre of power. Now she took to her bed, where in 705 – in the privacy and comfort of her own palace – she died peacefully in her sleep.

It took five more years for the Empress' grandson to eliminate the feckless Wei clan and restore the Tang dynasty. The grandson was Xuanzong, and before him lay nearly half a century of rule, the longest and most brilliant reign of any Tang monarch. His China had the glow of a golden age, of peace and prosperity, of

In a rustic setting favoured for literary retreats, a group of eighth-century scholars gather for contemplation and criticism. Two men of letters *(below, left)* debate the merits of a literary scroll. A colleague *(below, right)*, perhaps composing a new poem, is lost in thought as his servant grinds fresh ink for his brush. The unpredictable temperaments and unorthodox lifestyles of such scholars troubled traditional moralists, moving one bureaucrat to warn that the artists posed a threat to the maintenance of good order. Most Tang emperors ignored such prejudice, instead granting artists creative freedom and esteem.

successful politics at home and abroad. And still, as was often the case in Chinese history, Xuanzong would go down as a tragic figure. The years of power would corrupt and confuse; he would retreat into an obsessive study of esoteric doctrines. In the end, his grand edifice would crumble before the battering ram of revolt.

At the start and for many years, Xuanzong gathered about him the best and the brightest scholars and administrators in the land. Most ministers of importance were examination graduates, the sons of well-established official families rather than clannish aristocrats. A goodly number of them hailed from Luoyang, the secondary capital that the empress Wu had made the centre of her political power, and most had served their apprenticeships in her bureaucracy. Among the gifted elite were two of the greatest poets in Chinese history — Li Bo and Du Fu.

The Chinese assumed that a gentleman would be able to express himself in verse on any occasion. The Tang government tested poetic composition in its examinations, and all bureaucrats applied their poetic skills in celebration of imperial outings or auspicious events or the departure of officials. Such occasions did not encourage originality — rather, the Chinese admired poise and technical ability. Even the best poets used verse as other cultures might use the diary to record the minutiae of daily life as well as the epiphanies of intense feeling. All of which made the boldness and lyricism of the major Tang poets even more remarkable.

Li Bo was born in 701, somewhere in central Asia, where his people had been living for a century or more before returning and settling in Sichuan not long after 705. The family may have been involved in trade, which was regarded as an inferior occupation by the court and which may explain why Li Bo's civil service career languished. At any event, he was a rebel and a wanderer by nature, a romantic, mystic and libertine, addicted to wine, to love and to verse *(page 113)*.

月下獨酌
花間一壺酒
舉杯邀明月
月既不解飲
暫伴月將影
歌影月徘徊
醒時同交歡
永結無情遊

獨
行樂須及時
歌舞影零亂
醉後各分散
相期邈雲漢

Li Bo's friend Du Fu was an altogether more serious man, deeply committed to Confucianist humanism and to public service. He often used his poetry as a vehicle for political protest, attacking social injustice, perhaps by assuming the voice of a soldier or peasant, and setting his work in some distant era. Late in life, he witnessed the rebellion against Emperor Xuanzong and wrote of the famine and disorder that gripped China: *I remember when we first fled the rebels,/hurrying north over dangerous trails;/night deepened on the P'eng-ya Road,/the moon shone over White-Water Hills./A whole family endlessly trudging,/begging without shame from the people we met;/valley birds sang, a jangle of soft voices;/we didn't see a single traveller returning./The baby girl in her hunger bit me.*

Men such as these participated in a glorious explosion of literature and the arts. An early form of Chinese drama took shape and flourished under the Emperor's patronage. Throughout China, people began referring to him not by the official titles but by the fond name of Ming Huang, the "Brilliant Emperor". To his court flocked not just Chinese historians, scholars, poets, dramatists and entertainers, but foreign envoys, clerics and traders offering tribute from countries all over Eurasia.

There were ordinary visitors as well. Arab pearl divers, Mesopotamian adventurers, Turkish princes, Indian merchants, Japanese pilgrims, Malay pirates, Tibetan youths, all came seeking glory or riches or wisdom. Some found what they were looking for. A Sogdian merchant became the Protector of Annam. An Oman gem dealer returned home with a gold-lidded, black porcelain vase containing a golden fish, with ruby eyes, that smelt of musk and brought him 50,000 dinar. And an obese Turkish mercenary joined the Tang army, rose to the rank of general, and became military governor of two important outposts in the northeast. His name was An Lushan, and it would one day be written in Chinese blood.

In the meantime, however, he seemed little different from other foreigners who found their success in China. The newcomers were arriving in droves, especially in Guangzhou (Canton) and Yangzhou, the commercial centres of the nation. Guangzhou had a huge foreign quarter, which the Brilliant Emperor had set aside. And although it thrived, Guangzhou had a reputation for crime and corruption. Yangzhou, by contrast, was a jewel in Xuanzong's imperial crown. It lay at the junction of the Yangtze River and the Grand Canal, the hub of the great network of waterways built by the Sui dynasty. Yangzhou attracted Asian merchants, who came to ship their goods on canal boats up "The River of Transport", as the Chinese called the Grand Canal. For the same reason, the national salt monopoly established its headquarters in the city. Yangzhou was a banking centre, a gold market and an industrial town, greatly renowned for its metal work and textiles, as well as its refined sugar and its boat building.

Grander still were China's northern political centres – the biggest cities in the world. Luoyang boasted a population approaching a million, second only to Changan, which may have reached two million. Luoyang had a religious tradition stretching back thousands of years to the golden age of the Eastern Zhou and an atmosphere of ancient refinement and elegance, but Changan had the emperor.

Changan stretched just under 10 kilometres from east to west and eight from north to south. It had two large markets in the eastern and western sections of the city, one for foreign goods and one for domestic goods. The imperial palace complex occupied a large part of the city in the north, and some smaller areas had been taken over by religious orders or government agencies. Connecting them were

The hard-drinking poet Li Bo *(left)*, who often needed help to get home, was one of the Tang dynasty's most popular writer-scholars. Li Bo is said to have drowned while leaning out of a boat to kiss the moon's reflection on the water. His poem entitled "Drinking Alone with the Moon" appears on the opposite page in the artistic calligraphy of his era and below in translation.

From a pot of wine among the flowers
I drank alone. There was no one with me –
Till, raising my cup, I asked the bright moon
To bring me my shadow and make us three.
Alas, the moon was unable to drink,
And my shadow tagged me vacantly;
But still for a while I had these friends
To cheer me through the end of spring. . . .
I sang. The moon encouraged me.
I danced. My shadow tumbled after.
As long as I knew, we were boon companions.
And then I was drunk, and we lost one another.

THE EARTHLY PARADISE

The Tang imperial capital of Changan *(right),* a magnificent metropolis of two million people on the Wei River, was built to a divine blueprint. Its outer walls, enclosing an area 10 kilometres by eight kilometres, represented the rectangular shape of the land of the gods. Changan's sweeping boulevards and avenues formed a grid of perfect parallels, reflecting the harmonious proportions of paradise.

From the capital's south gate, a central thoroughfare led to the imperial city, an enclave of royal palaces and government ministries. The crowning jewel of the great complex was the wooden Hanyuan Hall *(above),* which was an architectural triumph of upcurved roofs, overhanging balconies and massive staircases where the Tang emperors were crowned and imperial armies passed in review.

The city's 109 neighbourhoods were bustling centres of everyday life. Residents could worship at the temples of five religions, shop at two large street markets, or celebrate with charming courtesans in the city's entertainment district.

On a flight that foreshadowed the Tang dynasty's downfall, Emperor Xuanzong *(above)* leads the imperial household through rugged Sichuan in 755 to escape a revolt by An Lushan, an upstart general. The General's ambitions had been encouraged by Yang Guifei, the Emperor's favourite concubine. This affair ended in tragedy; to retain the loyalty of his palace guard *(left),* the Emperor was forced to order the execution of his beloved mistress.

major avenues, some as wide as 150 metres. Between the avenues were the residential wards. Here, the citizens spent their days in a maze of lanes that passed among the houses and neighbourhood shops.

In their gardens and well-appointed houses, the rich and aristocratic indulged themselves by drinking tea with great formality from porcelain cups and made something of a fetish of the ceremony. Tea drinking had only just become popular in Changan, having travelled up the Grand Canal from the south some time during the seventh century. Sports-minded citizens might enjoy a hunt or a polo match or a form of football, while scholars found their pleasure in scrolls. The scrolls were made of sheets of paper, a Chinese invention, glued end-to-end, and the writing was usually in a fine calligraphy, though some scrolls were printed from blocks of wood using a recently developed printing technique.

As befitted a cosmopolitan capital, the cuisine of Changan was rich and varied. At meal times a person might sit down to wine-marinated white carp or steamed shoat in garlic sauce. The people doted on dumplings in the shape of 24 different flowers and ate quantities of fluffy wheat steamed in baskets. For dessert, they might have ice cream made of iced milk and rice, flavoured with camphor. After eating, they might play cards (which the Chinese invented), lotto, backgammon or *go,* or relax at home. The richest houses had artificial fountains and mechanical fans for cooling in summer and charcoal heaters to ease the winter chill.

For the well-to-do in Changan, these were the best of times. But as the years passed, the Emperor in the Great Luminous Palace high on the Dragon Head Plain would begin to change all this. At first, because he needed their support, Xuanzong appointed members of the northwestern aristocracy to be his close advisers. Like other emperors before him, he felt uncomfortable among those arrogant nobles and sharply reduced their number once he had consolidated his power. But he trusted not even the few who were left and began to rely on a corps of youthful, low-ranking scholars recruited directly through the palace examinations. The ensuing power struggles between the aristocrats and scholars increasingly disrupted the government, but Xuanzong only exacerbated the situation by using eunuchs from his harem as personal agents to circumvent the normal procedures of government.

As matters deteriorated, Xuanzong wearily began to withdraw altogether from the affairs of empire, finding solace in the pleasures of the harem and religious study. A few leading ministers handled matters, sometimes assuming unwonted dictatorial powers. To complicate everything, various wives and concubines began to meddle in public affairs. The most persistent among them was Yang Guifei, who had been the concubine of one of Xuanzong's sons before the Emperor took her for himself. And Yang Guifei looked to the empire's soldiers for her allies.

When China had expanded into central Asia, the Tang dynasts had reorganized their armed forces in order to deal with the fast-moving tribes of the steppes. The seventh-century reforms had created a professional standing army and given field generals fighting distant battles the autonomy they needed for victory. In the heady days of triumph, no one stopped to consider that the reforms would give the generals tremendous personal power as well.

Now, in the eighth century, the power of the field generals was greater still as a result of domestic disarray. The Emperor had appointed as his official adviser one Yang Guozhong, a favourite cousin of his omnipresent concubine. To check the adviser's growing influence, the powerful minister Li Linfu, the dominant man in the government, began to favour the generals of the northern armies, especially those of foreign descent, hoping that they would prove more tractable than Chinese officers. He invited them to court, wined and dined them, and sought to win them to his cause. One of those generals was An Lushan.

A capable soldier, though something of a social buffoon, the rotund An Lushan cut quite a figure at Changan. It was said that he was the lover of Yang Guifei – the Emperor's favourite concubine. When Li Linfu – the minister who had brought him to court – died, An Lushan and Yang Guozhong, his lover's cousin, began a bitter fight for the vacated prime ministerial post. The court seethed with intrigue and fury. The ageing emperor merely looked the other way.

In the meantime, China was undergoing profound yet unrecognized changes. Some time before, the government had introduced onerous new taxation designed to raise the huge revenue needed to defend the borders against the Turks, Tibetans and other northern tribes. But the taxes failed to provide the necessary funds, adding to the problems of bureaucratic conflict, a hothouse harem atmosphere, and a missing emperor at the top. At this point, Yang Guifei's cousin won the palace battle for prime minister, and the enraged An Lushan launched a rebellion.

The fighting lasted more than seven years, from December 755 to January 763, and it tore China asunder. At first, the revolt seemed to succeed. An Lushan marched on Changan from the Beijing area with 200,000 troops and, after a major battle, easily occupied the capital in 756. Xuanzong had already fled with his entourage, escorted by imperial guards. In a mutinous mood, the guards halted on the road and forced Xuanzong to execute both Yang Guifei, his concubine, and Yang Guozhong, her cousin the prime minister. It was the stuff of legend, and, some years later, the great poet Baijay would write a moving poem that enshrined the Emperor and his concubine forever in the mythology of tragic love. Meanwhile, Xuanzong established a court of exile at Chengdu in the Sichuan province.

In Changan, General An Lushan declared himself emperor of the Greater Yen dynasty, and a number of prominent Tang officials rushed to offer their support. A year later, in 757, the unfortunate general lay dead, killed by his own son, who took command of the rebellion. There followed a stupefying series of assassinations and successions, of resurgent loyalist attacks and rebel counterattacks, of mayhem and pillage across the face of North China. At one point, emboldened Tibetan raiders managed to sweep into Changan and occupy the city for two weeks, looting and burning the former metropolitan centre of Asia. The outcome of the awful civil war was in doubt almost to the end, but finally government forces were able to subdue the rebels. Xuanzong, nearing 80, exhausted and racked with grief over the death of Yang Guifei, returned to Changan to die in 762, while his son Daizong struggled to rebuild an empire that existed in name only.

It was a struggle that the Tang successors would wage throughout the following century. The great generals who had helped crush the An Lushan rebellion became warlords, ruling the provinces they had recovered and fighting constantly with one another. The remaining Tang emperors grappled to control the defiant provinces. Although the country enjoyed respites of relative peace and calm, the spectre of rebellion and chaos was seldom absent from the halls of the Tang courts.

The Tangs clung to the throne until 906. By then, the dynasty had lost real power and purpose, and another rebellion was gnawing at the state. The once rich, stable, far-flung empire had become a troubled, divided state, spinning into decline.

INSCRIBING THE SACRED WORD

issionary zeal abounded in the age that dawned with the rise of Islam. From Changan to Baghdad to the court of Charlemagne, rulers no less than religious leaders dedicated themselves to spreading the holy word. Empires were advancing on currents of faith, and the vessels that charted the way were sacred texts. The crafting of such manuscripts – many of them richly decorated – enlisted the skills of scribes, who pursued their tasks with the tenacity of soldiers and the patience of saints.

The scriptures disseminated during this period took various forms. In some parts of Asia, words of wisdom were still being penned on scrolls in the age-old way. But in the eighth century, Chinese artisans devised a method of printing that involved carving a text or a drawing on a woodblock; the raised lines of the image were then inked and stamped on to pages that could be sewn together to make a book. First used to produce Buddhist sutras, or discourses, this process enabled Chinese monks to turn out books at a pace that was unthinkable in the West, where hand-lettering remained the rule.

If the work of the Western scribes was excruciatingly slow, however, it at least endured – thanks to the sturdy parchment that replaced papyrus as the writer's medium of choice early in the Christian era. An English riddle set down in the 10th century – told from the point of view of the parchment itself – revealed how such vellum was made from the skin of a sheep or calf and used to produce a book: "An enemy ended my life . . . then he dipped me in water and drew me out again and put me in the sun, where I soon shed all my hair. After that, the knife's sharp edge bit into me, and all my blemishes were scraped away; fingers folded me, and the bird's feather often moved over my brown surface, sprinkling meaningful marks. . . . Then a man bound me, he stretched skin over me, and adorned me with gold."

However the scribes of the various faiths made their books, they had in common the desire to create a text as beautiful as it was edifying. Those who copied out the Koran laboured under a strict rule against representational art decreed by Muhammad, who reportedly told his wife Aisha that "angels refuse to enter a house in which there is a picture". There was no law against embroidering of typography, however, and pious scribes evolved ornate lettering that transformed the word itself into an art form. Objections to depicting sacred subjects were harboured by some early Buddhist monks and voiced periodically by Christian authorities, yet by and large the texts of both faiths proved fertile ground for illustrators.

Taken together, the scriptures of the age afford a prospect aptly described by a medieval scholar, who wrote in awe of an illustrated gospel in Ireland: "Look more keenly at it, and you will penetrate to the very shrine of art. You will make out intricacies so delicate and subtle, so exact and compact, so full of knots and links, with colours so fresh and vivid, that you might say that all this was the work of an angel and not of a man."

Penned on parchment from right to left, this passage from the Koran tells of salvation — and the judgment awaiting evildoers in the next life. The large gold disc on the far left marks the end of a chapter. The austerely elegant Kufic script used here was one of the earliest written forms of Arabic; it took its name from the Islamic cultural centre of Kufa, on the Euphrates River. The same script was later used to copy the Koran shown below. Those who created such texts were among the most respected of Islamic artisans, for they fulfilled Muhammad's saying: "Good writing makes the truth stand out."

SUTRAS FOR THE DEVOUT

Below: This treasured book of hinged gold leaves – found at the site of an eighth-century Buddhist temple in Korea – is inscribed with a scripture called Diamond Sutra. The Chinese text, arranged in pages of 17 vertical columns of up to 17 characters, calls on the devout to strive for *sunyata*, or the void – a blissful state likened to the timeless perfection of a diamond. Such sutras were brought back from China by Korean monks who had studied at Changan and other centres of Buddhist learning. Chinese characters constituted Korea's only written language until the 1600s.

Right: Discovered at Tun-huang – a stop on the Silk Road – this section of a ninth-century Diamond Sutra, produced with a wood block, is the world's oldest dated printed text. The illustration shows Buddha with the swastika – an ancient symbol of good fortune – on his chest, surrounded by shorn monks, fierce guardians and angelic attendants *(top)*.

凡欲讀經先念淨口業真言遍
脩唎 脩唎 摩訶脩唎 脩脩唎 娑婆訶
奉請除災金剛 奉請辟毒金剛 奉請黃隨求金剛
奉請白淨水金剛 奉請赤聲金剛 奉請定除災金剛
奉請紫賢金剛 奉請大神金剛
金剛般若波羅蜜經

This eighth-century Japanese scroll, using Chinese calligraphy, tells of Buddha's historical odyssey. On the right Buddha enters a monastery built for him by the Indian king Bimbisara; on the left Buddha accepts the monastery as the King prepares to pour perfumed water in a gesture of gift giving. Japanese monks, like Korean monks, disseminated Buddhist texts written in Chinese.

器不鼓自鳴門使更
廣門下更高一切丘
墟皆悉平坦𡏖穢塵
垢自然香淨聾者得
聽瘂者能言盲者得
視狂者得正拘癖疾
病普皆除愈枯木發
華腐草榮秀涸池曾
瀾香風清靡鳳雀孔
翠鳥鷹鴛鴦異類
衆鳥繽紛翔集出和
雅音有如是等種種
祥瑞既入城已與頻
比娑羅王俱往竹園
尒時諸天滿虛空中
時王即便手執寶瓶
盛以香水於如来前

Left: A portrait of Christ as a teacher, with book in hand, is the centrepiece for this gold-embossed, jewel-encrusted gospel cover crafted around 870 for the Carolingian emperor Charles the Bald.

Right: Astrological symbols adorn the capital letter *D* on this opening page from a Bible presented to Charles the Bald in 846. The page – illustrated in a manner so resplendent it was known as illumination – reproduces the opening words of a preface written more than four centuries earlier by the translator Saint Jerome and addressed to one Desiderius. Jerome's Latin version of the Greek and Hebrew scriptures – called the Vulgate because Latin was the more common, or vulgar, tongue – was copied countless times in palaces and monasteries, fulfilling his goal: to make God's word "accessible to our people".

INCP PFAT SCI
HIERONMI PRBI
ESIDERII
MEIDESI

28

Left: This page from the Lindisfarne Gospel, a late-seventh-century Hiberno-Saxon masterpiece, introduces Saint Matthew's account of Jesus' birth with an intricate chi-rho monogram, composed of the first three letters of the Greek word for Christ – *X* (chi), *P* (rho) and *I* (iota). The Latin text was copied out in colourful capitals by Eadfrith, one of the leading members of the Lindisfarne monastery.

Later, in the 10th century, a scholar by the name of Aldred, who described himself as an "unworthy and most miserable priest", translated the Latin discreetly into Old English. Above the Latin word *evangelium,* Aldred wrote in small letters the Anglo-Saxon equivalent – godspell *(top),* a compound meaning "good tale", which was contracted in time to the word *gospel.*

Below: A page from the Book of Kells, an eighth-century edition of the Gospels preserved at the Irish monastery of that name, introduces the Gospel of John with an anecdotal sketch of the evangelist. The richly illuminated line in the centre begins "*Hic est Johannis*" (Here is John). The monks who decorated the manuscript used motifs evolved by Celtic artists long before Christ's birth.

4 THE KINGDOM OF THE RISING SUN

Around the year 735, a deadly smallpox epidemic that had been sweeping through the island kingdom of Japan reached the capital of Nara and claimed many members of the aristocracy and notables of the imperial court. Clearly, the heavenly powers were for some reason angry with Japan, and to assuage their wrath the emperor Shomu announced he would build an enormous image of the Great Buddha, symbol of universal spiritual unity. The statue would be a national undertaking, and all Japanese people were encouraged to help, even those who could only offer "a twig or handful of dirt", as a chronicler of the day put it.

There were some formidable obstacles to overcome, chief among them obtaining the approval of Japan's traditional deities. Only two centuries before, the arrival of Buddhism in Japan had resulted in ferocious fighting between its converts and those who viewed it as a threat to the established pantheon. More recently, the two religions had coexisted in harmony, yet apprehensions persisted that the old gods might be annoyed by all the attention now paid to the Great Buddha.

In consequence, a venerable Buddhist priest named Gyogi was dispatched to the shrine of Amaterasu, the ancient sun goddess from whom all Japanese emperors claimed direct descent. There, after praying for seven days and seven nights, Gyogi received word from the goddess herself. Speaking in a clear, melodious voice, Amaterasu repeated a Chinese verse in which she said that she welcomed the imperial plan as she would a boat at a crossing or a torch in the darkness.

There were numerous distractions and problems before the great statue and its temple complex could be completed. A revolt flared in western Japan, causing the Emperor grave concern until it was put down. Funds ran short, and Japanese metal workers proved inadequate to the task. Finally, after eight failed castings, a Korean master was given the assignment. This expert created the body of the Buddha by pouring 40 bronze segments one on top of another after the layer below had cooled. Once that was done, the 365-centimetre neck and head were superimposed in a single, superb casting. There remained only the problem of acquiring gold for gilding the Great Buddha in a nation that had always lacked precious minerals. It was thus a sign of divine approval when gold was found in 749 in a northeastern province, whose governor immediately sent a large quantity to Nara.

In its final form, the Great Buddha, seated among the petals of a bronze lotus blossom, rose 16 metres in height and contained about half a million kilograms of copper, tin and lead, along with a couple of hundred kilograms of pure gold. The centrepiece of a cavernous hall that extended 86 metres in length and soared to a height of 46 metres, the giant statue was consecrated in 752 in a ceremony of great pomp and intense devotion. While the Indian ascetic Bodhisena gave the statue symbolic life by painting pupils into its eyes, 10,000 priests and other luminaries

Isolated from mainland Asia by nearly 200 kilometres of sea, the inhabitants of ancient Japan maintained their own ways without outside interference while gradually adopting influences from China – including Buddhism, which they espoused late in the sixth century. The insularity of the Japanese spawned distinctive art forms – among them was the ceramic style known as Jōmon, which embellished everyday objects, such as the storage jar on the left, with finely sculpted rims and typical herringbone decoration.

from across the Buddhist world joined in the occasion, which would stand both as symbol and substance of Japan's coming-of-age among Asian civilizations.

Behind that momentous event lay the extraordinary evolution of a people who had, within but a blink of recorded time, progressed from a primitive condition to an advanced culture. Obscure in their origins, insular in their geography, lacking in natural resources, devoted to an animist religion that offered no ethical or philosophical precepts whatsoever, bereft of a codified body of law, ruled but not governed by an emperor who owed his lofty position to the mystique of manufactured legends, the early Japanese had nonetheless shown an imitative and adaptive talent, which was to be their salvation and path to greatness.

The Great Buddha, for example, gave official status to a religion that had originated in India, spread to China, and come to Japan through Korea. Similarly, by the time the statue was dedicated, the Japanese used a written language borrowed from another people; their government's administrative apparatus, their legal system, and their social organization were all based on foreign models; their art and architecture had been taken from a great mainland culture; and even the name of Japan by which the rest of the world knew their land was of Chinese derivation.

None of this had occurred by chance. All of the importations were the result of a monumental effort undertaken by the leaders of a nation determined to emerge from the cultural mists that enshrouded it. Yet, both then and thereafter, it was the hallmark of the Japanese that they could place upon every one of these adopted institutions a stamp that was indelibly their own – and therein lay their genius.

More than most peoples, the early Japanese were compelled by the isolation of their environment to develop highly distinctive styles of living. They dwelt on a 3,200-kilometre-long chain of more than 1,000 islands, which had, aeons before, been thrust up from the ocean floor by monstrous volcanic eruptions to form a land area of about 370,000 square kilometres – only slightly larger than the British Isles. Arcing from the northeast towards the southwest, the Japanese archipelago extends from Arctic environs to subtropical latitudes; at its closest point to the Asian mainland, it is about 190 kilometres from southern Korea, while the nearest landfall in China is more than 725 kilometres across perilously stormy seas, which were the bane of ancient mariners in small vessels.

Like most of the others, the four main islands – from north to south, Hokkaidō, Honshū, Shikoku and Kyūshū – are crowded with steep mountains, which range in height from a couple of hundred metres to the 3,776 metres of snow-crowned Fuji in central Honshū. So rugged is the terrain that only 16 per cent of the land can be cultivated, and for that reason Japan's inhabitants gravitated naturally towards a few plains built up from rich soil deposited by rivers. Consequently, these fertile areas became centres of political power, economic activity and religious authority.

From the beginning Japan was a violent land, convulsed by active volcanoes, shuddering with earthquakes that sometimes took a frightful toll in human life, swept in late summer and early autumn by vicious typhoons that struck hardest at the most heavily populated areas – because those areas lay mainly along the exposed coast, unprotected by mountain barriers. But the people also found it beautiful and in many ways benign. Throughout much of the archipelago's reach, the inhabitants enjoyed a temperate climate that allowed each of the four seasons to run its characteristic course but permitted few extremes of heat or cold. An ample rainfall and the tumbling silver streams that laced the countryside provided an abundance of water. The mountains were heavily forested, with growths of native camphor and cypress clinging to the slopes, and in springtime the valleys exploded with the bright colour of their blooming flowers.

Looking in awe to their mountains, existing nowhere that was more than 110-kilometres from the sea, the people of Japan fell early into a rapturous and enduring love affair with their natural surroundings. As their society took form, they called their domain names such as "The Land of Fresh Rice Ears of a Thousand Autumns" or "The Land of Luxuriant Reed Plains", meanwhile bestowing upon some of their deities such beguiling titles as "Princess Blossoming-like-the-Flowers-of-the-Trees".

Although the Japanese islands were inhabited at least as early as 10,000 BC by people who used roughly chipped stone tools, it was not until after 8000 BC that a people with an identifiable culture appeared on the archipelago. Their origins would be mysterious to future generations; some may have migrated from northern Asia while others, perhaps, came northwards from the coastal areas of Southeast Asia or even from as far east as Polynesia.

For a Stone Age people, they were remarkably sophisticated. Their culture was later given the name Jōmon – cord pattern – after the graceful and intricate designs achieved by impressing twisted strands of fibre into the wet clay of their hand-shaped pottery. The Jōmon subsisted by hunting in the interior hill country and fishing and gathering shellfish along the coasts. To bring down deer and wild boar, which were especially favoured as game, they developed a laminated bow. And they hollowed out tree trunks in order to make canoes for venturing on to coastal waters. Gathered into small communities and dwelling in huts that they constructed in pits for the sake of both warmth and protection, the Jōmon people were the very picture of primitive domesticity – they even made a pet of the dog.

It is possible that the Jōmon period overlapped the arrival of the Ainu, a people of puzzling origin who migrated to the northern island of Hokkaidō and thence to part of Honshū at some prehistoric time. Short, robust and hairy, the Ainu bore a closer racial resemblance to Europeans than to other East Asians. Virtually no clues to their genesis would survive; perhaps they were ancient Caucasians who somehow wandered off the mainstream before the common characteristics of that racial group had had time to develop fully. At any rate, they would continue to exist on Hokkaidō into modern times as the lonely remnants of a lost tribe.

Whatever the ethnic mysteries surrounding the Jōmon and the Ainu, the next wave of immigrants to Japan was almost certainly of Mongol origin. Commencing in about 300 BC, the Jōmon culture was rapidly replaced by that of a people known as the Yayoi. This group settled first in northern Kyūshū, the region closest to the Korean peninsula jutting out from the Asian mainland, and then expanded northwards on to Honshū, probably reaching the Kantō Plain at the head of Tokyo Bay by the closing years of the first century BC.

Unlike the hunter-gatherer Jōmon, the Yayoi were sedentary farmers whose main crop was rice grown in irrigated paddies by the same techniques practised in southern China. In further testimony to contacts with East Asia's more advanced civilizations, the Yayoi had a rudimentary knowledge of how to smelt iron and forge it into weapons and tools; they also produced wheel-turned, fire-hardened pottery that, while it lacked the imaginative designs of the Jōmon, was undeniably superior in its ceramic quality. And although silk would not be known to them for several centuries, garments woven from hemp or paper-mulberry bark were worn from early times. Some costumes were decorated with belt buckles, necklaces and other ornaments made from such stones as agate and crystal.

Given their background, it is hardly surprising that the Yayoi sought to learn more about continental accomplishments. After 108 BC, when China's militant Han dynasty extended its rule to northern Korea, tribal leaders from western Japan sent delegations to the colonial administration near modern P'yŏngyang. In AD 57, an envoy was sent from Japan to China itself. By the middle of the third century, a two-way traffic in trade existed between Japan's islands and the Asian mainland. A document of that period from China's Wei dynasty, containing reports by Chinese travellers, offers a fascinating if fragmentary glimpse of life among the Yayoi.

To the sophisticated Chinese, Japan was the quaint land of Wa – for which they used an ideograph that meant dwarf. Its inhabitants, advised the travellers, were a backward folk who lived in small villages of thatch-roofed, wooden or bamboo huts secured by twisted vines and raised a metre or so off the ground to keep out the dampness. They went about barefoot, smeared their bodies with pink and scarlet pigments "just as the Chinese use powder", ate with their fingers, and were "fond of liquor" – doubtless sake, a rice derivative long known to the Japanese.

Yet for all their crude ways, they were a long-lived and generally content people. "All men of high rank have four or five wives; others have two or three," reported the travellers. "The women are faithful and not jealous. There is no robbery or theft, and litigation is infrequent." Strict social distinctions were already being observed: "When the lowly meet men of importance on the road, they stop and withdraw to the roadside where they either squat or kneel with both hands on the ground. This is the way they show respect."

The Yayoi, continued the travellers, "practise divination by burning bones, and by that means they ascertain good and bad luck and whether or not to undertake journeys." They also tried to ensure their good fortune through an unusual social institution – a sort of surrogate ascetic. According to the chroniclers, the Yayoi appointed a "mourning keeper", who was to lead a life of self-denial on behalf of the rest of them. "He is not allowed to comb his hair, to wash, to eat meat, or to approach women. When the people are fortunate, they make him valuable presents; but if they fall ill or meet with disaster, they set it down to the mourning keeper's failure to observe his vows, and together they put him to death."

Because of a terrain that kept relatively small communities isolated from one another by mountain barriers, political unity was hard to achieve. Yet in at least one region, whose location was not made clear, a queen of sorts was recognized. Her name was Himiko, wrote Chinese observers, and she "occupied herself with magic and sorcery, bewitching the people. Though mature in age, she remained unmarried. She had 1,000 women as attendants but only one man. He served her food and drink and acted as a medium of communication. She resided in a palace surrounded by towers and stockades, with armed guards in a state of constant vigilance." If the redoubtable Himiko was more than the product of a lively Chinese imagination, it is clear she would have held sway more as a sorceress than as the monarch of a duly constituted government.

Whatever the reality of her rule, Himiko may have been the precursor of a significant new phase in Japanese development: when she died, according to the Chinese accounts, Himiko was buried beneath an earthen mound more than 100

TOMBS FOR THE KOFUN LORDS

Watched over by a foreman and engineer, workers complete a scale model that will guide construction of the keyhole tomb and let the emperor see its design.

After the site is cleared and levelled, surveyors make a layout with a grid of wooden stakes. In surface area, Emperor Nintoku's tomb was larger than Cheops' pyramid in Egypt.

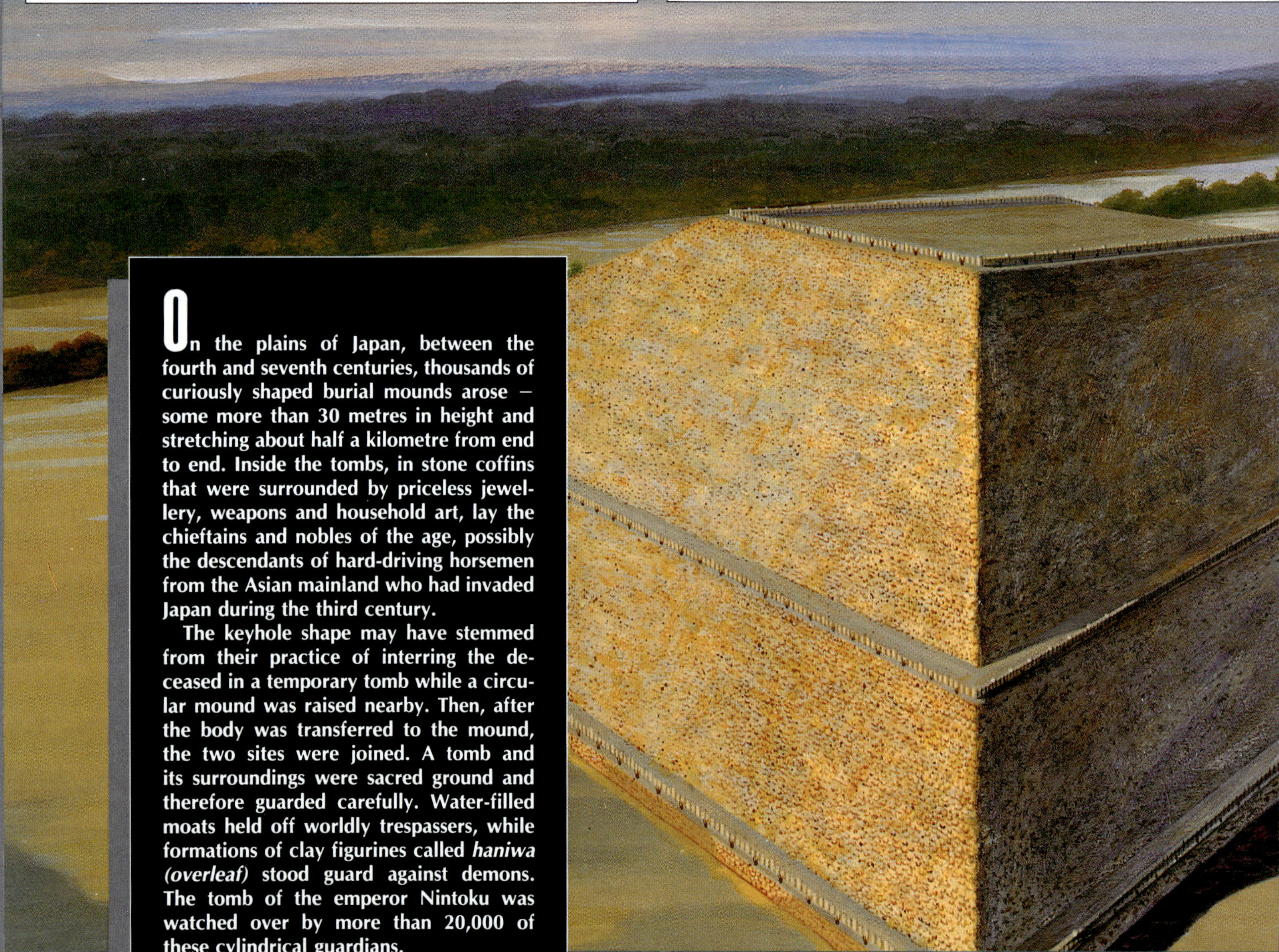

On the plains of Japan, between the fourth and seventh centuries, thousands of curiously shaped burial mounds arose – some more than 30 metres in height and stretching about half a kilometre from end to end. Inside the tombs, in stone coffins that were surrounded by priceless jewellery, weapons and household art, lay the chieftains and nobles of the age, possibly the descendants of hard-driving horsemen from the Asian mainland who had invaded Japan during the third century.

The keyhole shape may have stemmed from their practice of interring the deceased in a temporary tomb while a circular mound was raised nearby. Then, after the body was transferred to the mound, the two sites were joined. A tomb and its surroundings were sacred ground and therefore guarded carefully. Water-filled moats held off worldly trespassers, while formations of clay figurines called *haniwa* *(overleaf)* stood guard against demons. The tomb of the emperor Nintoku was watched over by more than 20,000 of these cylindrical guardians.

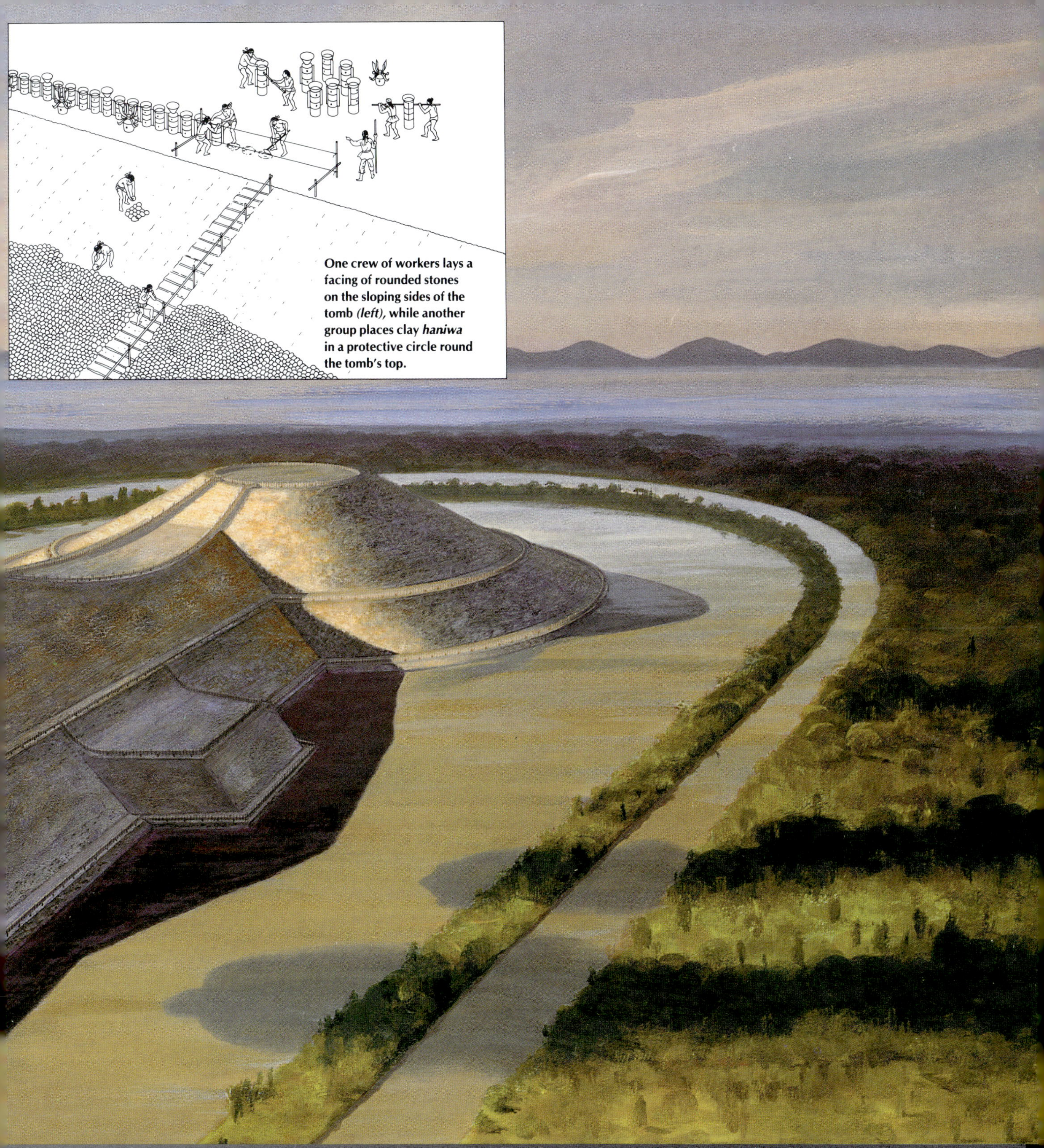

One crew of workers lays a facing of rounded stones on the sloping sides of the tomb *(left),* while another group places clay *haniwa* in a protective circle round the tomb's top.

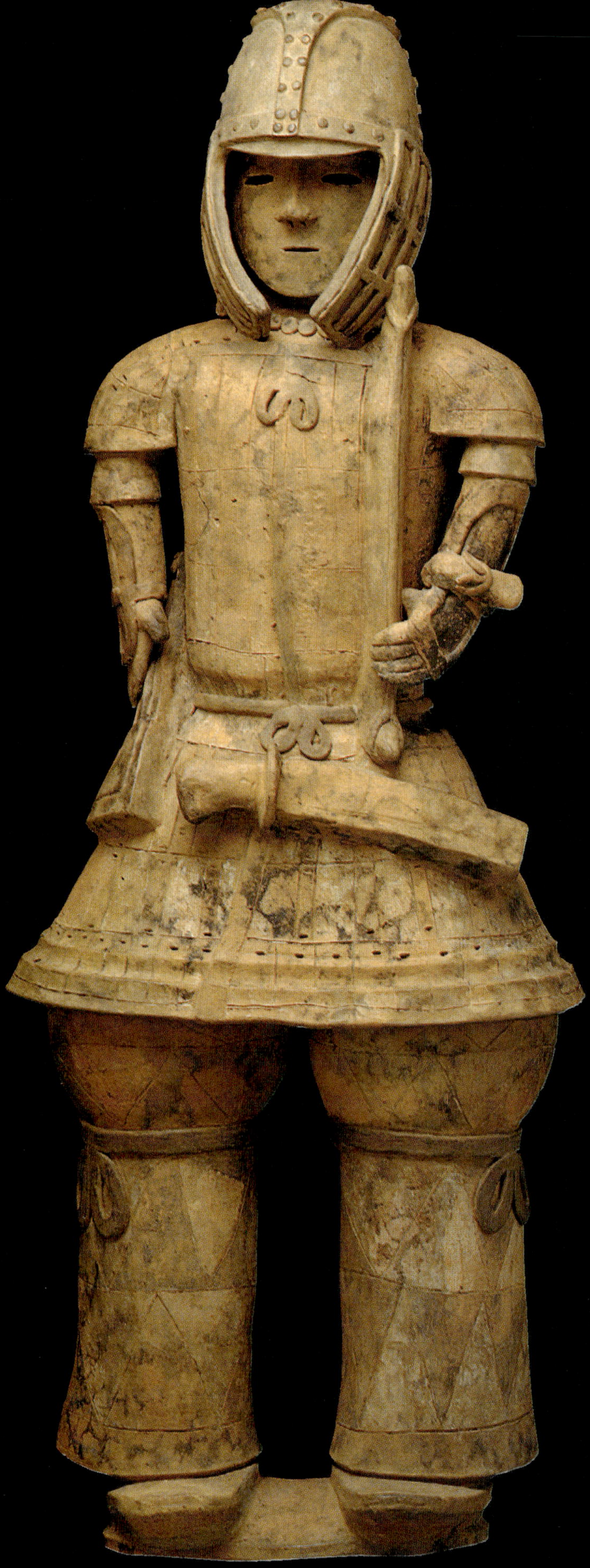

With a short sword dangling from his belt and a bow and quiver of arrows in his hands, a *haniwa* warrior wears the loose-fitting pants and tunic-style armour that permitted freedom of movement. Such figures were anchored on the sides of keyhole tombs. From head to toe, the warrior stood shoulder-high to a contemporary man *(box, above)*, a scale that emphasized his status over animals and inanimate objects.

A lavishly harnessed *haniwa* warhorse, with bells on its bit and breastplate and pendants adorning its hindquarters, reflects the equestrian origins of the Kofun nobleman whose tomb it adorned. Such animated *haniwa* evolved from unadorned clay cylinders initially designed to prevent erosion of steeply sloping tomb surfaces.

The intricate roof style and airy wings of this *haniwa* dwelling identify the spacious residence of a Kofun lord. These models accurately represented the architectural refinements affordable to Japan's elite. In contrast to the stuffy, earthen-floor shacks of their labourers, Kofun nobles walked on built-in floors and used numerous windows and high-ceilinged roofs to ventilate oppressive summer heat.

The shrines at Ise, on the island of Honshū, were built to honour Shinto deities and to exalt the ancient bond of the people with nature. The Inner Shrine, shown below, was dedicated to the ancestress of the imperial family, the sun goddess Amaterasu, whose spirit reigned over the seasonal rites of planting and harvest observed at Ise. The central structure on the right is thought to be modelled after an ancient grain storehouse and contains a sacred mirror symbolizing the goddess. Every 21 years, the shrine is razed and duplicated on an adjacent plot in a process that evokes the theme of seasonal degeneration and rebirth. During this time, a small shed on the old plot houses the "heart pillar", a remnant of the old building that will be preserved in the new shrine.

paces in diameter — and which also contained the remains of her 1,000 attendants, who followed her in death. By around AD 300, the traditional, simple and unpretentious Yayoi culture was giving way to a society distinguished by an aristocratic class that invested great effort and resources in building immense burial mounds, mysteriously shaped like keyholes.

The mound-building people, both men and women, wore jewellery and sleeved robes, affected elaborate hairstyles, and painted their faces with designs in red. Warriors wore armour, carried iron swords or longbows, and rode into battle on horses with decorative trappings and saddles with stirrups. Whether the mound-building culture was the result of indigenous evolution or was introduced by horseback-riding invaders from Asia's northern steppes is unknown. In either event, it offered fertile ground for Japan's institutional growth into a coherent community.

Probably during the third century, a tribal band whose patron deity was the sun goddess Amaterasu migrated from Kyūshū along the shores of Japan's Inland Sea to the Yamato Plain, a very fertile but small region — about 30 kilometres long and 15 kilometres wide — near where the city of Ōsaka would one day stand. There, by force of arms, by marital alliances with other leading clans, and especially by reason of the great reverence accorded to Amaterasu, the chieftains of the goddess' followers gradually established themselves as the dominant power in most of western Japan. In so doing, they founded an imperial dynasty — the Sun Line — that would reign in unbroken succession into the modern era.

Then and thereafter, the authority of the imperial family was inextricably tied to the native religion that came to be called Shinto — The Way of the Gods. As practised in those early days, Shinto was an unstructured body of beliefs, possessing no scriptures, offering no moral preachments, holding no promise of the soul's salvation, yet bursting with an enjoyment of nature. Its populous pantheon was filled with kami, a word that is usually equated with "gods" but actually comes closer to meaning something — almost anything — that is superior. In that particular sense, therefore, a remote ancestor or a departed hero might be considered a kami, but so too might a majestic mountain, a babbling brook, a dark and forbidding cave, a grain of sand, or a beautiful butterfly.

As befitted an agricultural society, growth and fertility were revered. Shinto rites, conducted in simple shrines that were, in general, one-room, thatched-roof wooden structures raised on stilts and approached by a ramp, often consisted of little more than offerings and prayers for the generous bestowal of nature's bounties. During one annual celebration, according to the Chinese, Shinto communities gave thanks for "crops in ears long and in ears abundant, things growing in the great moor-plain, sweet herbs and bitter herbs, things that dwell in the great sea-plain, the broad of fin and the narrow of fin, seaweed from the offing, seaweed from the shore, clothing, bright stuffs and shining stuffs, coarse stuffs and fine stuffs".

Disease, on the other hand, was evil, and death was a defilement whose corruptive consequences must be washed away by ritual ablutions. Outside every shrine stood a basin of water used by worshippers to cleanse their hands and mouths of the pollution that may have been caused by accidental or even unknowing contact with disease or death. Salt, as a purifying agent, was placed in small piles on the threshold of a house, next to the well, and in the corners of a wrestling ring. After a person had died, salt was strewn about the floor of the home as a purifying agent, and following a funeral, all the family survivors immediately repaired to bathe. Nor was the fear of being tainted confined to common folk; for many centuries, when an emperor died, his palace was deemed to be vile and was abandoned.

Naturally, some kami were more powerful than others, and according to the degree of their potency they offered protection to individuals, families, villages, regions and even the entire country. As goddess of the sun, which gave life to all things, Amaterasu was enormously powerful, and her stature was greatly elevated by legends that were carefully crafted by the earliest Japanese storytellers.

In the beginning, it seems, the primal god Izanagi and his goddess-wife, Izanami, created the Japanese islands. Izanami also gave birth to several other deities, but in producing a fire god she was tragically burnt to death. True to his troth, Izanagi sought and found her in the Land of Darkness, but by then she was so putrefied that he fled in horror to Japan. There, like any good Shintoist, he attempted to free himself from the taint of deathly corruption by bathing. In the process, he somehow washed the sun goddess Amaterasu out of his left eye, the moon god Tsuki-yumi from his right eye, and the storm god Susanowo from his nose.

Susanowo, as it turned out, was given to such devilry as making green mountains wither. Unhappily, a favourite butt of his nasty pranks was his sister Amaterasu, and when Susanowo defecated inside her heavenly palace she retired in anger to a cave, leaving the world in darkness.

Since that condition was intolerable, the other deities gathered before the cave and tried to coax Amaterasu from her hiding place. Finally, one goddess performed an erotic dance, inspiring such gleeful laughter that Amaterasu poked her head out from the cave to see what all the commotion was about. A muscular god pulled her the rest of the way, and light was restored to the earth.

Later, after many other adventures, Amaterasu dispatched her grandson Ninigi-no-Mikoto to rule Japan, and as the symbols of his majesty she gave him three items that would later constitute the official regalia of an emperor – a bronze mirror, a sword and a jewelled necklace. According to Japanese chronicles, it was Ninigi's grandson Jimmu Tenno (Divine Warrior) who led the imperial family on its march from Kyūshū to the Yamato Plain and who became Japan's first emperor.

Despite his divine blood, the power of the Sun Line emperor was far from absolute. He presided as a sort of first-among-equals over an unruly collection of chieftains who, in turn, held both political and religious authority over semi-autonomous groups called *uji,* which closely resembled clans. Although all the members of each *uji* were not necessarily related by blood, they were bound together by mutual interests and by their worship of a single god, known as an *uji-gami*. Within every *uji* was a number of *be,* or guilds, each with a specialized skill such as farming, fishing, weaving, pottery making or military service. Membership in the *be* was determined by heredity, and a son could no more abandon his father's vocation than he could desert the *uji* into which he was born.

Each major *uji*, therefore, was more or less self-sustaining, and its patriarch held supreme political sanction within his domain. Although the *uji* chieftains paid deference to the head of the Sun Line by reason of his status as the earthly descendant of Amaterasu, the Yamato emperor's position was in some ways more like that of a revered high priest than a secular ruler.

Whatever its virtues, this decentralized power structure undermined any ambitions of creating a state that could compete with the established kingdoms and empires of Asia. And so from this ambitious and energetic people there emerged a centralized authority in the form of a council of state, which was composed of the most powerful *uji* chieftains, to advise the Sun Line sovereign.

That body evolved into an organization led by two great ministers, one representing *uji* closely related to the imperial family, the other selected from *uji* sponsored by deities other than the sun goddess. Moreover, with the continuing evolution of the state, many of the more prominent *uji* took on specialized functions: the Nakatomi, for example, were court liturgists, the Imibe were experts in purification rituals, the Otomo were the emperor's bodyguards, the Mononobe supplied weapons, and the Kumebe provided soldiers.

In time, membership in a leading *uji* would become of such crucial importance that ambitious provincial families began forging their pedigrees, a transgression that brought an angry rebuke from all those in power at Yamato. "Single clans," they proclaimed, "have multiplied and formed 10,000 titles of doubtful authenticity." The rulers then decreed: "Let the people of the various clans and titles cleanse themselves and practise abstinence, and let them, calling upon the gods to witness, plunge their hands in boiling water." Those who survived the test were certified in their high rank, while those who failed or ran away in fear were stripped of their position. Although no record of the results of this searing trial of pedigrees was preserved, it is probable that the number of noble families was considerably diminished.

Unfortunately, the great *uji* were by no means always friendly, and in their constant jostling for power, they were far from fastidious about the use of violence. The situation was vastly exacerbated by the fact that there was no established formula for succession to the throne; the

Embellished with finely detailed butterflies and elaborate floral motifs, an eighth-century bronze mirror testifies to the perfectionism of its creators, craftsmen whose skills were passed from father to son. Along with two other objects, the sword and the jewel, the mirror was a token of imperial and divine authority in ancient Japan. The mirror was the most powerful of the three, however, since it was associated with the native Japanese sun goddess Amaterasu, who was the mythical ancestress of the imperial family.

only condition was that the ruler came from the imperial family. As a result, rival *uji* often engaged in bloody fights on behalf of opposing candidates for the crown.

Moreover, since all those in direct descent from Amaterasu were divinely qualified to rule, there were no great spiritual inhibitions about deposing or assassinating an incumbent emperor. This occurred with such distressing frequency that on one occasion when a vacancy existed and a great minister dispatched an armed guard to escort a Yamato prince to the throne, the prospective emperor saw the soldiers approaching, took to his heels, and was never seen again.

Yet despite their own unsettled conditions, the Japanese were sufficiently well organized to take an aggressive interest in the affairs of their nearest mainland neighbours, the contentious kingdoms of Korea – and Korea became the conduit for momentous innovations that would transform the Japanese culture.

By around the middle of the fourth century, Japanese warriors were fighting in Korea, where they established a base at Mimana on the southern extremity of the peninsula. From that foothold, they actively intervened in the ceaseless wars that took place among Korea's three kingdoms – Paekche, Silla and Koguryŏ – most often taking the side of Paekche. In 391, the Japanese forces marched northwards against Koguryŏ as far as P'yŏngyang (which centuries later would be the capital of North Korea) and, although forced to withdraw, these troops proved to be of inestimable help to the ruler of Paekche.

Paekche's ruler did not get round to expressing his gratitude formally for some years, but when he did he sent a treasure beyond price. Around the year 400, a delegation from Paekche arrived in Japan bearing gifts that included a copybook – *The Thousand Character Classic* – written in Chinese script. Despite their proximity to the mainland, the Japanese of that time were entirely illiterate. And it was out of a deep yearning that their leaders requested the Koreans to recommend a scholar who could teach one of their crown princes how to read and write Chinese. The man selected was a scribe named Wani, and his arrival in the year 405 signalled the official adoption of Chinese script as the written language of the Japanese.

The difficulties of converting Chinese writing to Japanese use were enormous, especially since the two spoken tongues were, and would remain, completely dissimilar. Chinese is largely monosyllabic, highly intonated, and tends towards terse sentence structures. Japanese, on the other hand, lends itself to long, complex sentences with grammatical usages defined by particles; the subject of a sentence, for example, is designated as such by the particle *wa,* which follows it. The polysyllabic words, mostly unaccented, consist of strings of solitary vowels preceded by single consonants, as in the syllables *sa, mi, ko, ru* and *te.* In their oral rendering of the Chinese characters, the two languages bear no phonetic resemblance. Thus, when the Japanese called their country Nippon – the Land of the Rising Sun – they used the Chinese characters for "sun" and "source". In Chinese, however, those characters would be pronounced as Jihpen – hence, in corrupted form, Japan.

Not until the ninth century would the Japanese find a solution to at least part of their written-language problem by developing a syllabary system called kana, in which phonetic sounds were assigned to simplified characters that could be used as particles, verb endings and the like. In the meantime, however, they managed to muddle through, putting their borrowed script to such vital purposes as issuing state documents, keeping public records, and producing all other forms of written communication necessary to the daily functioning of an organized government.

Before very long, they would even be capable of creating a considerable body of historical and poetic literature – written in Chinese characters but very distinctly Japanese in both its feeling and form.

During the period when the Japanese were making their first struggling attempts to master the script presented to them by the king of Paekche, that country remained embroiled in strife with its Korean neighbours. In 552, another Paekchean monarch felt so menaced that he sent envoys to Japan with a desperate plea for renewed military assistance. This time the delegation bore with it some volumes of Buddhist scripture and a bronze image of the Buddha, together with a letter recommending that the Yamato court give serious consideration to that faith, which had already pervaded Korea. To be sure, wrote Paekche's ruler, Buddhism was extremely difficult to understand, but once comprehended it was doubtless the world's most excellent doctrine.

As it happened, the Paekchean proposal suited perfectly the purposes of a man named Soga no Iname, who had risen to the rank of great minister largely through his family's shrewd habit of marrying off its daughters to princes of the Yamato court. Soga no Iname was statesman enough to realize that only through a massive infusion of Chinese culture, as reflected by Buddhism, could his backward nation advance. Beyond that, he saw in Buddhism a chance to undermine such powerful rival clans as the Nakatomi and the Mononobe, whose influence as court ritualists and military armourers was based on the potency of their Shinto kami.

Confronted by the conflicting factions, the reigning emperor temporized over Soga no Iname's proposal to adopt Buddhism, going only so far as to allow him to install and worship the bronze Buddha in his own house. Then, however, Japan was swept by disease – which the Nakatomi and the Mononobe immediately attributed to the anger of the ancient deities at the presence of an alien god. The emperor agreed, and Buddha's image was mutilated and then hurled into a canal.

But the struggle was far from over. By 575, Soga no Iname's son, Soga no Umako, was great minister to another emperor, Bidatsu, who – though no adherent of Buddhism – was an ardent admirer of Chinese culture. Presumably with Bidatsu's permission, Sogo no Umako set about establishing a Buddhist clergy. To start, he found a former monk from Korea who had come to Japan and retired to secular life. Required by Soga no Umako to return to his religious calling, the monk duly enrolled as nuns three young girls of unimpeachable virtue. "From this," records an early Japanese chronicle, "arose the beginning of Buddhism."

Yet it was a tentative, troubled birth. Again there was an epidemic of disease, again the enemies of Soga no Umako blamed it on Buddhism, and again the Emperor banned the religion. The Nakatomi and the Mononobe had the pleasure of razing a temple Soga no Umako had erected, while the unfortunate nuns were stripped of their habits and lashed in a marketplace. Still, Soga no Umako was both persistent and persuasive; before long, the Emperor allowed him to conduct private Buddhist devotions, for which he built a small chapel and summoned the nuns to resume their religious endeavours.

To the vast consternation of the Nakatomi and Mononobe leaders and their conservative allies, Bidatsu's successor was the emperor Yomei, a ruler of equable mind who believed in the law of Buddha yet also revered the way of the Shinto gods. Yomei, however, died after a brief reign, and quarrels over the imperial succession between the Soga family and its enemies soon turned to civil war. The short but bloody contest ended in 587 with a Soga victory at Shigisen, in central Honshū, during which the Mononobe family was annihilated.

Soga no Umako now held undisputed power behind the throne, and the way was open to the phenomenal growth of the religion he espoused. By his death in 626, the Buddhist establishment that he founded with a Korean monk and three nuns would burgeon to 46 monasteries, 816 monks and 569 nuns. By the century's end, there were 545 monasteries, with a priesthood numbering in the thousands.

Yet with Soga no Umako, first things always came first, and after his triumph in battle, his most pressing task was to enthrone an acceptable emperor. He selected a prince of the imperial family who was also, and by no coincidence, his own nephew. But when the new emperor Sajun for some reason incurred his displeasure, Soga no Umako coolly engineered his assassination. For a replacement, he picked one of his royal nieces, a 39-year-old widow and mother of seven sons, who reigned as the empress Suiko. Then, to guide the lady along proper lines, Soga no Umako designated as regent and heir apparent a 21-year-old prince with the formidable name of Umayado-no-toyotomimi-no-mikato, who would become known to posterity simply as Shōtoku, meaning "Sovereign Moral Power".

Although the crown prince Shōtoku was no blood kin to Soga no Umako, he had the redeeming virtues of being married to a Soga woman, of having fought on the Soga side in the recent civil war, and of being a Buddhist. During the three decades he would hold power, he would become one of the most renowned figures in the annals of Japan – not so much because of his specific achievements but because, using Chinese civilization as his model, he would set his land on a calculated course of cultural borrowing that was without previous parallel in world history.

Shōtoku was an intellectual prodigy. One chronicle stated that, "He was able to speak as soon as he was born and was so wise when he grew up that he could attend to the suits of 10 men at once and decide them all without error." Even if that description inflated his talent, Shōtoku was undoubtedly studious, fond of writing commentaries on Buddhist scripture, and steeped in the concepts of Confucianism.

When the two creeds came into conflict, as they often did, Shōtoku settled the issue with great wisdom: Buddhist thought had precedence in religious matters, and Confucian principles were best applied to secular policy. For example, while Buddhism was imbued with the timelessness of nirvana, Confucianism held that for efficient government, events on earth must be in tune with heavenly time. Shōtoku therefore adopted the Confucian-based Chinese calendar.

In 604, the crown prince Shōtoku issued the so-called Constitution of Seventeen Articles, which was, in fact, not a proper constitution at all but rather a compendium of such Buddhist and Confucian homilies as "Harmony is to be valued" and "Chastise that which is evil and encourage that which is good", along with more down-to-earth strictures, which included, "Let the ministers and functionaries attend the court early in the morning and retire late". For all its platitudes, the document was significant in that it was the first attempt to apply an ethical code of responsible service and establish an ideological basis for rule.

Admiring the orderly dignity of the Chinese court, Shōtoku followed its model by introducing a system in which Japanese court officials could be identified as to rank by the colour of their caps. Each of 12 ranks was named after a human virtue; a courtier who had reached the grade of greater righteousness wore a red cap, while someone at the level of lesser benevolence had to be content with blue headwear.

According to their rank, the court officials were rewarded with grants from the crown in the form of either land or produce.

Yet it was in the area of conscious cultural contact with China that Shōtoku made his most enduring contribution to Japanese civilization. In 607, he sent a large delegation to the court of the Sui dynasty under the leadership of One no Imoko, the first envoy ever to represent the ruler of a united Japan in China. As it turned out, the mission almost came to disaster before it began. Imoko bore with him a letter, apparently written by Shōtoku on behalf of his empress, that began, with a fine disregard both for gender and Chinese sensibilities: "The Son of Heaven of the Land of the Rising Sun to the Son of Heaven of the Land of the Setting Sun."

It was an odd lapse for the normally thoughtful Shōtoku, and it so offended the Chinese emperor that he at first refused to accept the delegation, declaring that he had no need to deal with barbarians. However, matters were soon patched over. Imoko remained in China for a year and returned in the company of two Chinese envoys, who were grandly welcomed in Japan.

One no Imoko's pioneer mission had set a pattern that would endure for the next two-and-a-half centuries, with China playing host to a veritable deluge of Japanese delegations. As a rule, the groups were composed of young Japanese who were skilled in the arts or who had shown promise in Confucian or Buddhist studies.

Their journey to and from China was fraught with danger. On one expedition, a ship ran aground before it ever cleared the mouth of the Yangtze; finally extricated, it made landfall in Kyūshū after a 40-day trip. The other ships in the group were buffeted by a storm that wrecked one of them on the shores of Quelpart Island off Korea, where its passengers and crew were captured by natives. A few of the captives managed to escape and make their way back to Japan. On another ship, about 40 Japanese and 25 Chinese, including the leaders of both parties, drowned after being swept overboard by waves that engulfed the vessel. One or two days later, the same ship broke in half; clinging to the separate sections, about 50 bedraggled survivors on each were washed ashore on the coast of Kyūshū.

Yet the experience of studying in China was worth the risks of the voyage. For upon returning to Japan, sometimes after spending as many as three decades absorbing the accumulated wisdom of the ancient empire, the scholars were awarded positions of great influence in a court and a society that valued Chinese knowledge above all else. In fact, within a generation after the crown prince Shōtoku passed from the scene, some of the scholars would be involved in a conspiracy that brought Japan even more closely within China's cultural embrace.

Shōtoku died in the year 622, at the age of 49; four years later, he was followed to the grave by the great minister Soga no Umako, who had remained as a grey eminence during the years of Shōtoku's administration; and in 628, the empress Suiko, perhaps the least of the triumvirate that had wrought such vast change upon Japan, joined her ancestors. Effective power then passed into the hands of Soga no Umako's son, Soga no Yemishi, a man who was every bit as ruthless as his sire but who possessed far less subtle cunning.

As a first order of business – after arranging several murders in order to consolidate his power – Yemishi placed on the throne a grandson of the old emperor Bidatsu, and when that figurehead ruler died some years later in 641, Yemishi saw to it that his successor was an empress who had ties with the Soga family. Meanwhile, and with increasing blatancy, he made it clear that his intention was

Attended here by his two sons, Prince Shōtoku earned a place in Japanese history for the masterful blend of wisdom and foresight he demonstrated as imperial regent between 593 and 622. Although best known for his promotion of Buddhist teachings and temples, Shōtoku wrote a new constitution, compiled a history of Japan, and reorganized the imperial court's administrative system. Despite his achievements, he seems to have become disillusioned with political life and in the end sought solace in religion: "The world is empty and false," he lamented, "Buddha alone is real."

eventually to take possession of the crown himself – an unthinkable act that would have brought to an end the long, deeply revered tenure of the Sun Line.

Among his transgressions, Yemishi claimed his sons and daughters to be of imperial blood, and set them up in fortified palaces, guarded by moats and soldiers. Further, he trod on imperial appointive rights by giving an odious son, Iruka, whom he used as a bully boy, a purple cap of highest rank. Watching this with dismay was Nakatomi no Kamatari, leader of an *uji* that had fought the Soga ascent to power when recognition of Buddhism was being so bloodily debated.

After the defeat of his faction in battle, Nakatomi no Kamatari had retired from the court to meditate upon the teachings of Chinese wise men. Now, however, he began casting about among the princes of the imperial family for one who would join him in a conspiracy to topple the Soga. He found his man in Prince Naka no Oye, who seemed to have the qualifications to become a successful ruler. To ingratiate himself with his candidate, with whom he had never been on close terms, Nakatomi no Kamatari watched while the Prince played kickball – a popular game of the day in court circles. Then, claimed one account, he observed Naka no Oye's shoe fall off as he kicked the ball. "Placing it on the palm of his hand, he knelt before the Prince and humbly offered it to him."

From then on, the two were as thick as only plotters can be. Their ambitions were realized in 645 when a band of conspirators, headed by the Prince himself, burst in on a state ceremony and assassinated the detested Soga no Iruka before the very eyes of the empress. Just a few days later, Soga no Yemishi was also slain, Soga palaces were put to the torch, and the era of Soga power was ended forever.

Murder was amply rewarded – within a few years, Prince Naka no Oye became the emperor Tenchi, and his chief accomplice, Nakatomi no Kamatari, given the honorary name of Fujiwara Kamatari, founded a family dynasty that would abide as the power behind the throne for five centuries.

Throughout their scheming, the leaders of the conspiracy against the Soga had been advised by scholars who had returned from China, eager to reform Japan's government along Chinese lines. Their efforts bore fruit: early in 646, the heads of Japan's mightiest *uji* were summoned to attend the imperial court in order to hear the new year proclaimed as *Taika* – Great Transformation – and also to absorb the principles of the so-called Taika Reform, which took as its model for rule the system that was practised by China's mighty Tang dynasty.

At the heart of the Taika Reform was the imperial court's determination to wrest power from the *uji* and place it in the hands of the central government. Thus, first and foremost, the emperor was decreed an absolute sovereign, his status deriving from his descent from Amaterasu. Gathered under a giant *tsuki* tree, the assembled nobles swore their allegiance, calling down terrible consequences upon violators: "Heaven will send a curse and earth a plague, demons will slay them, and men will smite them." In theory, the emperor was now the fount of all secular as well as religious authority; in practice, he was still a creature of his closest advisers.

Under the Taika edict, ownership of all rice lands, the source of wealth in Japan, would pass to the Crown, presumably for redistribution to the peasants who worked in the paddies. The land allotments would be made according to the size of the household, or number of "mouths", on a scale adjusted for age, sex and status as freeman or slave; a slave counted for only two thirds as much as a freeman.

Towards those ends, a population census and a survey of arable lands would be taken. The workers' guilds, or *be*, which had traditionally been subservient to the *uji*, were to be abolished. Throughout Japan, provinces, districts and villages (there were no cities) would be overseen by officials appointed by and responsible to the central government, whose own administrative apparatus would be expanded. As an inevitable accompaniment to government reforms, land and head taxes would be imposed, with payment made either in crops – usually 10 sheaves of rice per hectare – in textiles, or through military service or forced labour.

To show the way, the Crown Prince turned over his own estate to the throne. In fact, the reforms were by no means what they seemed – and if they had been real, the nobles would have undoubtedly risen in armed wrath. Although the state assumed ownership of their lands, in most cases the nobles maintained actual possession. They were more than compensated by appointments to high position in the government, for which they received generous emoluments. The land redistribution was extremely limited; peasants who were granted land were so heavily taxed for it that many had to give up their new holdings and resume vassalage.

Despite its shortcomings, the Taika Reform largely accomplished its main purpose – that of removing the fundamental power in the realm from the unruly *uji* and placing it in the hands of a sovereign authority. In that sense, the edict came close to satisfying the Chinese concept that, "Under the heavens there is no land that is not the king's land. Among holders of land there is none who is not the king's vassal." In addition, the oath taken under the *tsuki* tree paved the way for the more explicit and extensive reforms that came about half a century later.

Issued in 702 after many years of study, the code of Taihō – Great Treasure – consisted of two major sections: the *ryo*, containing more than 900 articles in 30 chapters, dealt elaborately with administrative institutions; the *ritsu* was Japan's first formal enunciation of penal law. Predictably, the Taihō was patterned after Chinese precedents – and yet bore a stamp that was unmistakably Japanese.

According to the *ryo*, responsibility for rule was shared by two major branches of government – the Department of State, controlled by the Great Council of State, and the Department of Religion. But, in a departure from the Chinese way, the Department of Religion was considered the more important, and it concerned itself not with imported Buddhism but with the native Shinto faith. Given that franchise, the Department of Religion observed and reported on oracular pronouncements and divinations, presided over religious celebrations of such major significance as the rites of enthronement and the Festival of the First Fruits, and supervised the maintenance of Shinto shrines and the discipline of shrine wardens.

The Department of State was divided into eight main units: the Mediate Office and the ministries of Aristocratic Affairs, Popular Affairs, Ceremonies and Personnel, War, Justice, Treasury and the Imperial Household. Among those, the senior was the Mediate Office with its prestigious Bureau of Yin-Yang, which immersed itself deeply in the cosmological study of the polar extremes – light and dark, positive and negative, active and passive – that Confucian principles held to control the unfolding course of human events.

For administrative and tax purposes, Japan was divided into provinces and, within them in a descending order of size, districts, villages and hamlets. According to one document of the early eighth century, there were 67 provinces, 555 districts, 4,012 villages and 12,036 hamlets. The census was extremely thorough. The village of Mira, for example, was recorded as having 50 households that were placed in one of three different tax grades according to the amount of land each one worked. Actual taxes were determined by the number of taxable males present in each household; of Mira's total of 899 people, 14 were slaves, 463 were females, and 422 were males. Due to various exemptions because of age, infirmity or military service, 121 able-bodied adult males and 38 able-bodied minor males in Mira were listed as taxable.

Each village was governed by a headman chosen from among the people. The districts – each covering perhaps 20 villages or about 20,000 people in all – were likewise supervised by leaders who, for the most part, were chosen from

In a pair of scroll paintings illustrating the Buddhist reverence for all forms of life, Buddha's cousin *(top)* demonstrates his strength by cruelly pushing an elephant to the ground; the master then makes a point by holding the beast aloft *(right)*, with the admonition that it is more important to respect life than to quash it. Such Buddhist sentiments appealed to the Japanese, as did the religion's flexibility: rather than rejecting the traditional Shinto deities and rituals, Buddhism incorporated them, transforming the Shinto spirits into guides in the eternal quest for enlightenment.

The Holiest Temple

Soaring 33 metres skywards, a five-storey pagoda dominates the most sacred Buddhist temple in Japan, at Hōryūji, near the imperial city of Nara. Originally a modest temple dedicated to the Buddha of Healing, the complex was rebuilt after a fire at the end of the seventh century and was gradually enlarged into a monastery that became famous for Buddhist studies. Tile-roofed walkways enclose the central compound, joining the steeply pitched main gate *(inset, front)* to the elongated Lecture Hall *(rear)*. The pagoda and the Golden Hall *(right)*, which houses the temple's altar and bronze icons, are among the world's oldest examples of wooden architecture. Although heavily influenced by Chinese prototypes, the temple design includes some quite distinctively Japanese touches. The pagoda's centre post *(cut away, left)*, carved from a single tree trunk, is loosely fastened to the structure's horizontal supports, allowing the building to sway during Japan's frequent earthquakes.

among the local gentry. But provincial governors were almost without exception chosen from among the elite of the Yamato court.

Unlike the Chinese government, in which many bureaucratic appointments were based on merit as determined by examinations, the Japanese made little pretence about respecting anything other than family pedigree. The institutions of government were shaped to enable a hereditary aristocratic oligarchy to exercise direct control over a land whose population may have exceeded five million.

The top officials often grew wealthy. While provincial governors had modest base salaries, they were also entitled to a share of the taxes they collected and often lined their coffers in other ways. An imperial edict in 775 complained: "It has come to our ears that while the functionaries of the capital are poorly paid and cannot escape the hardships of cold and hunger, provincial governors make great profits. In consequence, all officials openly covet posts in the provinces." Another memorandum advised: "Those who govern a province are excessively prosperous. Their storehouses are full of gold and cloth, their tables piled with wine and meat."

Japan's legal code, *ritsu*, specified that justice should be dispensed with an even hand and in precise degree. Killing a man in a fight, for example, was one degree worse than slaying him in a sport in which swords or other lethal weapons were used – and that, in turn, was one degree more serious than causing death in an unarmed contest such as a wrestling match. The five basic penalties, also assessed by degree, were beatings with a light rod or a heavy one, both in five degrees as calculated by the number of strokes; penal servitude in five degrees and ranging from one to three years; exile in three degrees based on the distance a culprit was sent; and death in two degrees – strangulation or beheading.

But this carefully wrought system was still inequitable, for the privileged classes could generally avoid such punishments through payments of copper; 600 grams of the metal was the equivalent of 10 strokes with a light rod, while about 6 kilograms of copper was sufficient to escape the death penalties.

Yet not even the elite could hope to get off so lightly if they were found guilty of one of "the Eight Outrages", as defined by the *ritsu*. Among them, the political crimes of plotting rebellion, sedition or treason were invariably punished by death and frequently by family extermination and the confiscation of all property as well. Only marginally less outrageous in official eyes were the terrible felonies of "depravity" (which might be anything from killing three or more members of the same family to possessing magical poisons), "great irreverence" (which included stealing from a shrine and acts of lese-majesty), and "unrighteousness" (a covering clause for which even a widow who failed to mourn her husband might be prosecuted). And, finally, there was lack of filial behaviour, and contumacy, which covered the full range of Confucian notions about family morality, such as cursing one's parents or failing to provide for them.

The Japanese now possessed an extensive administrative machine and a maturing system of government, and they determined to add another element of stability to their country – a capital, a permanent home for their monarch and a base of operations for his expanding bureaucracy. The ancient Shinto law calling for the relocation of the imperial house on the death of an emperor to avoid pollution was no longer considered imperative. The Chinese example proved powerful – they, after all, had a fixed capital and effective ways of avoiding ritual uncleanliness other than abandoning the palace. In the effort to find a site, there were lengthy consultations with experts in Chinese geomancy — the pseudoscience of choosing an auspicious homestead based on the arrangement of its surrounding hills and the character of its "wind and water". Finally, it was decided that Japan's new capital should be located squarely in the middle of the Yamato Plain.

Japan's first true city, Nara, was laid out as a smaller copy of Changan, the capital of Tang China. Of rectangular shape, covering an area approximately five kilometres long by four kilometres wide, the city boasted broad avenues set at right angles and lined by homes of the wealthy aristocracy. Just north of its centre sat the Imperial Palace, with its red pillars and tiled roof, amid stately Buddhist temples and monasteries. Although Nara's population would grow to some 200,000, there was plenty of open space. Its parks and pagodas made it a lovely city, which reminded one Japanese poet of "many-petalled cherry blossoms" — a description appropriate to the place where the civilization of early Japan would bloom.

During the relatively few but glorious years of Nara's golden era, the cultural influence of China in general and Buddhism in particular was beyond measure. The long period of tutelage by the Chinese was beginning to pay dividends. Japanese scholars who had studied in China now returned to bestow the gifts of their experience. Notable among them were Gembo, who brought back more than 5,000 sutras, or Buddhist scriptures, for the enlightenment of his people, and Kibi no Makibi, who, after steeping himself for 17 years in the knowledge of Buddhist ceremonial rites, military science and Confucianism, returned to Japan to establish a training programme for prospective government officials.

At the same time, Japan had become a magnet for Buddhist priests and artists and artisans from China and Korea, all eager to sow the seeds of their faith or their craft in the fertile Land of the Rising Sun. In their enthusiasm, they were willing to endure all manner of hardships, as witness the case of Ganjin, a Chinese monk and renowned savant. When he first attempted to make the journey in 742, his ship was captured by pirates and he himself was held prisoner for a time. Twice more he set forth, and twice more he was turned back by storms. Next, his plans were thwarted by Chinese officials who were reluctant to have so eminent a scholar leave their land. Once that obstacle was overcome, Ganjin set out again; this time his ship was wrecked, and one of his party drowned. But Ganjin survived, and in 753, 11 years after he had first ventured forth from China, he at last made landfall in Kyūshū. By then, he was 66 years old — and blind.

Still, the results of the trip were worth the ordeal. Upon his arrival he was greeted by a message from the Japanese emperor giving him the exclusive privilege of conducting the Buddhist rituals of ordination, and upon his death at the age of 77, he left 17 disciples as leading lights of Buddhism in Japan.

Despite such missionary zeal, Buddhism miraculously managed to dwell in harmony with the native Shintoism of the Japanese islands. For the imperial family and its followers, coexistence of the two religions was a matter of simple necessity. They recognized the cultural benefits that Buddhism could bestow upon their land; but because the Sun Line derived its authority from the divine descent attributed to it by Shintoism, the ruling class could under no circumstances forsake the native cult. As for Japan's common folk, they were willing as always to respect the beliefs of their betters — as long as they were still able to worship their own gods of nature.

And so, most Japanese saw nothing contradictory in embracing both religions, though at different levels — Buddhism because of its enlightened philosophy, its civilizing endowments and its magical powers and Shintoism as sign and symbol of the love the Japanese held for their homeland.

That open acceptance of the two faiths took practical forms. Most of the Nara monarchs gave generously and even-handedly to Buddhist and Shinto endowments alike. Their religious proclamations combined Buddhist and Shinto ideas and some Confucian precepts as well. Shinto shrines and Buddhist temples sometimes shared the same land, and one Buddhist monk was moved to build a temple on the advice, he said, of a Shinto kami who spoke to him through an oracle. When the pious emperor Shomu called on his people to contribute towards the casting of the Rushana Buddha, at least one Shinto sect responded with money; and after the installation of that Great Buddha in the Golden Hall of Nara's Tōdaiji monasterial complex, Buddhist priests, perhaps motivated by their gratitude for the cooperative intercession of the goddess Amaterasu, regularly participated in Shinto rites.

Within that benign atmosphere, both religions flourished, Shintoism in its simple shrines and Buddhism, particularly in Nara, in its elegant temples and monasteries. To those Buddhist establishments the migrant priests from the mainland brought all the trappings of their trade: brightly coloured vestments, magical incantations, sutras rich in language and profound in thought, incense to effuse the aroma of sanctity, and bells, gongs, chimes and drums to provide a divine cacophony.

But the Buddhist holy men transported much more than mere paraphernalia. They carried with them the learning for which the Japanese felt an insatiable hunger, and through their presence the Japan of the Nara age achieved remarkable advances in art and literature, imitative at first but gradually assuming forms that fully reflected Japanese tastes and skills.

In their basic style, both Japanese painting and sculpture followed the art of the Tang dynasty, and when, for example, Tang renderings of court women changed from the slim, languid forms of the previous era to a more curvaceous type, so did the Japanese depictions. Even then, however, the Japanese displayed more of a tendency towards realism, a desire to portray the subject as an individual instead of a stereotype. Moreover, for some of their painted artwork, the Japanese developed their own special technique for using lacquer with lead colours mixed in oil.

Unlike the Chinese, Japanese sculptors usually shunned working in stone, preferring more malleable materials such as clay, wood and dry lacquer. To create their dry-lacquer forms, they began with a wooden or clay frame, then filled out their desired shapes with alternating layers of fabric and lacquer. It was a laborious process, yet with it the Japanese were able to achieve remarkably realistic detail; dry lacquer was the medium for the four menacing deities who stood guard at the Tōdaiji and for the famed sculpture of the priest Ganjin, who had experienced such difficulty in reaching Japan. As Japan's oldest surviving portrait of an actual person, the statue almost brings the blind Ganjin to life as he sits in deep meditation, his features those of a man who has found tranquillity after much travail.

Yet if art was a pleasure to the Nara Japanese, poetry was a joy. With the exception of two histories that were contrived to fit the genealogy of the imperial family into the framework of legend, Japanese prose forms had yet to develop in any notable way. Poetry, however, suited both their inclinations and their language, and they proceeded with boundless enthusiasm and astonishing results. In the year 760, an anthology called the *Man'yoshu (Collection of Ten Thousand Leaves)* was issued, containing 4,500 poems of a quality that would never be surpassed in

Japan. Although many entries purportedly dated from antiquity, it is likely that all were written in the century preceding the year of publication; in that case they represent the true voice of Japan immediately before and during the Nara period.

The difficulties of applying Chinese script to Japanese verse were of course formidable, and for their outpourings the Japanese poets employed characters that could be rendered phonetically. Even so, the system did not lend itself to lengthy narratives or to coping with complex philosophical themes. Of the myriad poems in the *Man'yoshu,* only 260 were *choka,* or "long poems", while by far the prevailing form was the *waka,* consisting of 31 syllables in five lines. In a very short time, the *choka* would disappear almost entirely, while the *waka* would survive for centuries as the forerunner of the modern, 17-syllable haiku.

Although the debt was far less obvious than in the case of Japanese art, the poets undeniably owed a great deal to the Chinese, and certain Chinese themes kept creeping into their work. Most noticeable among these, perhaps, was the *Tanabata* myth of those celestial lovers Altair (the Herdsman) and Vega (the Weaving Maiden), who, unhappily being separated by the Milky Way, could meet only on the seventh night of the seventh month of each year.

The poetry in the *Man'yoshu* reflected all classes of Japanese society, ranging from the imperial family to peasants and even beggars. The princesses of the court wrote feelingly of love among the elite, and a school of delicate verse extolling the wonders of nature emerged among the aristocracy. Yet the literate few also set down the folk songs and verses favoured by those of humbler station. Thus, a frontier guard expressed his loneliness in terms of his remote surroundings: *I will think of you, love, / On evenings when the grey mist / Rises above the rushes, / And chill sounds the voice / Of the wild ducks crying.*

Poets whose work would shine through the centuries appeared in the pages of the *Man'yoshu.* One of the most versatile was Otomo no Yakamochi, who wrote of his travels, of his love for a prodigious number of women, of the grandeur of mountains, and of his grief at the death of a pet hawk. Yamanoue no Okura, who

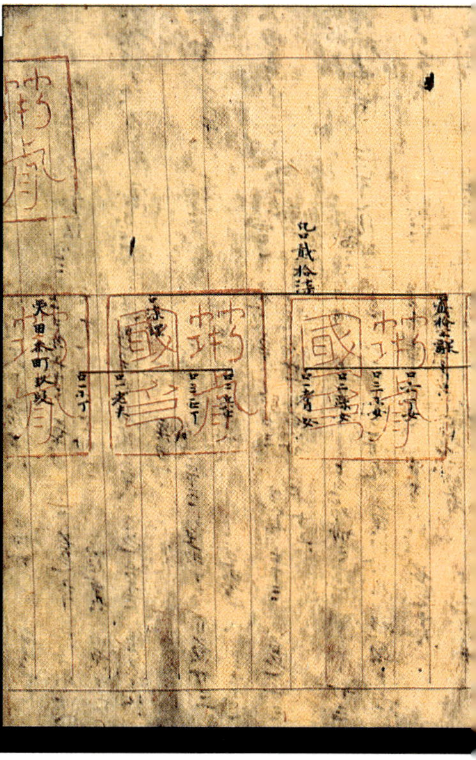

After seizing power in a coup d'état in 645, the emperor Tenchi began a sweeping programme of land reforms – the Taika – aimed at breaking the power of Japan's hereditary provincial clans by nationalizing their vast estates. First, Tenchi dispatched swarms of surveyors to inventory each property's topography and natural resources. They drew maps such as the one below, which shows an estate owned by the Tōdai temple in the Settsu Province, an expanse bounded by mountains and traversed by a river and subdivided by the cartographer into farm-sized rectangles. Peasant farmers were granted plots of land corresponding in size to the number of mouths they had to feed – but not without obligation. To finance his government, Tenchi levied various stiff taxes on the new landowners, including a tariff on all adult males. There was no escaping the taxman's reach: imperial census takers compiled detailed registers on each family. The document on the right below lists the 27 members of the Mononobe family of the Chikuzen Province, giving the name, age and tax status of each person. The tax burden finally grew so heavy that many peasants abandoned the land, compelling the government to return it, tax free, to its original aristocratic owners.

appears to have been a curmudgeonly sort — gruff and outspoken, yet fond of small children — was an aristocrat, but he possessed a genuine social conscience and was capable of putting himself in the place of a wretched peasant: *Here I lie on straw / Spread on bare earth, / With my parents at my pillow, / My wife and children at my feet, / All huddled in grief and tears. / No fire sends up smoke / At the cooking place, / And in the cauldron / A spider spins its web.*

Among the most outstanding of these poets was Kakinomoto no Hitomaro, a courtier of lesser rank who served variously in provincial posts and as a court poet. Even in his dutiful descriptions of imperial hunts and in his eulogies to deceased imperial cousins, Hitomaro somehow soared above the ordinary, and on those occasions when he had the opportunity to sing fully of life's mystery, of human sadness, and of death's stillness, he had no peer. Thus, in the simple eloquence of his own grief, he eulogized his wife: *I cherished her in my heart, / Looking to aftertime when we should be together, / And lived secure in my trust / As one riding a great ship. / Suddenly there came a messenger / Who told me she was dead — / Was gone like a yellow leaf of autumn, / Dead as the day dies with the setting sun, / Lost as the bright moon is lost behind the cloud.*

For the poets as for the priests, for the artists and the artisans alike, for the imperial family and for its courtiers, the ceremonial dedication of the emperor Shomu's Great Buddha in the year 752 was a culminating event in which their accomplishments were dramatically recognized through the assemblage of distinguished guests who had gathered from the sophisticated societies of continental Asia. Yet even then, most of the people of Japan were with good reason growing discontent, and the days of Nara as Japan's capital and cultural centre were already numbered.

While the elite of Nara pursued their intellectual pastimes and indulged in their pleasures, peasants in the Japanese countryside continued to toil in their paddies, subsist on rice, cultivate mulberry trees to nourish their silkworms, worship their beloved native gods — and groan under the burden of a tax system that had become increasingly onerous with the expansion of Buddhism.

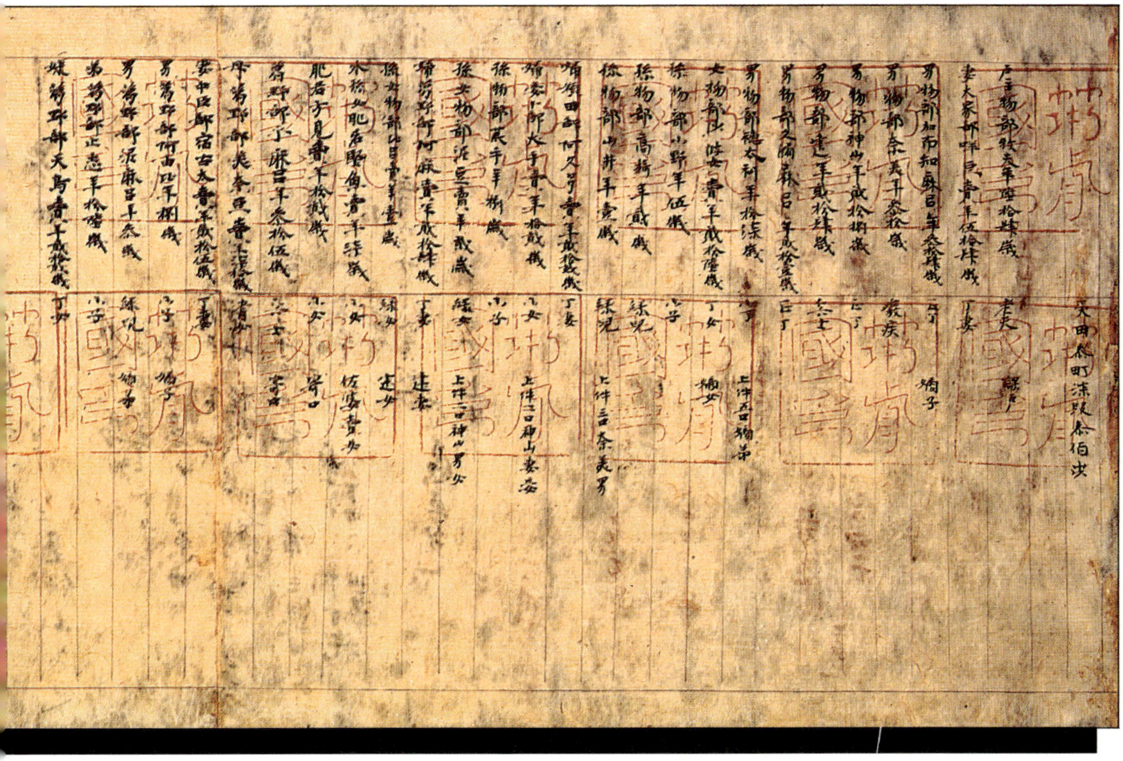

In an earlier day, imperial officials had dutifully gathered taxes from the Buddhist temples and monasteries. But as Buddhism grew more influential in the government, the church became officially immune from taxation. Thus with the explosive growth of Buddhist establishments, the strain on state resources could only be relieved by squeezing the long-suffering peasants, and their plight was dire. In one province, a survey found that 412 of 414 households lived in abject poverty. Many impoverished peasants were therefore forced to abandon their little plots of land, while others, in sheer desperation, took mortgages and signed over the women of their families to serve as security.

For Buddhism, wealth was accompanied by an increasing thirst for power, and Buddhist leaders came increasingly to meddle in Nara's secular affairs, even to the point of playing a role in the selection of emperors and empresses. Moreover, the good life led by Nara's affluent clergy was attractive to many ambitious men who, far from being pious, were downright scoundrels. Such a man was a faith-healing Buddhist monk by the name of Dokyo, and his ruinous liaison with a Japanese empress would hasten the end of the Nara era.

Crowned in 749 as the empress Koken, the daughter of the good emperor Shomu eventually wearied of her worldly life, abdicated her throne, shaved her head, and put on the habit of a Buddhist nun. At precisely what point she encountered the monk Dokyo is unclear, but meet they did, and since he was by all accounts a handsome energetic fellow, he ingratiated himself not only into the confidence of the Empress but also into her heart.

When this liaison was consummated, a tragic sequence of events unfolded. Renouncing her abdication, Koken deposed the young sovereign who had succeeded her and sent him into exile on a faraway island, where a short time later he was strangled. Then she appointed the cunning Dokyo as chancellor of the realm, a position of secular supremacy, and further designated him as *hoo,* an important title that might be freely translated as pope.

But Dokyo's ambition was by no means sated: he aspired to nothing less than the throne, and eventually he produced an oracular pronouncement to the effect that a Shinto war god named Hachiman had promised that Japan would have everlasting peace only if he, Dokyo, were proclaimed emperor. Even to the Empress this manoeuvre seemed excessive. According to one account she dispatched an emissary to Hachiman's shrine to ask the god if Dokyo's claim was true. Supposedly the god responded that the monk could never be emperor because he lacked imperial lineage. In any event, the scheming cleric soon fell into disfavour, and after the death of the Empress in 770, Nara's wrathful nobility stripped the monk of his titles. Banished to the small island of Awaji, Dokyo could only consider himself fortunate that his punishment had been no worse.

From those unseemly events, Japan's ruling class drew a dramatic conclusion: it was obvious that females could no longer be trusted to reign – and for many centuries to follow none did. In addition, the emperor Kammu, backed by the powerful Fujiwara clan, now determined to remove his nation's government from the clutches of Nara's proliferating Buddhist clergy, and in 784, the gracious city was abandoned as Japan's national capital.

For a while, the imperial family and its court occupied the nearby city of Nagaoka, but apparently it was deemed to be an ill-omened place. Therefore, in 795, the government was once again relocated in a newly built capital, which, though only 50 kilometres north of the city of Nara, was considered sufficiently distant to keep Buddhism's leaders at arm's length.

In a spirit of heady optimism, the new centre of government was christened Heian-kyo, the "capital of peace and tranquillity". However, that name soon gave way to Kyoto, which meant simply "the capital", and it was from Kyoto that Japan would be ruled for the next millennium.

SHOMU'S ECLECTIC TREASURES

In June of 756, precisely 49 days after the death of the Japanese emperor Shomu, his widow Komyo brought to an end her official period of mourning by donating the Emperor's prized belongings to the Universal Buddha at the Tōdaiji in Nara – the giant statue of the Enlightened One that Shomu had consecrated in a spectacular ceremony four years earlier. "For the sake of the late emperor," the empress Komyo proclaimed, "these various articles that he handled – girdles, ivory sceptres, bows and arrows, collection of calligraphy, musical instruments and the rest, which are in truth rare national treasures – I donate to the Tōdaiji as a votive offering." A personal motive lay behind this generous bequest to the Buddha, as the heartsick Komyo revealed in a note attached to the index of donated items: "These objects remind me of the bygone days, and the sight of them causes me bitter grief."

The treasures of the lamented Shomu were kept with assorted relics of the religious community at the Tōdaiji, in a large storehouse known as the Shoso-in. Built of Japanese cypress and raised above the ground on pilings, the building and most of its contents withstood natural hazards and political upheavals through the centuries. The finely crafted articles preserved in this way – illustrated on the following pages – tell of an era in which Japan was drawing artistic inspiration not just from China but from every civilized quarter of Asia *(map)*. Many of the items were imported, but others were the work of Japanese artisans who had mastered foreign styles. From the lands along the Mediterranean came a technique for making cut-glass bowls with shimmering facets and an alluring grapevine motif to adorn the silk gowns of Japanese dancers. Persia contributed rich floral designs for carpets and vases; India provided patterns for the devotional objects important in Buddhist ceremonies; Southeast Asia furnished precious raw materials such as ivory, sandalwood and mother-of-pearl. Many finished objects arrived in Japan from China, whose Tang rulers received a steady stream of ambassadors from the Japanese court and saw them off with gifts crafted in Changan or garnered in trade from round the continent. Thus, like Buddhism itself, which arrived in Japan bearing the stamp of every Asian society through which it had passed, the treasures

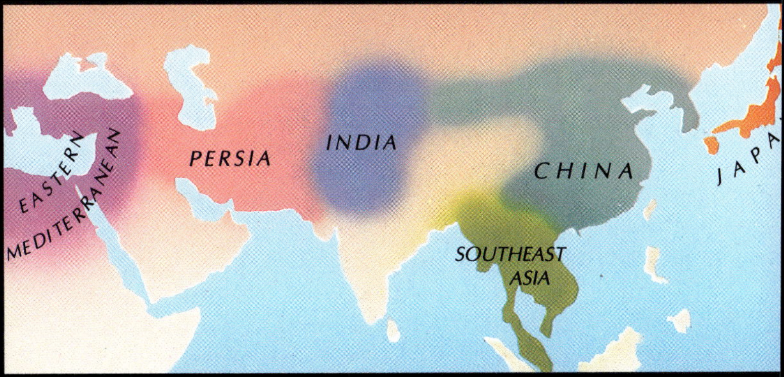

DESIGNS FROM THE MIDDLE EAST

The cut-glass bowl below, with its precise facets, may have been manufactured in that part of the Middle East once occupied by the Romans: such work was common there and was known by the name of Roman glass. Transported eastwards to Changan along the Silk Road, prizes such as this were eventually dispatched to Japan from the Tang court.

Although the bronze back of this mirror frame *(left)* was probably fashioned in China, it bears a design from the Mediterranean: animals – in this case, lions and birds – amid twisting grapevines. The Mediterranean artists who popularized the motif tended to portray animals realistically, but here an Oriental designer has given the lions a reptilian look.

This silk coat, with its grapevine pattern, was worn at the court of the emperor Shomu by a performer in the ceremonial dances known as *bugaku*. In Greece and Asia Minor, this same vine-scroll motif was an emblem that was associated first with the revels of the wine god Bacchus and later with the Christian communion.

PERSIAN CONTRIBUTIONS

Woven in Japan using techniques derived from China, this silk fabric is decorated with a Persian hunting motif. Persian artists often portrayed kings and nobles slaying animals with a Parthian shot such as the one shown here; the theme was readily picked up by court artists in China, whose emperors indulged in similar sport on their preserves.

A rug of felted sheep's wool bears a Persian floral pattern. During the seventh and eighth centuries, Persian craftsmen migrated along the Silk Road to set up shop in Changan and other Far Eastern centres of commerce; soon, their designs were being assimilated by artisans native to the region.

This ewer with its bird-shaped lid was modelled after Persian-style vessels using methods peculiar to the Far East. The body of the pitcher was woven of bamboo strips, covered with cloth and coated with lacquer. Elegant flora-and-fauna patterns were then cut from thin silver foil and affixed to the surface.

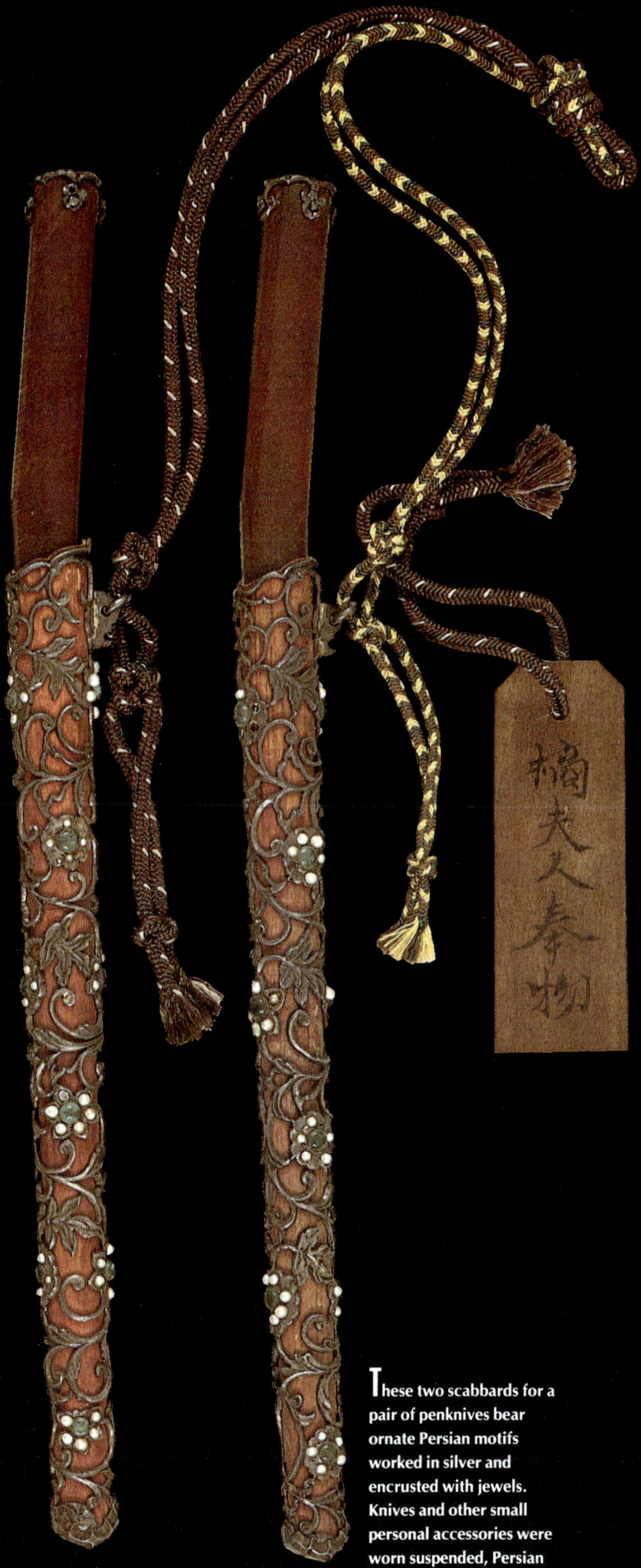

These two scabbards for a pair of penknives bear ornate Persian motifs worked in silver and encrusted with jewels. Knives and other small personal accessories were worn suspended, Persian style, from the girdles of Japanese dignitaries.

The sutra cover on the left, made of fine strands of bamboo woven together with silk thread, was used to envelop Buddhist scrolls at the Tōdaiji. The curious winged figure with a long tail portrayed amid the wreath of leaves is Kalavinka, a human-headed bird from Indian mythology. As Buddhism's birthplace, India developed not only its principal doctrines but also many of the motifs that illustrated the sacred texts and adorned their covers.

This rope of twisted silk dangled from the brush of the Indian high priest Bodhisena as he painted in the eyes of the immense bronze Buddha at the Tōdaiji during Shomu's consecration ceremony in April of 752. By grasping the rope, selected members of the audience were able to take part directly in the eye-opening ritual, which endowed the statue with spiritual life.

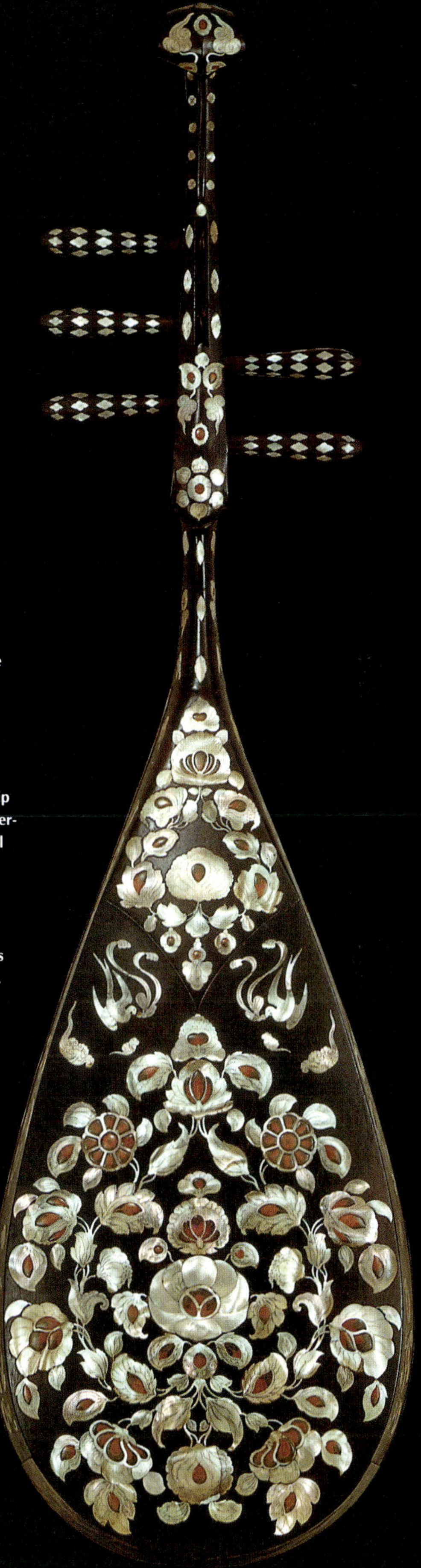

A classic example of the eclectic nature of the crafted goods reaching Japan in the eighth century, this Indian-style five-string lute – shown front and back – is decorated with Persian floral motifs in a style typical of China's Tang court. Chinese artisanship is suggested by the mother-of-pearl and tortoiseshell ornamentation – and by the Oriental look of the musician on the camel. Such lutes were played both in court ceremonies and at Buddhist services.

The leering mask on the right, representing a slave from the tropical lands to China's south, was worn by a performer in the dramatic spectacles known as *gigaku*, a tradition that spread from China to Korea, and thence to Japan. The play in which this mask figured told of the slave's infatuation with a noblewoman at the Tang court. Other *gigaku* masks portrayed roaring lions and fire-breathing birds, pompous Indian priests and drunken Persian kings.

Among the exotic creatures of South Asia that were portrayed fondly by artists of the realms to the north was the peacock, shown below on a lacquered Chinese chest. Lacquer, a varnish obtained from the sap of a sumac tree native to both China and Japan, was applied straight or mixed with gold dust or red pigment to provide lustrous coatings for objects, including furniture, utensils, masks, and images of the Buddha.

Ivory from elephant herds in Indochina furnished the material for the measuring rule on the left – shown from both sides – and the inlay for the sandalwood board below, used at Shomu's court for the game of *go*. One side of the rule was decorated with units that divided the measure into tenths *(far left)*, while the board was incised with 18 rows of 18 squares; its pieces were kept in drawers fitted with tortoise-shaped receptacles.

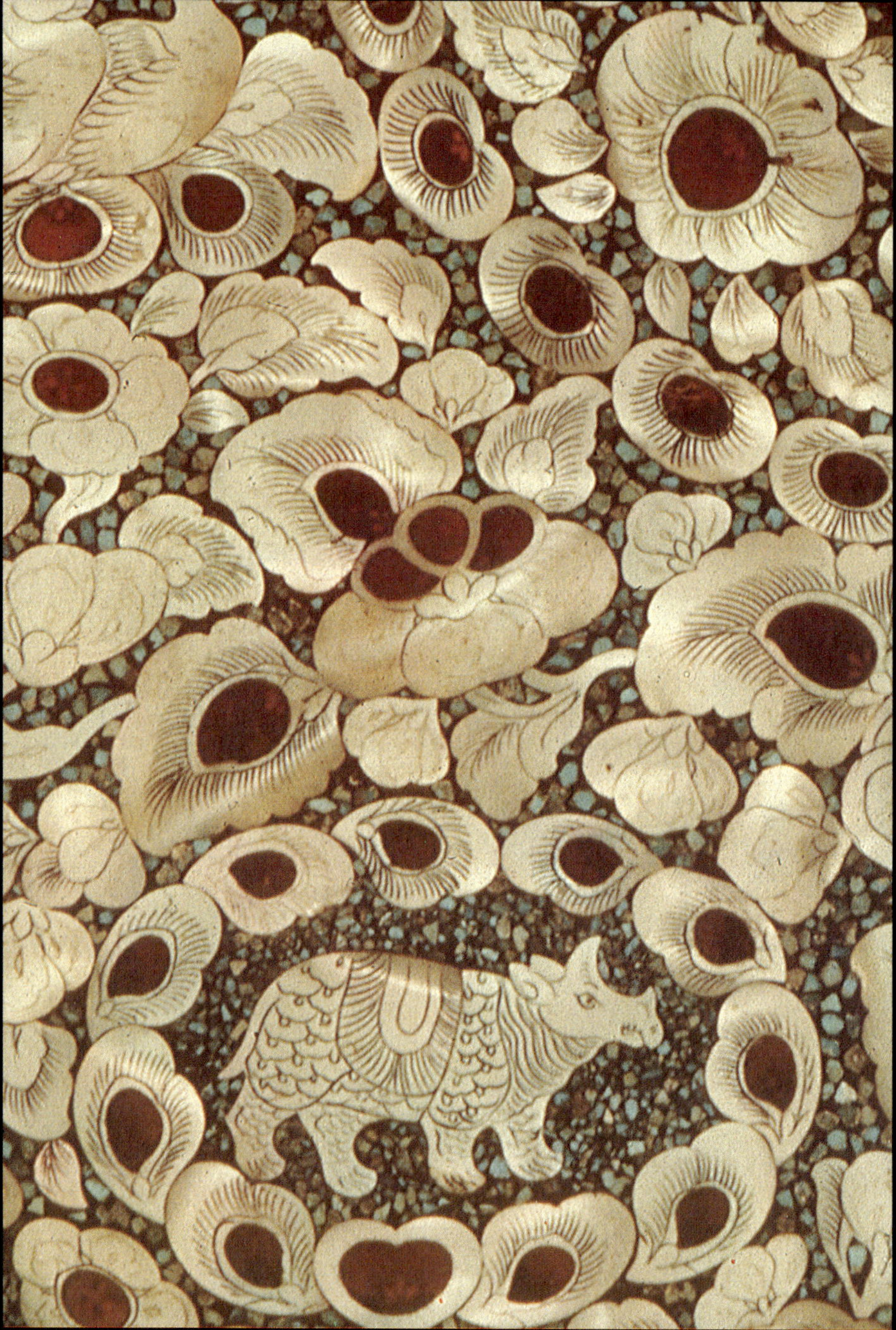

A hulking rhinoceros appears to be hemmed in by delicate petals in this detail from a Chinese mirror-back decorated with mother-of-pearl, amber and tortoiseshell. Rhinoceroses, which ranged along the upper Yangtze and Yellow rivers, were prized for their horn, used to adorn such beguiling objects as the *nyoi* below — a ceremonial staff carried by Buddhist priests. Both ends of this example were fashioned of rhinoceros horn, fringed with carved ivory.

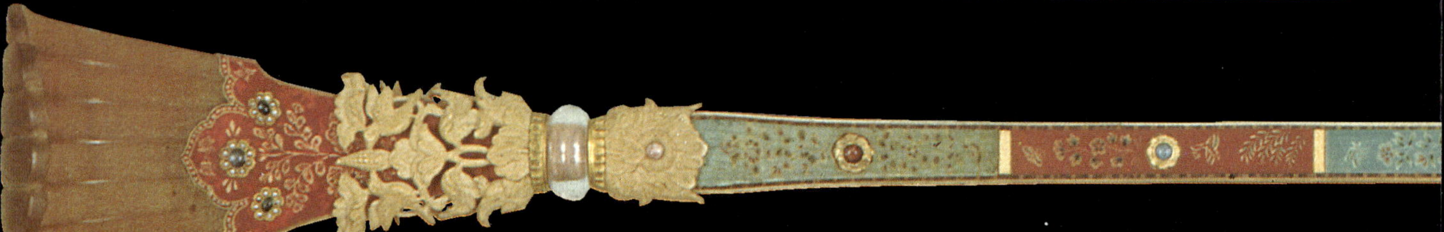

The copper vase on the lower left, alongside wooden darts painted with imitation feathers, served as the target in a game of Chinese origin that must have proved equally diverting to those at the Japanese court. Contestants attempted to fling their darts from some distance into the mouth of the vase – a task made fiendishly difficult by the vessel's narrow opening.

This saddle pad, whose leather was artfully decoloured to portray a mandarin duck with a flowering sprig in its beak, was among the eighth-century trappings preserved in the Shoso-in. The store also housed numerous swords, bows and arrows, and suits of armour – many of which were plundered during an uprising eight years after Shomu's death.

Coated with lacquer and trimmed with gold leaf, the wooden petals of a lotus blossom open round a bronze censer used in Buddhist services at the Tōdaiji. The lotus, revered in many lands for its ability to rise fresh from the water to greet each dawn, was memorialized in Buddhist art as the seat of the Enlightened One; among the most influential scriptures in Japan was the Lotus Sutra, which told of the ceaseless vitality of the Buddha's spirit.

600 | 650 | 700

ARABIA

The prophet Muhammad begins to preach publicly, advocating the worship of a single god.

In the *hijrah*, or exodus, Muhammad and his followers emigrate from Mecca to Medina. The Islamic calendar begins.

After repeated fighting between Meccans and Muhammad's followers, Mecca's leaders accept Islam.

Muhammad dies. Muslim leaders choose Abu Bakr as first caliph; he subdues dissident Bedouins, and all Arabs acknowledge the Islamic faith.

Abu Bakr dies and is succeeded by Umar.

The Muslims begin conquests outside Arabia and gain Byzantine territory with the capture of Damascus.

Egypt falls to the Muslims. Islam expands into North Africa.

Umar is assassinated, and Uthman becomes the third caliph.

The Muslims continue their conquest and gain Persia.

Rebels murder Uthman. Ali is declared the fourth caliph. Islam splits into factions of Sunnis and Shiites. A civil war ensues, pitting Muslim against Muslim in the Battle of the Camel.

Ali is assassinated. His son Hasan abdicates in favour of Muawiya of Syria, whose rule begins the Umayyad dynasty from Damascus.

The Muslims invade Turkish territory across the Oxus River in Transoxiana.

A four-year Muslim siege begins on Constantinople.

Husayn, son of Ali and Shii Imam, and his followers are slaughtered by the army of the caliph Yazid. "Martyrdom" of Husayn is commemorated as a major Shiite religious ritual.

The Arabs push to the farthest corners of their empire and conquer Sind in India and Spain in the West.

A new Arab siege on Constantinople is dispelled by the Byzantines.

The Muslims advance from Spain into southern France.

Charles Martel and the Franks defeat the Arabs in the Battle of Tours.

BYZANTIUM AND EUROPE

Heraclius seizes the throne of Byzantium.

Jerusalem is captured by the Persians, but the Byzantines regain the territory.

The Avars unsuccessfully besiege Constantinople.

King Edwin of Northumbria and his Anglo-Saxon followers are converted to Christianity.

Carthage, the last Byzantine stronghold in Africa, falls to the Muslims.

Charles Martel becomes the Frankish mayor of the palace under a weak Merovingian king.

In another siege on Constantinople, the Muslims are defeated by Byzantine emperor Leo III.

The iconoclastic controversy begins.

The Muslims advance from Spain into Frankish territory, and Charles Martel defeats them in the Battle of Tours.

INDIA, SOUTHEAST ASIA AND CHINA

Wendi founds the Sui dynasty in China and reunites the country. Harsha founds a kingdom in northern India, taking over much of the land the Guptas had held. After his death, other small, independent states, the Rajput kingdoms, rise in the north and thrive for 400 years.

The Tang dynasty is founded in China by Li Yuan.

The greatest Tang emperor, Taizong, ascends the throne and begins expansion of the empire.

Empress Wu, as regent, becomes the power behind the Chinese throne until she proclaims herself empress in her own right in 690.

The Arabs conquer Sind, bringing Muslim rule to India. The Pāndya and Pallava dynasties rule in southern India. Hindu philosopher Shankara begins to teach.

Xuanzong begins a 54-year reign, a period of Tang power and high literary attainment.

JAPAN

The regent Prince Shôtoku issues the "Seventeen Article Constitution".

The first Japanese emissaries to the Sui court embark for China, to be followed eventually by 15 further missions to the Sui and the Tang.

The Taika reforms are promulgated.

The Tang-type Taihō (law) code is adopted.

Nara, the first permanent capital, is founded.

The earliest Japanese histories, the *Kojiki* and the *Nihonshoki*, are compiled.

Shomu ascends the throne and maintains his influence during the apogee of the Nara period.

A Chronology of Major Events AD 600-800

750

800

The Abbasids overthrow the Umayyads and establish a new dynasty in Iraq. They found Baghdad as their new capital.

Caliph Harun al-Rashid rules while the Muslim empire is at its zenith, in a time of unparalleled economic prosperity.

Pepin is crowned king of the Franks, beginning the Carolingian line. The Lombards capture Ravenna, the last of the Byzantine holdings in northern Italy.

Pepin's son Charlemagne becomes king of the Franks, together with his brother Carloman, who resigns in 770.

Charlemagne defeats the Saxons and the Lombards.

Constantine VI becomes emperor of Byzantium.

In the seventh ecumenical council in Nicaea, iconoclasm is condemned as heresy, and icons are once again permitted in churches.

In Constantinople Irene installs herself as "emperor" after blinding her own son, Constantine VI.

Charlemagne is crowned imperator in Rome.

The rebellion led by An Lushan plunges China into civil war.

The statue of the Great Buddha at Tōdaiji is dedicated.

The *Man'yoshu*, a collection of more than 4,500 poems is compiled.

Kammu becomes emperor of Japan and moves the capital from Nara to Nagaoka.

The capital is moved to Heiankyo, near present-day Kyoto.

ACKNOWLEDGEMENTS

The translated lines appearing on page 44 are reprinted from "A letter from the governor of Egypt to the king of Nubia and Muquarra concerning Egypt-Nubian relations in 141/758" by Martin Hinds and Hamdi Sakkut in *Studia Arabica et Islamica*, a Festschrift for Ihsan Abbas published by Wadad al-Qadi, A.U.B., Beirut, 1981.
The poetry appearing on the following pages is reprinted with the kind permission of the publishers: Page 113: ("I remember when . . ." *Chinese Lyricism: Shih Poetry from the Second to the Twelfth Century*, by Burton Watson, New York: Columbia University Press, 1971. ("From a pot of wine . . .") *The Jade Mountain: A Chinese Anthology, Being Three Hundred Poems of the T'ang Dynasty 618-960*, translated by Witter Brynner from the texts of Kiang Kang-hu, New York: Alfred A. Knopf, © 1929, renewed 1957. Page 154: ("I will think of you . . .") *Anthology of Japanese Literature from the Earliest Era to the Mid-Nineteenth Century*, by Donald Keene, New York: Grove Press, 1955, and Iwanami Shoten Publishers, 1940. Page 155: ("Here I lie . . . ") *Anthology of Japanese Literature from the Earliest Era to the Mid-Nineteenth Century*, by Donald Keene, New York: Grove Press, 1955, and Iwanami Shoten Publishers, 1940. ("I cherished her . . .") *Japanese Culture: A Short History*, expanded edition, by H. Paul Varley, New York: © H. Paul Varley, 1977, by Henry Holt & Company, Inc.

The editors also wish to thank the following individuals and institutions for their valuable assistance in the preparation of this volume.
Egypt: Cairo – Ni'mat Abou Bakr, Director of the Islamic Museum; Gloria Karnouk, Curator of the Creswell Library, The American University in Cairo; George Scanlon, Professor of Islamic Art and Architecture, The American University in Cairo.
England: Gloucestershire – Graham Speake. London – Janet Backhouse, Curator of Illustrated Manuscripts, British Library; Michael Brett, Department of History, School of Oriental & African Studies, University of London; Yu-Ying Brown, Japanese Curator of Oriental Collections, British Library; Beth McKillop, Chinese Curator of Oriental Collections, British Library; Lyn Rodley, Society for Hellenic Studies; Michael Rogers, Department of Oriental Antiquities, British Museum; Brian A. Tremain, Photographic Service, British Museum; Leslie Webster, Medieval and Later Antiquities Department, British Museum; Yun Kil Yang, Cultural Attaché, Korean Embassy; Sandra Doble. Suffolk – R. W. Hamilton. Potton, Bedfordshire – Kate Cann.
Federal Republic of Germany: Aachen – Michael Jansen, Institut für Baugeschichte und Denkmalpflege, Universität; Georg Minkenberg, Domschatz Kammer. Berlin – Klaus Brisch, Direktor, Museum für Islamische Kunst, Staatliche Museen Preussischer Kulturbesitz; Heidi Klein, Bildarchiv Preussischer Kulturbesitz; Jens Kröger, Museum für Indische Kunst, Staatliche Museen Preussischer Kulturbesitz; Lore Sander, Museum für Indische Kunst, Staatliche Museen Preussischer Kulturbesitz; Hans-Georg Severin, Direktor, Frühchristlich-Byzantinische Abteilung, Staatliche Museen Preussischer Kulturbesitz; Marianne Yaldiz, Direktor, Museum für Indische Kunst, Staatliche Museen Preussischer Kulturbesitz. Bonn – Christine Weidlich, Handschriftenabteilung, Universitätsbibliothek. Frankfurt – David King, Institut für Geschichte der Naturwissenschaften, Universität. Stockdorf – Klaus Hansmann and Liselotte Hansmann; Matthias Holzapfel. Stuttgart – Klaus-J. Brandt, Linden Museum; Ursula Didoni, Linden Museum; Ingeborg Krekler, Handschriftenabteilung Württembergische Landesbibliothek.
France: Irène Aghion, Curateur, Cabinet des Médailles, Bibliothèque Nationale; François Avril, Curateur, Département des Manuscrits, Bibliothèque Nationale; Christophe Barbotin, Conservateur du Département des Antiquités Egyptiennes, Musée du Louvre; Pascale Barthélemy, Curateur, Département des Manuscrits, Bibliothèque Nationale; Laure Beaumont-Maillet, Conservateur en Chef du Cabinet des Estampes, Bibliothèque Nationale; Catherine Bélanger, Chargée des Relations Extérieures du Musée du Louvre; Jeannette Chalufour, Archives Tallandier; Béatrice Coti, Directrice du Service Iconographique, Éditions Mazenod; Antoinette Decaudin, Documentaliste, Département des Antiquités Orientales, Musée du Louvre; Michel Fleury, Président de la IV Section de l'École Pratique des Hautes Études; Marie-Françoise Huygues des Étages, Conservateur, Musée de la Marine; François Jestaz, Conservateur, Cabinet des Estampes, Bibliothèque Nationale; Marie Montembault, Documentaliste, Département des Antiquités Grecques et Romaines, Musée du Louvre; Marie-Odile Roy, Service Photographique, Bibliothèque Nationale; Jacqueline Sanson, Conservateur, Directeur du Service Photographique, Bibliothèque Nationale.
German Democratic Republic: Berlin – Arne Effenberger, Direktor Früchristlich-Byzantinische Sammlung, Staatliche Museen zu Berlin; Volkmar Enderlein, Direktor, Islamisches Museum, Staatliche Museen zu Berlin.
India: Bombay – Amrita Shah, Journalist; Trustees of the Prince of Wales Museum of Western India.
Israel: Jerusalem – Israel Department of Antiquities, Rockefeller Museum; Hadassa Shy, Department of Hebrew Language and Literature, Ben Gurion University.
Italy: Florence – Brigitte Baumbusch, Scala. Milan – Mons. Enrico Galbiati, Il Prefetto, Biblioteca Ambrosiana; Luisa Ricciarini. Monza – Roberto Conti, Il Conservatore, Museo del Duomo. Rome – Biblioteca Apostolica Vaticana.
Japan: Tokyo – J. Edward Kidder, International Christian University; Mari Koide, Tokyo National Museum; Machiko Morita, Tokyo National Museum.
Peoples' Republic of China: Beijing – Beijing Cultural Relics Publishing House; Research Institute of Music, Academy of Chinese Arts.
U.S.A.: New York: New York City – Michael L. Bates, Curator of Islamic Coins, The American Numismatic Society; Priscilla P. Soucek, Hagop Kevorkian Professor of Islamic Art, Institute of Fine Arts, New York University. Washington, D.C. – Esin Atil, Arthur M. Sackler Gallery, Smithsonian Institution; Shōjō Honda, Senior Reference Librarian, Asian Division, Library of Congress; Lily Kecskes, Arthur M. Sackler Library, Smithsonian Institution; Bob Kimberlin, Reference Librarian, The American Institute of Architects; Thaddeus Y. Otah, Senior Reference Librarian, Asian Division, Library of Congress; Kathryn Phillips, Arthur M. Sackler Library, Smithsonian Institution.
Wales: Gwynedd – William Watson.

The index for this volume was prepared by Roy Nanovic.

BIBLIOGRAPHY

BOOKS

Andaya, Barbara Watson, and Leonard Y. Andaya, *A History of Malaysia*. (MacMillan Asian Histories series). London: MacMillan, 1985.

Bary, William Theodore de, ed., *Sources of Indian Tradition*. New York: Columbia University Press, 1964.

Beckwith, John, *The Art of Constantinople*. London: Phaidon, 1968.

Bingham, Woodbridge, *The Founding of the T'ang Dynasty*. New York: Octagon Books, 1970.

Borgen, Robert, *Sugawara no Michizane and the Early Heian Court*. London: Harvard University, 1986.

Boussard, Jacques, *The Civilization of Charlemagne*. Transl. by Frances Partridge. London: Weidenfeld & Nicolson, 1968.

Buchanan, Keith, Charles P. FitzGerald, and Colin A. Ronan, *China*. New York: Crown, 1981.

Campbell, James, Eric John, and Patrick Wormald, *The Anglo-Saxons*. Oxford: Phaidon Press, 1982.

Ch'en, Kenneth K. S., *Buddhism in China: A Historical Survey*. Guildford, England: Princeton University Press, 1964.

Clarke, Helen, *The Archaeology of Medieval England*. Oxford: Basil Blackwell, 1986.

Coedès, G., *The Making of South East Asia*. Transl. by H. M. Wright. London: Routledge & Kegan Paul, 1966.

Creswell, K. A. C., *Early Muslim Architecture*. 2 vols. Oxford: Oxford University Press, 1969, 1940.

Crone, Patricia, *Meccan Trade and the Rise of Islam*. Oxford: Basil Blackwell, 1987.

Dasgupta, Surendranath, *A History of Indian Philosophy*. Vol. 1. Cambridge: Cambridge University Press, 1969.

Donner, Fred McGraw, *The Early Islamic Conquests.* Guildford, England: Princeton University Press, 1981.
Dunlop, D. M., *Arab Civilization to A.D. 1500.* Harlow, England: Longman, 1971.
Durliat, Marcel, *Des Barbares à l'An Mil.* Paris: Éditions Mazenod, 1985.
Duus, Peter, *Feudalism in Japan.* New York: Alfred A. Knopf, 1976.
Ebrey, Patricia Buckley, ed., *Chinese Civilization and Society.* London: Collier MacMillan, 1981.
Egami, Namio, *The Beginnings of Japanese Art.* Transl. by John Bester. New York: Weatherhill, 1978.
Esposito, John L., *Islam and Politics.* Syracuse, N.Y.: Syracuse University Press, 1984.
Ettinghausen, Richard, and Oleg Grabar, *The Art and Architecture of Islam: 650-1250.* Harmondsworth, England: Penguin Books, 1987.
Fairbank, John K., Edwin O. Reischauer, and Albert M. Craig, *East Asia Tradition and Transformation.* Boston: Houghton Mifflin, 1978.
Frazer, Margaret English:
Age of Spirituality. New York: The Metropolitan Museum of Art, 1977.
Medieval Church Treasuries. New York: The Metropolitan Museum of Art, 1986.
Gernet, Jacques, *A History of Chinese Civilization.* Transl. by J. R. Foster. Cambridge: Cambridge University Press, 1985.
Gibb, Sir Hamilton A. R.:
Arabic Literature. Oxford: Oxford University Press, 1974.
Studies on the Civilization of Islam. Guildford, England: Princeton University Press, 1982.
Green, Charles, *Sutton Hoo: The Excavation of a Royal Ship Burial.* London: Merlin Press, 1980.
Hall, D. G. E., *A History of South-East Asia.* London: MacMillan Press, 1981.
Hall, John W., and Jeffrey P. Mass, eds., *Medieval Japan.* London: Yale University Press, 1974.
Hamilton, R. W., *Khirbat Al Mafjar.* New York: Oxford University Press, 1959.
Hayashi, Ryoichi, *The Silk Road and the Shoso-in.* Transl. by Robert Ricketts. New York: Weatherhill, 1976.
Hayes, John R., ed., *The Genius of Arab Civilization.* Oxford: Phaidon Press, 1978.
Hitti, Philip K., *History of the Arabs.* London: MacMillan, 1970.
Hoag, John D., *Islamic Architecture.* London: Faber, 1987.
Holt, P. M., ed., *The Cambridge History of Islam.* Vol. 1. Cambridge: Cambridge University Press, 1977.
Ienaga, Saburo, *Japanese Art: A Cultural Appreciation.* Transl. by Richard L. Gage. New York: Weatherhill, 1979.
Inoue, Mitsusada, *Introduction to Japanese History Before the Meiji Restoration.* Tokyo: Japan Cultural Society, 1968.
Ishii, Ryōsuke, *A History of Political Institutions in Japan.* Tokyo: University of Tokyo Press, 1980.
James, Edward, *The Origins of France.* London: MacMillan Press, 1982.
Kageyama, Haruki, *The Arts of Shinto.* Transl. by Christine Guth. New York: Weatherhill, 1973.
Keene, Donald, ed., *Anthology of Japanese Literature From the Earliest Era to the Mid-Nineteenth Century.* New York: Grove Press, 1955.
Kidder, J. Edward: *The Art of Japan.* London: Century Publishing Co., 1985.
Early Buddhist Japan. London: Thames & Hudson, 1972.
Japan Before Buddhism. New York: Frederick A. Praeger, 1966.
Kitzinger, Ernst: *Byzantine Art in the Making.* London: Faber, 1987.
Kobayashi, Takeshi, *Nara Buddhist Art: Todai-ji.* Transl. by Richard L. Gage. New York: Weatherhill, 1975.
Kodansha Encyclopedia of Japan. Tokyo: Kodansha Ltd., 1983.
Krautheimer, Richard, *Early Christian and Byzantine Art.* Harmondsworth: Penguin Books, 1975.
Lasko, Peter, *The Kingdom of the Franks.* London: Thames & Hudson, 1971.
Leacroft, Helen, and Richard Leacroft, *The Buildings of Early Islam.* London: Hodder & Stoughton, 1976.
Lewis, Bernard, et. al., *Islam and the Arab World.* London: Thames & Hudson, 1976.
Lu, David John, *Sources of Japanese History.* Vol. 1. New York: McGraw-Hill, 1974.
McCormick, Michael, *Eternal Victory.* Cambridge: Cambridge University Press, 1986.
McLanathan, Richard, *The Pageant of Medieval Art and Life.* Philadelphia: The Westminster Press, 1966.
Majumdar, R. C., *Ancient India.* Delhi: Motilal Banarsidass, 1982.
Martin, Richard C., *Islam: A Cultural Perspective.* Hemel Hempstead, Herts. Prentice-Hall, 1982.
Meyer, Milton W., *Japan: A Concise History.* Boston: Allyn and Bacon, 1966.
Miki, Fumio, *Haniwa.* Transl. by Gina Lee Barnes. New York: Weatherhill, 1974.
Mizuno, Seiichi, *Asuka Buddhist Art: Horyu-ji.* Transl. by Richard L. Gage. New York: Weatherhill, 1974.
Paine, Robert Treat, and Alexander Soper, *The Art and Architecture of Japan.* Harmondsworth, England: Penguin Books, 1985.
Papadopoulo, Alexandre, *Islam and Muslim Art.* Transl. by Robert Erich Wolf. London: Thames & Hudson, 1980.
Pope, Arthur Upham, *A Survey of Persian Art From Prehistoric Times to the Present.* Vol. 4. Oxford: Oxford University Press, 1938.
Porter, Arthur Kingsley, *The Crosses and Culture of Ireland.* New York: Benjamin Blom, 1971.
Reischauer, Edwin O., *Ennin's Travels in T'ang China.* New York: The Ronald Press Co., 1955.
Rice, Tamara Talbot, *Byzantium.* London: Rupert Hart-Davis Educational Publications, 1969.
Richée, Pierre, *Daily Life in the World of Charlemagne.* Transl. by Jo Ann McNamara. Philadelphia: University of Pennsylvania Press, 1979.
Rodinson, Maxime, *Mohammed.* Transl. by Anne Carter. Harmondsworth, England: Penguin Books, 1974.
Salibi, Kamal, *A History of Arabia.* Delmar, N.Y.: Caravan Books, 1980.
Sansom, G. B., *Japan: A Short Cultural History.* London: Cresset Library, 1987.
Sastri, K. A. Nilakanta, *A History of South India.* Madras, India: Oxford University Press, 1976.
Schafer, Edward H., *The Golden Peaches of Samarkand.* Guildford, England: University of California Press, 1985.
Smith, Bradley, and Wang-go Weng, *China: A History in Art.* London: Studio Vista, 1973.
Stanley-Baker, Joan, *Japanese Art.* London: Thames & Hudson, 1986.
Terukazu, Akiyama, *Japanese Painting.* London: MacMillan, 1977.
Thapar, Romila, *A History of India.* Vol. 1. Harmondsworth, England: Penguin, 1969.
Tsunoda, Ryusaku, William Theodore de Bary, and Donald Keene, comps., *Sources of the Japanese Tradition.* Oxford: Oxford University Press, 1958.
Twitchett, D. C., *Financial Administration Under the T'ang Dynasty.* Cambridge: Cambridge University Press, 1970.
Twitchett, Denis, ed., *Sui and T'ang China, 589-906.* Part I, Vol. 3 of *The Cambridge History of China.* Cambridge: Cambridge University Press, 1979.
Varley, H. Paul, *Japanese Culture.* Honolulu: University of Hawaii Press, 1986.
Von Grunebaum, Gustave E., *Medieval Islam.* Cambridge: Cambridge University Press, 1953.
Vryonis, Speros, Jr., *Byzantium and Europe.* London: Thames & Hudson, 1967.
Watanabe, Yasutada, *Shinto Art.* Transl. by Robert Ricketts. New York: Weatherhill, 1974.
Watters, Thomas, *On Yuan Chwang's Travels in India.* New York: AMS Press, 1971.
Wechsler, Howard J., *Mirror to the Son of Heaven.* London: Yale University Press, 1975.
Wiencek, Henry, *The Lords of Japan.* Chicago: Stonehenge Press, 1982.
Winston, Richard, *Charlemagne from the Hammer to the Cross.* Andover, England: Eyre & Spottiswoode, 1956.
Wolpert, Stanley, *A New History of India.* Oxford: Oxford University Press, 1982.
Wright, Arthur F.:
Buddhism in Chinese History. Oxford: Oxford University Press, 1959.
The Sui Dynasty. New York: Alfred A. Knopf, 1978.
Wright, Arthur F., and Denis Twitchett, eds., *Perspectives on the T'ang.* London: Yale University Press, 1981.
Yanagi, Munemoto, et al., *Byzantium.* Transl. by Nicholas Fry. London: Cassell, 1978.
Yoshikawa, Itsuji, *Major Themes in Japanese Art.* Transl. by Armins Nikovskis. New York: Weatherhill, 1976.

OTHER SOURCES
Ford, Barbara Brennan, *The Arts of Japan.* New York: The Metropolitan Museum of Art, 1987.
A Thousand Cranes. Seattle, Wash./San Francisco: Seattle Art Museum/ Chronicle Books, 1987.
Treasures of Ireland. Edited by Michael Ryan. Dublin: Royal Irish Academy/ Museum of Ireland/Trinity College, 1983.

INDEX

L

M

N

O

P

Q

R

S

T

U

V

W

X

Y

Z

PICTURE CREDITS

The sources for the illustrations that appear in this book are listed below. Credits from left to right are separated by semicolons; from top to bottom by dashes.

Cover: Composite portrait, art by John Rush. **2, 3:** Maps by Alfred T. Kamajian – background map by R. R. Donnelley. **8, 9:** Background © 1981 Si Chiko from The Image Bank. Art by John Rush, based on paintings by Angus McBride in *The Armies of Islam: 7th-11th Centuries* (Men at Arms series), Osprey Publishing, 1982. **10, 11:** Background André Martin, Neuilly-sur-Seine, France. Art by John Rush, based on paintings by Angus McBride, in *The Age of Charlemagne* (Men at Arms series), Osprey Publishing, 1984. **12, 13:** Background © Hiroji Kubota from Magnum Photos, Inc. Art by John Rush, based on paintings by Angus McBride in *The Barbarians: Warriors and War of the Dark Ages,* Blanford Press, 1985. **14, 15:** Background © Dennis Stock from Magnum Photos, Inc. Art by John Rush. **16:** Detail of a composite window, stucco, palace at Khirbat al-Mafjar, Umayyad eighth century, photo by Zev Radovan, Jerusalem, courtesy Department of Antiquities, Jerusalem. **18:** © Photo Bibliothèque Nationale, Paris; American Numismatic Society Photographic Department; The Al Sabah Collection, Dar Al Athar Al Islamiyyah, Kuwait National Museum(2) – map by Alfred T. Kamajian. **22, 23:** Art by Lloyd K. Townsend. **24, 25:** Art by Lloyd K. Townsend. **26, 27:** Art by Lloyd K. Townsend. **30:** M. Babey/Artephot-Ziolo, Paris; Musical Institute, Academy of Chinese Arts, Beijing. **31:** Bibliothèque Nationale, Paris. **32:** Matthieu Ravaux, Paris/Musée Guimet, Paris. **34, 35:** Arabic calligraphy by M. U. Zakariya. **36, 37:** M. Babey/Artephot-Ziolo, Paris. **41:** Ole Woldbye/The David Collection, Copenhagen. **42:** Drawing by Fred Holz, mosaic © Zev Radovan, Jerusalem. **44:** Barry Iverson, Cairo, courtesy The Islamic Museum, Cairo. **46:** Zev Radovan, Jerusalem, courtesy Department of Antiquities, Jerusalem. **49:** Detail of Khirbat al- Mafjar, art by Dante Kristoff. **50, 51:** Diagrams by Fred Holz(2); art by Dante Kristoff. **52, 53:** Art by Dante Kristoff – diagram by Fred Holz. **54, 55:** Art by Dante Kristoff – diagram by Fred Holz. **56:** St. Gregory the Great writing, detail of an ivory panel, Trier, FRG, ninth-10th century, photo courtesy Kunsthistorisches Museum, Vienna. **58:** Badisches Landesmuseum, Karlsruhe, FRG – map of Europe and Byzantium by Alfred T. Kamajian. **62:** © Trustees of the National Museums of Scotland, Edinburgh. **63:** Biblioteca Apostolica Vaticana, Rome. **64**: Pope Gregory the Great, detail of an ivory diptych, Monza, Italy, ca. 900, photo by SEF/Art Resource/Museo del Duomo di Monza (Lombardia). **65:** A priestly donor, detail of a fresco, Oratory of San Benedetto, Malles Venosta, Italy, ninth century, photo by Scala, Florence, courtesy S. Benedetto, Malles Venosta, Italy. **67:** Courtesy Trustees of the British Museum, London (1939.10-10.160,205 (55)). **68:** Courtesy Trustees of the British Museum, London (1939.10-10.94(51)). **69:** Michael Holford, Loughton, Essex/ British Museum, London – courtesy Trustees of the British Museum, London (1939.10-10.4,5(66)). **71:** Photoresources, Canterbury, Kent. **72:** Michael Holford, Loughton, Essex. **74:** Frühchristlich-Byzantinische Sammlung, Staatliche Museen zu Berlin, GDR. **75:** Collection Millet, École Pratique des Hautes Études, Paris. **76:** Scala/Art Resource. **77:** Scala, Florence, courtesy Museo del Bargello, Florence. **78:** Bibliothèque Nationale, Paris – S. Rebsamen/Bernisches Historisches Museum, Bern – Württembergische Landesbibliothek, Stuttgart, photo by Werner Schüring. **80:** Art by John Batchelor. **81:** Art by John Batchelor. **82:** Raban Maur and Alcuin, detail from the frontispiece of Maur's *De Laudibus Sanctae Crucis,* illuminated parchment, ca. 840, photo © Edimedia, Paris, courtesy Bibliothèque Nationale, Paris. **83:** Stiftbibliothek, St. Gall, Switzerland. **84, 85:** Bibliothèque Nationale, Paris. **86:** Celestial tomb guardian, detail of pottery statue, Tang dynasty, China 618-906, photo British Museum, London (1932.10-10.2). **88:** Map by Alfred T. Kamajian – courtesy of the Cultural Attaché, Korean Embassy, London/Kyongju National Museum, Korea. **90, 91:** Fujita Art Gallery, Ōsaka; © The British Museum, London. **92:** Ashok Gupta, Bombay/The Trustees of the Prince of Wales Museum of Western India, Bombay – Robert Lautman. **96, 97:** © 1987 All Rights Reserved, Museum of Fine Arts, Boston, Keith McLeod Fund; The Cultural Relics Publishing House, Beijing. **98:** Leonard von Matt/ Rapho Guillumette, courtesy Royal Ontario Museum, Toronto, Canada. **99:** © Wan-go H. C. Weng, courtesy Seattle Art Museum. **102, 103:** Art by Don Ivan Punchatz. **105:** Portrait of the emperor Tai Zong, anonymous, 14th-17th century copy of seventh-10th century original, National Palace Museum, Taipei, (Takeyoshi Tanuma). **106:** The Cultural Relics Publishing House, Beijing – © Wan-go H. C. Weng, courtesy Palace Museum, Beijing; © Wan-go H. C. Weng, courtesy The Metropolitan Museum of Art, New York. **107:** © Wan-go H. C. Weng, courtesy Palace Museum, Beijing. **108:** Ōsaka Municipal Museum, Abe Collection, Ōsaka. **111:** © Wan-go H. C. Weng, courtesy Palace Museum, Beijing. **112:** Chinese calligraphy by Henry H. Wang, inset, E. T. Archive, London, courtesy The British Museum, London. **114, 115:** Art by Dante Kristoff. **116:** National Palace Museum, Taipei (Wan-go H. C. Weng) – Lowell Georgia/Photo Researchers. **119:** Beginning of the Argumentum of Matthew, illuminated M from The Book of Kells, ink on parchment, Dublin, photo courtesy The Board of Trinity College, Dublin. **120, 121:** Werner Forman Archive, London/Mrs. Bashir Mohammed Collection, inset, Biblioteca Ambrosiana, Milan. **122, 123:** © The British Library, London – courtesy of the Cultural Attaché, Korean Embassy, London/National Museum of Korea, Seoul-National Treasure No. 123. **124, 125:** Tokyo Geijutsu Daigaku, Tokyo. **126:** Bayerische Staatsbibliothek, München. **127:** Bibliothèque Nationale, Paris. **128:** The Bridgeman Art Library, London/The British Library, London. **129:** The Board of Trinity College, Dublin. **130:** Statue of Chinese priest Ganjin, hollow dry lacquer sculpture, Japan, eighth century, photo Tōshōdai-ji, Nara. **132:** The Metropolitan Museum of Art, The Harry G. C. Packard Collection of Asian Art, Gift of Harry G. C. Packard and Purchase, Fletcher Rogers, Harris Brisbane Dick, and Louis V. Bell Funds, Joseph Pulitzer Bequest and The Annenberg Fund, Inc. Gift, 1975 (1975.268.182); map by Alfred T. Kamajian. **136, 137:** Art and drawings by Fred Holz. **138:** The Seattle Art Museum, Eugene Fuller Memorial Collection, 62.44; drawing by Fred Holz. **139:** The Tokyo National Museum, Tokyo. **140:** Shrine at Ise, art Fred Holz. **142:** Tokyo National Museum, Tokyo. **147:** Imperial Household Agency, Tokyo. **149:** Laurie Platt Winfrey, Inc. **150:** Hōryūji Pagoda, art Fred Holz; Manabu Watabe, Tokyo. **154, 155:** Shōsō-in Hōmotsu, Nara; Nara National Museum, Nara. **157:** Map Alfred T. Kamajian. **158-169:** Shōsō-in Hōmotsu, Nara.

Typeset by A.J. Latham Limited, Dunstable, Bedfordshire.
Printed and bound by Brepols S.A. – Turnhout, Belgium.